EXAM C

CW00957262

The CCNA Cram Sheet

This Cram Sheet contains the distilled, key facts about Exams 640-821, 640-811, and 640-801. Review this information as the last thing you do before you enter the testing center, paying special attention to those areas where you feel that you need the most review. You can transfer any of these facts from your head onto a blank sheet of paper immediately before you begin the exam.

1. The primary advantage of bridging is increased bandwidth available on a segment because of the decreased number of devices in the collision domain.

2. Switches are high-speed, multiport bridges. Switches support the same functionality as bridges but usually have a greater port density. Each switch port is a separate collision domain, and each port provides dedicated bandwidth.

3. Virtual local area networks (VLANs) can be used to make a group of switch ports into a separate, isolated LAN. Routing is required for communication between VLANs.

4. VLANs can function across multiple switches when they are connected by a trunk connection. Inter-switch linking (ISL) is used to create a trunk connection between Fast Ethernet ports on Cisco switches.

5. Switches make it possible to run Ethernet devices in full-duplex mode. In full-duplex mode, two devices share the Ethernet wire simultaneously and exclusively, enabling faster throughput because no collisions are possible.

6. Store-and-forward switching reads the entire frame before making a forwarding decision; cut-through switching reads only the first six bytes—the destination media access control (MAC) address—to make a forwarding decision. Store-and-forward switching performs error checking; cut-through switching does not.

7. The primary advantages of routers are

   ➤ They allow you to connect dissimilar LANs.

   ➤ They provide multiple paths to a destination network.

   ➤ They allow the interconnection of large and complex networks.

8. Connection-oriented communication uses a nonpermanent path for data transfer. It involves three steps: establish the connection, transfer the data, and terminate the connection. A practical example of a connection-oriented communication would be a walkie-talkie conversation in which the connection has to be established each time to the receiver by pressing a button, and after you are finished talking, you release the button until you want to talk again. Connectionless communication uses a permanently established link. An example of a connection-oriented protocol is TCP, and an example of connectionless communication protocol is UDP. Again, a practical example would be that of a telephone conversation in which a connection is made and maintained throughout the duration of the call.

9. The layers of the OSI model are as follows:

   7. Application
   6. Presentation
   5. Session
   4. Transport
   3. Network
   2. Data Link
   1. Physical

10. Encapsulation, or tunneling, takes frames from one network system and places them inside frames from another network system.

11. The Presentation layer concerns itself with data representation, data encryption, and data compression. It supports different protocols for text, data, sound, video, graphics, and images, such as ASCII, MIDI, MPEG, GIF, and JPEG.

12. The Session layer establishes, manages, and terminates sessions between applications. Network file system (NFS), structured query language (SQL), and remote procedure calls (RPCs) are examples of Session layer protocols.

13. The Transport layer sits between the upper and lower layers of the OSI model. It performs flow control by buffering, multiplexing, and paralleli- tion. It provides end-to-end data transport

46. A list of the important access list numeric identifiers follows:

 ➤ 1 through 99: IP standard access list
 ➤ 100 through 199: IP extended access list
 ➤ 800 through 899: IPX standard access list
 ➤ 900 through 999: IPX extended access list
 ➤ 1000 through 1099: Service Advertisement Protocols (SAP) access list

47. Two rules for applying a wildcard mask to an IP address are

 ➤ A 1 bit in the wildcard mask indicates that the corresponding bit in the IP address can be ignored. Thus, the IP address bit can be either 1 or 0.
 ➤ A 0 in the wildcard mask indicates that the corresponding bit in the IP address must be strictly followed. Thus, the value must be exactly the same as specified in the IP address.

48. The difference in the capabilities of IP-extended access lists in comparison with IP standard access lists is that standard access lists filter IP traffic based on source IP address or address range. IP extended access lists filter traffic based on source and destination addresses, ports, and many other fields.

49. Know that the last line of any access list is deny any any (implicit).

50. A standard access list can be configured on a router using the following command:

```
Router(config)#access-list <1-99>
<permit/deny> <source IP> <wild-
card mask>
```

51. An extended access list can be configured on a router using the following command:

```
Router(config)#access-list
<100-199> <permit/deny> <protocol>
<source IP> <wildcard mask>
<destination IP> <wildcard mask>
eq <port number>
```

52. Network Address Translation (NAT) allows internal IP addresses to be translated to external IP addresses.

53. The three forms of NAT include

 ➤ Static NAT
 ➤ Dynamic NAT
 ➤ NAT Overload

54. The most popular form of NAT is the NAT Overload configuration, which translates many internal IP addresses to a single external IP address. The commands to configure NAT Overload are as follows:

```
Router(config-if)#ip nat inside
Router(config-if)#ip nat outside
Router(config)#ip nat inside
```

```
source list <access list identify-
ing inside addresses> interface
<external interface> overload
```

55. A single physical interface can be configured with several virtual subinterfaces. Each subinterface can be configured with different addressing information. Subinterfaces can be created and accessed using the serial interface number followed by a period and a number (such as serial 0.78).

56. The commands to configure frame relay on a router are

```
Router (config)# encapsulation
frame-relay cisco
```

```
Router (config)# frame-relay
lmi-type cisco
```

```
Router (config)# interface serial 0
```

```
Router (config-if)# frame-relay
interface-dlci <dlci number>
```

57. The basic commands to monitor frame relay activity on a router are show frame-relay pvc, show frame-relay lmi, show frame-relay map, and debug frame-relay lmi.

58. The commands to configure PPP on a router are

```
Router (config)# username <name>
password <password>
```

```
Router (config)# interface serial
0 Router (config-if)# encapsula-
tion ppp
```

```
Router (config-if)# ppp
authentication chap
```

59. The basic commands to monitor PPP activity on a router are show interface and debug ppp chap.

60. The commands to configure ISDN on a router are

```
Router (config)# isdn switch-type
<switch-type>
```

```
Router (config)# dialer-list
<dialer-group> protocol
<protocol-name> permit
```

```
Router (config-if)# interface
bri 0 Router (config-if)#
encapsulation PPP
```

```
Router (config-if)# dialer-group
<number>
```

```
Router (config-if)# dialer map
<protocol> <next-hop address>
name <hostname> speed <number>
<dial-string>
```

```
Router (config-if) dialer
idle-timeout <seconds>
```

61. The basic commands to monitor ISDN and DDR activity on a router are show controller bri, show interface bri, and show dialer.

services by segmenting upper-layer applications, establishing an end-to-end connection, sending segments from one end host to another, and ensuring reliable data transport.

14. The primary functions of the Network layer of the OSI model are path determination and logical addressing. In addition, remember that the Network layer is the domain of routing.

15. The primary functions of the Data-Link layer of the OSI model are

    ➤ It allows the upper layers of the OSI model to work independently of the physical media.

    ➤ It performs physical hardware addressing.

    ➤ It provides optional flow control.

    ➤ It generates error notification.

16. Convergence occurs when all routers in an internetwork agree on optimal routes. A routing loop occurs when a packet bounces back and forth between two or more routers.

17. Distance vector routing protocols send their entire routing tables to their neighbors. Link state protocols send the state of their own interfaces to every router in the internetwork.

18. Counting to infinity is a problem for distance vector routing protocols. This problem can be eliminated or mitigated by using the following techniques: maximum hop count, split horizon, route poisoning, and hold-down timers.

19. TCP provides a connection-oriented and reliable service to the applications that use its services with the use of acknowledgments, sequence number checking, error and duplication checking, and the TCP three-way handshake. User Datagram Protocol (UDP) provides a connection-less and best-effort service to the applications that use its services.

20. Well-known port numbers include

    ➤ File Transfer Protocol (FTP) 21

    ➤ Telnet 23

    ➤ Simple Mail Transfer Protocol (SMTP) 25

    ➤ Domain Name System (DNS) 53

    ➤ TFTP 69

    ➤ Simple Network Management Protocol (SNMP) 161, 162

    ➤ HTTP 80

21. Address Resolution Protocol (ARP) maps a known IP address to a physical address. Reverse Address Resolution Protocol (RARP) maps a known physical address to a logical address.

22. You should understand the basic concepts of IP addressing. Dotted-decimal notation is the decimal representation of a 32-bit IP address. The dotted-decimal notation represents the four octets of bits by performing binary-to-decimal conversion for each octet and providing a decimal value for each octet.

23. You should know the decimal representation of classes A, B, and C addresses as well as the number of networks and nodes each supports as follows:

    ➤ Class A: 1 through 126

    ➤ Class B: 128 through 191

    ➤ Class C: 192 through 223

24. You should be able to recognize the default mask for each class of IP address as follows:

    ➤ Class A: 255.0.0.0

    ➤ Class B: 255.255.0.0

    ➤ Class C: 255.255.255.0

25. The network number and broadcast address for a given subnet are the first and last IP addresses, respectively. The range of usable IP addresses is all addresses between the network number and broadcast address. In binary format, the network number has all of the host bits of the address set to 0. The broadcast address has all of the host bits set to 1.

26. You should know how to do subnetting tasks very quickly. This capability will save you valuable time in the end.

27. The interface between the customer network and the WAN provider network occurs between the data terminal equipment (DTE) and the data communication equipment (DCE). DTE devices are usually routers. DCE devices are usually modems, channel service units/data service units (CSUs/DSUs), and terminal adapter/network terminations 1 (TA/NT1s).

28. Frame relay is a high-speed, packet-switching WAN protocol that operates at the Data-Link layer. It runs on nearly any type of serial interface, uses frame check sequence (FCS) as its error-checking mechanism, and relies on a discard eligibility bit for congestion management. A virtual circuit must connect two DTE devices within a frame relay network. Permanent virtual circuits (PVCs) are more widely used than switched virtual circuits (SVCs) in frame relay networks.

29. Data link connection identifier (DLCI) serves as the addressing scheme within a frame relay network. Local Management Information (LMI) is a set of enhancements to frame relay that was developed by Cisco, StrataCom, Northern Telecom, and DEC. Cisco routers support LMI variations for American National Standards Institute (ANSI), Q933a, and Cisco.

30. DLCIs are mapped to network layer addresses through inverse ARP or by using the frame-relay map command.

31. Committed Information Rate (CIR) is the rate, in bits per second, at which data is transferred across the frame relay network.

32. Password Authentication Protocol (PAP) uses a two-way handshake to authenticate Point-to-Point Protocol (PPP) connections and transmits username/password information in clear text. Challenge Handshake Authentication Protocol (CHAP) uses a three-way handshake and relies on secret, encrypted passwords and unique IDs to authenticate PPP.

33. Integrated Services Digital Network (ISDN) can be ordered as either basic rate interface (BRI) or primary rate interface (PRI). ISDN functions represent devices or hardware functions within ISDN. Reference points describe the logical interfaces between functions.

34. ISDN can be used to add bandwidth for telecommuting, improve Internet response time, carry multiple network layer protocols, and encapsulate other WAN services.

35. Dial-on-demand routing (DDR) works with ISDN to establish and terminate connections. It uses access lists to look for interesting traffic.

36. EXEC includes the following:

  ➤ Context-sensitive help for syntax checking, command prompting, and keyword completion. Use the question mark (?) to activate context-sensitive help.

  ➤ Command history that provides a record of recent commands. Use the up- and down-arrow keys to scroll through the history list. Tab completes a partially entered command.

  ➤ Enhanced editing that enables commands retrieved from the command history to be changed quickly and then reexecuted. The `terminal editing` and `terminal no editing` commands enable and disable enhanced editing.

  ➤ Use the Tab key to allow the router to complete commands after you get a `%incomplete command%` message.

37. Examine the status of a router with the following commands: show `version`, show `memory`, show `protocols`, show `running-config` (or `write terminal`), show `startup-config` (or `show configuration`), show `interfaces`, and show `flash`.

38. The Cisco Discovery Protocol (CDP) displays summary information about directly connected devices and operates at the Data Link layer. The show `cdp neighbors` command displays ID, local and remote port, holdtime, platform, and capability information. The show `cdp entry <device id>` command displays information about a specific device, including all Layer 3 addresses and Internetwork Operating System (IOS) versions.

39. The command to back up a router configuration file (copy a configuration file from a router to a Trivial File Transfer Protocol [TFTP] server) is copy `running-config tftp`. The command to restore a configuration file (copy a configuration file from a TFTP server to a router) is copy `tftp running-config`.

40. The commands to set the enable secret, console, and auxiliary passwords on a router are as follows:

```
Router(config)#enable password
Router(config)#enable secret
password
Router(config)#line aux 0
Router(config-line)#login
Router(config-line)#password
password
Router(config)#line con 0
Router(config-line)#login
Router(config-line)#password
password
Router(config)#line vty 0 4
Router(config-line)#login
Router(config-line)#password
password
```

41. To create a banner for a router and a description for an interface, use the `banner motd` (message of the day) and `description` commands.

42. Router resource usage, bandwidth consumption, and update synchronization are problems for link state routing protocols. They can be eliminated or reduced by using the following techniques:

  ➤ Lengthening update frequency

  ➤ Exchanging route summaries

  ➤ Using time stamps or sequence numbers

43. Routing Information Protocol (RIP) can be configured on a router with the following commands:

```
Router (config)# router rip
Router (config-router)# network
<network>
```

44. Enhanced Interior Gateway Routing Protocol (EIGRP) can be configured on a router with the following commands:

```
Router (config)# router eigrp
<autonomous system number>
Router (config-router)# network
<network>
```

45. The most important basic commands used to monitor IP with Cisco routers are show `ip interface`, show `ip protocol`, and sh `ip route`.

EXAM CRAM™

CCNA
Practice
Questions

2nd Edition

Jeremy D. Cioara

Chris Ward

que®

CERTIFICATION

CCNA Practice Questions Exam Cram, 2nd Edition

Copyright © 2006 by Que Publishing

All rights reserved. No part of this book shall be reproduced, stored in a retrieval system, or transmitted by any means, electronic, mechanical, photocopying, recording, or otherwise, without written permission from the publisher. No patent liability is assumed with respect to the use of the information contained herein. Although every precaution has been taken in the preparation of this book, the publisher and author assume no responsibility for errors or omissions. Nor is any liability assumed for damages resulting from the use of the information contained herein.

International Standard Book Number: 0-7897-3529-6

Library of Congress Catalog Card Number: 2005934728

Printed in the United States of America

First Printing: December 2005

08   07   06   05   4   3   2   1

Trademarks

All terms mentioned in this book that are known to be trademarks or service marks have been appropriately capitalized. Que Publishing cannot attest to the accuracy of this information. Use of a term in this book should not be regarded as affecting the validity of any trademark or service mark.

Warning and Disclaimer

Every effort has been made to make this book as complete and as accurate as possible, but no warranty or fitness is implied. The information provided is on an "as is" basis. The authors and the publisher shall have neither liability nor responsibility to any person or entity with respect to any loss or damages arising from the information contained in this book or from the use of the CD or programs accompanying it.

Bulk Sales

Que Publishing offers excellent discounts on this book when ordered in quantity for bulk purchases or special sales. For more information, please contact

> **U.S. Corporate and Government Sales**
> **1-800-382-3419**
> **corpsales@pearsontechgroup.com**

For sales outside the U.S., please contact

> **International Sales**
> **international@pearsoned.com**

Publisher
Paul Boger

Executive Editor
Jeff Riley

Acquisitions and Development Editor
Carol Ackerman

Managing Editor
Charlotte Clapp

Project Editor
Andy Beaster

Copy Editor
Chuck Hutchinson

Proofreader
Suzanne Thomas

Technical Editors
Matthew J. Miller
Michelle Plumb

Publishing Coordinator
Cindy Teeters

Multimedia Developer
Dan Scherf

Interior Designer
Gary Adair

Cover Designer
Anne Jones

Page Layout
Brad Chinn
Toi Davis

About the Authors

Jeremy D. Cioara (CCIE, MCSE, CNE) is the owner of AdTEC Networks and works as a network consultant, instructor, and author. He has been working in network technologies for more than a decade and has deployed networks worldwide. His current consulting work focuses on network and Voice over IP (VoIP) implementations. Jeremy has written many books on Cisco network technology but has a true passion for educating individuals both in the classroom and through e-learning environments. He is married to a stunningly beautiful, talented, and witty woman who has recently attained the coveted Certified Best Wife in the World (CBWW) certification.

Chris Ward is a Senior Technical Instructor for a Web-based ILT company and a pastor of a small church. He is certified as a CCSI, CCNP, CCDP, and MCSE. He has worked for companies such as IntegrationWorks, Salem Communications, and his own company, NightFall Productions, over the past 10+ years. He has written for several publications, as well as co-authored a book on Windows Server 2003. His most important achievement, however, is being a good husband and dad to his wife and two children.

About the Technical Editors

Matthew J. Miller is a senior network engineer with Derive Technologies, LLC, in New York. He is a CCDP with more than 10 years of experience designing, implementing, and troubleshooting LAN/WAN solutions in corporate environments. You can reach Matthew at mmiller@derivetech.com.

Michelle Plumb is a full-time instructor focusing on Cisco and the Cisco IP telephony track with more than 15 years in the field as an IT and telephony specialist. Michelle maintains a high level of Cisco and Microsoft certifications, including CCNP, CCVP, Cisco IP Telephony Support Specialist, Unity, and MCSE NT/2000. Michelle has technically reviewed numerous books for the Cisco CCNP track and Microsoft 2000.

Contents at a Glance

Table of Contents

We Want to Hear from You!

As the reader of this book, *you* are our most important critic and commentator. We value your opinion and want to know what we're doing right, what we could do better, what areas you'd like to see us publish in, and any other words of wisdom you're willing to pass our way.

As an executive editor for Que Publishing, I welcome your comments. You can email or write me directly to let me know what you did or didn't like about this book—as well as what we can do to make our books better.

Please note that I cannot help you with technical problems related to the topic of this book. We do have a User Services group, however, where I will forward specific technical questions related to the book.

When you write, please be sure to include this book's title and author as well as your name, email address, and phone number. I will carefully review your comments and share them with the author and editors who worked on the book.

Email: feedback@quepublishing.com

Mail: Jeff Riley
Executive Editor
Que Publishing
800 East 96th Street
Indianapolis, IN 46240 USA

For information about the Exam Cram series, visit www.examcram.com. Type the ISBN (excluding hyphens) or the title of a book in the Search field to find the page you're looking for.

Introduction

What Is This Book About?

Welcome to the *CCNA Practice Questions Exam Cram, 2nd Edition*! The sole aim of this book is to provide you with practice questions, complete with answers and explanations, that will help you learn, drill, and review for the CCNA exam.

Who Is This Book For?

If you have studied the CCNA exam's content and feel you are ready to put your knowledge to the test, but aren't sure you want to take the real exam yet, this book is for you! Maybe you have answered other practice questions or unsuccessfully taken the real exam, reviewed, and want to do more practice questions before going to take the real exam—then this book is for you, too!

What Will You Find in This Book?

As mentioned before, this book is all about practice questions! This book is separated according to the topics you will find in the CCNA exam. Each chapter represents an exam topic, and in each chapter you will find three elements:

- **Practice Questions**—These are the numerous questions that will help you learn, drill, and review.
- **Quick Check Answers**—After you have finished answering the questions, you can quickly grade your exam from this section. Only correct answers are given here—no explanations are offered yet!

• **Answers and Explanations**—This section offers you the correct answers, as well as further explanation about the content posed in that question. Use this information to learn why an answer is correct and to reinforce the content in your mind for exam day.

You will also find a Cram Sheet at the beginning of this book specifically written for this exam. This is a very popular element that is also found in *CCNA Exam Cram, Second Edition* (Que Publishing, ISBN 0-7897-3502-4). This item condenses all the necessary facts found in this exam into one easy-to-handle tear card. The Cram Sheet is something you can carry with you to the exam location and use as a last-second study aid. Be aware that you can't take it into the exam room, though!

Hints for Using This Book

As this book is a paper practice product, you might want to complete your exams on a separate piece of paper so that you can reuse the questions over and over without having previous answers in your way. Also, a general rule of thumb across all practice question products is to make sure you are scoring well into the high 80 to 90% range in all topics before attempting the real exam. The higher percentages you score on practice question products, the better your chances for passing the real exam. Of course, we can't guarantee a passing score on the real exam, but we can offer you plenty of opportunities to practice and assess your knowledge level before entering the real exam.

Need Further Study?

Are you having a hard time correctly answering these questions? If so, you probably need further review. Be sure to see the sister products to this book, *CCNA Exam Cram, Second Edition* (Que Publishing, ISBN 0-7897-3502-4) and *CCNA Exam Prep* (Que Publishing, ISBN 0-7897-3519-9) for further review. If you need even further study, check out the many offerings from Que's sister company, Cisco Press, at www.ciscopress.com.

Cisco Network Fundamentals

Quick Check

1. You need to establish an EXEC session and access the command-line interface of your Cisco router. Which of the following access methods meet your requirements? (Choose three.)
   - ❑ A. Console connection
   - ❑ B. TFTP session
   - ❑ C. Telnet session
   - ❑ D. Modem connection
   - ❑ E. FTP session

Quick Answer: **11**
Detailed Answer: **12**

2. When you start a Catalyst 2950 switch for the first time, where does it receive its initial configuration?
   - ❑ A. The switch downloads a configuration from a TFTP server.
   - ❑ B. The switch begins to perform basic functionality and enters a setup menu.
   - ❑ C. The switch autosenses the local area network configuration and configures itself accordingly.
   - ❑ D. The switch must have its configuration unlocked with a password.

Quick Answer: **11**
Detailed Answer: **12**

3. What is the first action performed when a Cisco router starts up?
   - ❑ A. Load the Cisco IOS image
   - ❑ B. POST test
   - ❑ C. Configure IP address on the interfaces
   - ❑ D. Implement access list restrictions

Quick Answer: **11**
Detailed Answer: **12**

4. What configuration requirements are necessary when communicating over the console port of your router?
   - ❑ A. 9600bps, 8 data bits, no parity, 1 stop bit, hardware flow control
   - ❑ B. 9600bps, 8 data bits, no parity, 1 stop bit, no flow control
   - ❑ C. 56000bps, 8 data bits, no parity, 1 stop bit, hardware flow control
   - ❑ D. 56000bps, 8 data bits, no parity, 1 stop bit, no flow control

Quick Answer: **11**
Detailed Answer: **12**

. . . .

5. You need to configure a remote device via a modem. To which interface should the modem be connected?

   ❑ A. `Console`

   ❑ B. `Eth0/0`

   ❑ C. `AUX`

   ❑ D. `Ser0/0`

Quick Answer: **11**
Detailed Answer: **12**

6. After initial startup, which of the following are valid ways to access and configure your Cisco router? (Choose three.)

   ❑ A. Terminal session via Telnet

   ❑ B. Configuration download via TFTP

   ❑ C. Command-line session via TFTP

   ❑ D. Configuration download via CiscoWorks2000

Quick Answer: **11**
Detailed Answer: **12**

7. Which of the following is a configuration mode that allows a person to access only a limited number of basic monitoring commands?

   ❑ A. User EXEC level

   ❑ B. Restricted EXEC level

   ❑ C. Guest EXEC level

   ❑ D. Anonymous EXEC level

Quick Answer: **11**
Detailed Answer: **12**

8. Which of the following is a command mode that allows a person to access all router commands?

   ❑ A. Admin EXEC level

   ❑ B. Root EXEC level

   ❑ C. Privileged EXEC level

   ❑ D. Unrestricted EXEC level

Quick Answer: **11**
Detailed Answer: **12**

9. Which key is used to parse and execute CLI commands?

   ❑ A. Tab

   ❑ B. Esc

   ❑ C. Enter

   ❑ D. F1

Quick Answer: **11**
Detailed Answer: **13**

10. Which of the following prompts indicates a router in User EXEC mode?

   ❑ A. `hostname`

   ❑ B. `hostname>`

   ❑ C. `hostname#`

   ❑ D. `hostname:`

Quick Answer: **11**
Detailed Answer: **13**

11. Which of the following is a security concern when configuring a device using Telnet?

Quick Answer: **11**
Detailed Answer: **13**

- ❑ A. Passwords are sent in clear text
- ❑ B. Passwords are sent using reversible encryption
- ❑ C. Passwords cannot be changed in a Telnet session
- ❑ D. Passwords are not used during a Telnet session

12. Which of the following prompts indicates a router in Privileged EXEC mode?

Quick Answer: **11**
Detailed Answer: **13**

- ❑ A. `hostname`
- ❑ B. `hostname>`
- ❑ C. `hostname#`
- ❑ D. `hostname:`

13. You are unsure of the command to use while configuring a router. How can you access the context-sensitive help to see a list of commands available to you?

Quick Answer: **11**
Detailed Answer: **13**

- ❑ A. `help`
- ❑ B. `/help`
- ❑ C. `?`
- ❑ D. `-?`

14. After working in a router in Privileged EXEC mode, how can you return to User EXEC mode?

Quick Answer: **11**
Detailed Answer: **13**

- ❑ A. `exit`
- ❑ B. `esc`
- ❑ C. `disable`
- ❑ D. `quit`

15. Which of the following commands lists all the commands that start with the letter c?

Quick Answer: **11**
Detailed Answer: **13**

- ❑ A. `show c`
- ❑ B. `c?`
- ❑ C. `c ?`
- ❑ D. `show c?`

16. You need to specify a name for your Catalyst 2950 Series switch. Which command assigns the name "branch" to your Catalyst 2950 switch?

Quick Answer: **11**
Detailed Answer: **13**

- ❑ A. `name branch`
- ❑ B. `hostname branch`
- ❑ C. `set name branch`
- ❑ D. `set hostname branch`

17. You need to configure a switch from a remote subnet. Which of the following must be configured on the switch?

    ❏ A. Console port
    ❏ B. Default gateway
    ❏ C. Hostname
    ❏ D. SNMP

Quick Answer: **11**
Detailed Answer: **13**

18. You are examining the functionality of your switch. Which of the following commands displays the configuration of the system hardware, as well as the software version, configuration filenames, and boot images?

    ❏ A. `show version`
    ❏ B. `show running-config`
    ❏ C. `show running-configuration`
    ❏ D. `show startup-configuration`

Quick Answer: **11**
Detailed Answer: **14**

19. You are attempting to isolate a configuration error on your switch. Which of the following commands displays the current active configuration of the switch?

    ❏ A. `show active-configuration`
    ❏ B. `show running-config`
    ❏ C. `show running-configuration`
    ❏ D. `show startup-configuration`

Quick Answer: **11**
Detailed Answer: **14**

20. You want to examine the performance of your switch. Which of the following commands displays the statistics for the switch's interfaces?

    ❏ A. `show version`
    ❏ B. `show stats`
    ❏ C. `show interfaces`
    ❏ D. `show results`

Quick Answer: **11**
Detailed Answer: **14**

21. You failed in attempting to access a switch remotely. You need to confirm the IP configuration of the switch to determine whether there was an entry error. Which of the following commands displays the IP address and subnet mask configured for the switch?

    ❏ A. `show ip config`
    ❏ B. `ipconfig`
    ❏ C. `show config`
    ❏ D. `show interface vlan 1`

Quick Answer: **11**
Detailed Answer: **14**

22. You have received a new router. When you initially start the device, how does it receive its initial configuration?

Quick Answer: **11**
Detailed Answer: **14**

❑ A. The router uses a default configuration.
❑ B. The router enters a setup mode.
❑ C. The router downloads a configuration from a TFTP server.
❑ D. The router autosenses the local area network configuration and configures itself accordingly.

23. You are working on your router, and after you enter a command, the router returns the error message % Ambiguous command. What does the message mean?

Quick Answer: **11**
Detailed Answer: **14**

❑ A. You did not use the proper command syntax.
❑ B. You mistyped the command.
❑ C. You did not enter enough characters to specify a single command.
❑ D. You are attempting to configure a nonexistent interface.

24. You want to review the last command you entered. Which key sequences will display the last command entered on your router? (Choose two.)

Quick Answer: **11**
Detailed Answer: **14**

❑ A. Ctrl+P
❑ B. Up arrow
❑ C. Esc
❑ D. Tab

25. You have been entering a complex router configuration and would like to review the prior commands. However, when you do so, the oldest commands do not appear. You would like to increase the number of prior commands available to you to 150 for your current session. What command can you use?

Quick Answer: **11**
Detailed Answer: **15**

❑ A. buffer size 150
❑ B. command buffer 150
❑ C. terminal history size 150
❑ D. history size 150

26. You are creating a report that will include performance statistics for your routers. You need to determine how long each router has currently been running. Which command should you use?

Quick Answer: **11**
Detailed Answer: **15**

❑ A. show running-config
❑ B. show statistics
❑ C. show version
❑ D. show uptime

27. Which of the following stores routing tables and the running configuration?

    ❑ A. NVRAM
    ❑ B. Flash
    ❑ C. RAM
    ❑ D. IOS

Quick Answer: **11**
Detailed Answer: **15**

28. Which of the following locations is used to store the startup configuration?

    ❑ A. NVRAM
    ❑ B. Flash
    ❑ C. RAM
    ❑ D. IOS

Quick Answer: **11**
Detailed Answer: **15**

29. Which of the following locations is used to store the backup configurations and IOS?

    ❑ A. NVRAM
    ❑ B. Flash
    ❑ C. RAM
    ❑ D. IOS

Quick Answer: **11**
Detailed Answer: **15**

30. Which prompt displays the configuration mode that allows you to configure multiple virtual interfaces on a single physical interface?

    ❑ A. `router(config-if)#`
    ❑ B. `router(config-subif)#`
    ❑ C. `router(config-line)#`
    ❑ D. `router(config)#`

Quick Answer: **11**
Detailed Answer: **15**

31. You need to configure the hostname of your router. Which command allows you to enter Global Configuration mode to make this change?

    ❑ A. `configure terminal`
    ❑ B. `configure global`
    ❑ C. `configure hostname`
    ❑ D. `configure network`

Quick Answer: **11**
Detailed Answer: **15**

32. Which prompt displays the configuration mode that allows you to configure virtual terminal ports?

    ❑ A. `router(config-if)#`
    ❑ B. `router(config-subif)#`
    ❑ C. `router(config-line)#`
    ❑ D. `router(config)#`

Quick Answer: **11**
Detailed Answer: **15**

Quick Check

33. You have made changes in your router's configuration that are causing communication problems. You want to restore the configuration the router was using when it powered up. What command should you enter?

Quick Answer: **11**
Detailed Answer: **16**

- ❏ A. `restore startup`
- ❏ B. `copy running-config startup-config`
- ❏ C. `copy startup-config running-config`
- ❏ D. This cannot be done from the command line.
- ❏ E. `Reload`

34. You are concerned about unauthorized access and configurations to the Privileged EXEC mode of your router. You want to implement an encrypted password for access to the device. Which command will accomplish this?

Quick Answer: **11**
Detailed Answer: **16**

- ❏ A. `enable password`
- ❏ B. `enable secret`
- ❏ C. `enable password encrypted`
- ❏ D. `enable encryption`

35. You want to create a message for users who connect to the router, indicating that only authorized access is allowed. Which command creates this message?

Quick Answer: **11**
Detailed Answer: **16**

- ❏ A. `banner # Authorized access only! #`
- ❏ B. `banner motd # Authorized access only! #`
- ❏ C. `motd # Authorized access only! #`
- ❏ D. `login motd # Authorized access only! #`

36. You want to protect Telnet sessions with a login password. Which series of commands will create a password of `cisco` to protect access to the router through Telnet?

Quick Answer: **11**
Detailed Answer: **16**

- ❏ A. `line console 0`
      `login`
      `password cisco`
- ❏ B. `line vty 0 4`
      `login`
      `enable secret cisco`
- ❏ C. `line console 0`
      `login`
      `enable secret cisco`
- ❏ D. `line vty 0 4`
      `login`
      `password cisco`

37. While you are working on the router, your session is interrupted by the interjection of feedback from the router. You
would like to make it easier to read your input and the messages. Which command accomplishes this?

  ❑ A. `logging synchronous`
  ❑ B. `no interrupt`
  ❑ C. `enable continuous`
  ❑ D. `display on`

Quick Answer: **11**
Detailed Answer: **16**

38. While working with your router, you receive a phone call.
You return to your session to find you have been disconnected
by the timeout feature of the router, and you want to disable
it. What command accomplishes your goal?

  ❑ A. `no timeout`
  ❑ B. `exec-timeout 0 0`
  ❑ C. `timeout disable`
  ❑ D. `no disconnect`

Quick Answer: **11**
Detailed Answer: **16**

39. You have just installed a module with additional interfaces
into your router. The module was installed in slot 1, and you
need to configure the module's first Ethernet interface. What
command do you use to access Interface Configuration mode
to perform the configuration?

  ❑ A. `interface ethernet 1/0`
  ❑ B. `ethernet 1/0`
  ❑ C. `ethernet 1/1`
  ❑ D. `interface ethernet 1/1`

Quick Answer: **11**
Detailed Answer: **16**

40. You are configuring a serial link between two routers. You
need to configure one router as the DCE device. The clock
rate needs to be set to 2400bps. Which command do you use?

  ❑ A. `clock 2400`
  ❑ B. `clock rate 2400`
  ❑ C. `clock 2.4`
  ❑ D. `clock rate 2.4`

Quick Answer: **11**
Detailed Answer: **17**

41. You have disabled a serial interface temporarily. Which command will allow you to re-enable serial interface 0/1?

  ❑ A. `no shutdown`
  ❑ B. `enable`
  ❑ C. `no shutdown serial 0/1`
  ❑ D. `enable serial 0/1`

Quick Answer: **11**
Detailed Answer: **17**

42. Which of the following indicates that `Ethernet0/1` has a cable or interface problem?
    - ❑ A. `Ethernet0/1` is up, line protocol is up
    - ❑ B. `Ethernet0/1` is down, line protocol is up
    - ❑ C. `Ethernet0/1` is up, line protocol is down
    - ❑ D. `Ethernet0/1` is down, line protocol is down

Quick Answer: **11**
Detailed Answer: **17**

43. Which of the following indicates that `Ethernet0/1` has a clock rate or encapsulation problem?
    - ❑ A. `Ethernet0/1` is up, line protocol is up
    - ❑ B. `Ethernet0/1` is down, line protocol is up
    - ❑ C. `Ethernet0/1` is up, line protocol is down
    - ❑ D. `Ethernet0/1` is down, line protocol is down

Quick Answer: **11**
Detailed Answer: **17**

44. Which of the following indicates that `Ethernet0/1` has been turned off from the command-line interface?
    - ❑ A. `Ethernet0/1` is administratively down, line protocol is down
    - ❑ B. `Ethernet0/1` is down, line protocol is up
    - ❑ C. `Ethernet0/1` is up, line protocol is down
    - ❑ D. `Ethernet0/1` is down, line protocol is down

Quick Answer: **11**
Detailed Answer: **17**

45. You are connected to a remote router, and you need to determine the type of serial cables connected to the interface. What command should be issued?
    - ❑ A. `show cable`
    - ❑ B. `show interface`
    - ❑ C. `show running-config`
    - ❑ D. `show controller`

Quick Answer: **11**
Detailed Answer: **17**

46. Which command specifies the Ethernet interface physical connection on your router?
    - ❑ A. `media-type`
    - ❑ B. `connection-type`
    - ❑ C. `media`
    - ❑ D. `connection`

Quick Answer: **11**
Detailed Answer: **17**

47. On which interface should the clock rate be set when one router acts as the DCE and one router acts as the DTE?
    - ❑ A. Both
    - ❑ B. Neither
    - ❑ C. DTE
    - ❑ D. DCE

Quick Answer: **11**
Detailed Answer: **17**

48. You want to ensure that passwords are encrypted over the network so that they are not easily discovered by packet sniffing. Which command accomplishes this?

Quick Answer: **11**
Detailed Answer: **17**

- ❑ A. `encrypt network`
- ❑ B. `encrypt all`
- ❑ C. `encrypt passwords`
- ❑ D. `service password-encryption`

49. Which prompt displays a configuration mode that allows you to change an IP address on the router?

Quick Answer: **11**
Detailed Answer: **18**

- ❑ A. `router(config)#`
- ❑ B. `router(config-if)#`
- ❑ C. `router(config-ip)#`
- ❑ D. `router(config-line)#`

50. Which prompt displays a configuration mode that allows you to set the message of the day?

Quick Answer: **11**
Detailed Answer: **18**

- ❑ A. `router(config)#`
- ❑ B. `router(config-if)#`
- ❑ C. `router(config-ip)#`
- ❑ D. `router(config-line)#`

Quick Check Answer Key

1. A, C, D
2. B
3. B
4. B
5. C
6. A, B, D
7. A
8. C
9. C
10. B
11. A
12. C
13. C
14. C
15. B
16. B
17. B
18. A
19. B
20. C
21. D
22. B
23. C
24. A, B
25. C

26. C
27. C
28. A
29. B
30. B
31. A
32. C
33. E
34. B
35. B
36. D
37. A
38. B
39. A
40. B
41. A
42. D
43. C
44. A
45. D
46. A
47. D
48. D
49. B
50. A

Answers and Explanations

1. **Answers: A, C, and D.** Command-line interfaces can be established through a Telnet session, modem connection, and console connection. B is incorrect. Although TFTP is used to load a new IOS image onto a router, it does not allow you to establish a command-line interface session. E is incorrect, as FTP sessions are not used to establish command-line interface sessions with Cisco routers.

2. **Answer: B.** All Catalyst switches perform basic switching functions. However, a setup menu similar to a router shows up on the screen. A is incorrect because the switch does not have an IP address or a default gateway installed in order to contact a TFTP server. C is incorrect because Catalyst switches rely on their default configuration on power-up and do not autosense the LAN configuration. D is incorrect because no passwords are set on the switch when it is turned on for the first time.

3. **Answer: B.** When a Cisco router is first powered on, it performs a Power On Self Test, or POST, to ensure that its hardware is functioning properly. A is incorrect, as the Cisco IOS image is loaded after the post. C and D are incorrect, as they both take place after the IOS image is loaded.

4. **Answer: B.** Communications software should be configured to communicate at 9600bps, with 8 data bits, 1 stop bit, no parity, and no flow control. A is incorrect because hardware flow control should not be configured. C and D are incorrect; the bps setting should be 9600, not 56000.

5. **Answer: C.** For remote configuration, you connect a modem to the device's AUX port. A is incorrect; the console port is used for local configuration changes. B is incorrect, as the Eth0/0 interface does not support remote configuration via a modem. D is incorrect, as the Ser0/0 interface does not support remote configuration via a modem.

6. **Answers: A, B, and D.** Configuration changes can be made through a Telnet session established with the router. B is correct, as configuration files can be downloaded from a TFTP server. Additionally, D is correct; network management applications such as CiscoWorks2000 also facilitate the downloading of configuration files. C is incorrect, as command-line sessions cannot be established through TFTP.

7. **Answer: A.** User EXEC level contains a limited number of commands to allow basic monitoring. B, C, and D are incorrect, as they are not actual EXEC levels.

8. **Answer: C.** The command mode that allows full access to all router commands is the Privileged EXEC level. A, B, and D are all fictitious command modes.

9. **Answer: C.** The Enter key is used when configuring a router to parse and execute the typed command. A is incorrect, as the Tab key doesn't submit the command to the router; it merely autocompletes a partially entered command. B and D are incorrect, as neither the Esc key nor the F1 key is used to parse and execute commands.

10. **Answer: B.** The `hostname>` prompt indicates the router is in User EXEC mode. A and D are incorrect, as they are not valid indicators of an EXEC mode. C is incorrect, as it indicates the user is in Privileged EXEC mode.

11. **Answer: A.** Telnet traffic is not encrypted, so passwords are sent in plain text. B is incorrect, as Telnet uses no encryption. Passwords can be changed in a Telnet session, so C is incorrect. D is incorrect as well, as passwords are indeed usable during a Telnet session.

12. **Answer: C.** The `hostname#` prompt indicates the router is in Privileged EXEC mode. A and D are incorrect, as they are not valid indicators of an EXEC mode. B is incorrect, as it indicates the user is in User EXEC mode.

13. **Answer: C.** Entering `?` at the prompt reveals the command options available to the user. A is incorrect, as entering `help` explains how to use the help feature. B and D are invalid commands.

14. **Answer: C.** The `disable` command returns a user from Privileged EXEC mode to User EXEC mode. A is incorrect and typically ends the Telnet session. B is an invalid command. D is also incorrect and ends the Telnet session without returning the user to User EXEC mode.

15. **Answer: B.** The proper syntax to show all commands beginning with the letter c is c?. A is incorrect, as entering `show  c` attempts to execute a command; however, c is ambiguous, and the device returns an error message. C is also incorrect and has the same result; entering c ? attempts to show help, but c by itself is not specific enough to indicate a single command on the device and returns an error message. D is incorrect, as it is an invalid command.

16. **Answer: B.** To assign a name to your switch, use the `hostname` command, followed by the name you want to assign. A is incorrect and is an invalid command. C and D are also incorrect and result in error messages on the device.

17. **Answer: B.** Unless the switch is configured as an IP router, a default gateway must be configured. A is incorrect; your connection is not using the console port. C is correct, as a hostname is not required to configure the switch. D is incorrect; SNMP is used for remote management but is not required for you to configure a switch from a remote subnet.

18. **Answer: A.** The `show version` command displays the switch's hardware configuration, as well as configuration files in use and boot images. The `show version` command also shows the switch's uptime. B is incorrect, but it is a valid command for showing the active configuration of the switch. C and D are invalid commands and result in error messages.

19. **Answer: B.** The `show running-config` command displays the device's current active configuration. A is incorrect and results in an error message on the device. C and D are invalid commands that return error messages when entered.

20. **Answer: C.** The `show interfaces` command displays statistics and status information on the interfaces of a switch. A is incorrect; the `show version` command displays the switch's hardware configuration, as well as configuration files in use and boot images. B and D are invalid commands.

21. **Answer: D.** On a Catalyst switch, the `show interface vlan 1` command displays information such as the IP address and subnet mask. A and C are incorrect and result in error messages. B is used on Microsoft operating systems to show the IP configuration.

22. **Answer: B.** A new router enters a setup mode initially on its first boot. This creates a configuration file to be used when the router starts up again. A is incorrect. Although a switch can function with a default configuration, router configurations vary too greatly to allow a default configuration to work in most networks. C is incorrect, as the router initially looks in NVRAM for its configuration. D is incorrect because the router does not autosense and configure itself; it requires user interaction.

23. **Answer: C.** `Ambiguous command` indicates that you are using an abbreviation but did not specify enough characters for the IOS to determine which command you intended. A is incorrect. If you do not specify enough parameters, for instance, you receive the `% Incomplete command` error. B is incorrect, as typographical mistakes result in the `% Invalid input detected at '^'` error. D is incorrect, as attempting to configure a nonexistent interface results in an `% Invalid input detected at '^'` error, as well.

24. **Answers: A and B.** Ctrl+P and the up arrow both display the last command entered. Continue to use these keys to scroll through prior commands entered before the most recent command. Esc does not display prior commands, and the Tab key completes a command that you have begun typing, as long as it is not ambiguous.

25. **Answer: C.** The `terminal history size` command sets the buffer for the current session only. A and B are invalid commands. D is incorrect; `history size` is a valid command, but it permanently changes the buffer size instead of changing it for the session only.

26. **Answer: C.** The `show version` command shows the device's uptime. A is incorrect because `show running-config` shows the router's current active configuration. B and D are incorrect as well; `show statistics` and `show uptime` each display errors for invalid commands.

27. **Answer: C.** RAM stores routing tables and the running configuration. A is incorrect, as NVRAM stores the startup configuration and is writable permanent storage. B is incorrect because flash memory is used for storage of the Cisco IOS, backup configurations, and other files. D is incorrect, as the IOS is the operating system of the router.

28. **Answer: A.** NVRAM stores the startup configuration and is writable permanent storage. B is incorrect; Flash memory is used for storage of the Cisco IOS, backup configurations, and other files. C is incorrect because RAM stores routing tables and the running configuration. D is incorrect, as the IOS is the operating system of the router.

29. **Answer: B.** Flash memory is used for storage of the Cisco IOS, backup configurations, and other files. A is incorrect because NVRAM stores the startup configuration and is writable permanent storage. C is incorrect, as RAM stores routing tables and the running configuration. D is incorrect because the IOS is the operating system of the router.

30. **Answer: B.** Sub-interface mode allows you to configure virtual interfaces on a physical interface. A is incorrect because Interface mode supports commands on a per-interface basis. C is incorrect, as Line mode supports commands that configure the operation of a terminal line. D is incorrect; this prompt indicates that you are in Global Configuration mode.

31. **Answer: A.** `configure terminal` is the correct command to enter Global Configuration mode. B and C are invalid commands and result in error messages. D is incorrect; this is a valid command, but it seeks configuration information from a network source instead of taking you into Global Configuration mode.

32. **Answer: C.** Line mode supports commands that configure the operation of a terminal line as well as virtual terminal ports. A is incorrect, as Interface mode supports commands on a per-interface basis. B is incorrect, as Sub-interface mode allows you to configure virtual interfaces on a physical interface. D is incorrect, as this prompt indicates that you are in Global Configuration mode.

33. **Answer: E.** As long as you haven't saved the `running-config` and any changes, reloading the router causes it to reboot and load the `startup-config` without any changes. C is a valid command, but incorrect. Copying the `startup-config` to the current `running-config` restores the router's configuration; however, if you have made a new configuration setting that won't be overwritten by the conflicting `startup-config` setting, it remains and is not overwritten. Instead, it is merged. A is an invalid command. B is a valid command, but it's the opposite of what you want to accomplish: It takes the current configuration in use and makes it the default startup configuration. D is incorrect because you can perform the desired operation from the command line.

34. **Answer: B.** `enable secret` is the command used for creating encrypted passwords for Privileged EXEC mode. A is incorrect; `enable password` creates an unencrypted password. C and D are not valid IOS commands and result in error messages.

35. **Answer: B.** The `banner motd` command creates a login message. The # symbol is a delimiter, indicating the start and end of your message. A is incorrect and results in an invalid command error message; it is missing the `motd` portion of the command. C is incorrect, as it does not follow the proper syntax by using the banner portion of the command. D is invalid, as there is no `login` command to create a login banner.

36. **Answer: D.** `line vty` controls Telnet access, and `password cisco` is the correct syntax to set the password to `cisco`. A is incorrect, as `line console` controls console access. B is incorrect because `enable secret` is used not for Telnet access, but to control access to Privileged EXEC mode. C is incorrect, as `line console` is for console sessions, and `enable secret` is for setting the Privileged EXEC mode password.

37. **Answer: A.** The `logging synchronous` command keeps console messages from interrupting, resulting in a more readable console session. B, C, and D are invalid commands that all result in error messages.

38. **Answer: B.** `exec-timeout 0 0` disables the timeout feature for sessions. A is incorrect; although using `no` with a command often disables it, there is no `timeout` command. C is incorrect as well, resulting in an invalid command error. D also is an invalid command. Although `disable` is a valid command for exiting Privileged EXEC mode, `no disable` does not achieve the desired goal.

39. **Answer: A.** The proper format is `interface type slot/port`. B is incorrect; the correct syntax includes the term `interface`. C is incorrect, as `interface` is not used, and port numbering starts with 0. D is incorrect because although it uses the `interface` command, the port should be 0, not 1.

40. **Answer: B.** The correct syntax of the command is `clock rate bps`. A and C are incorrect, as they do not use the proper syntax. D is incorrect because although the proper syntax is used, 2.4 does not set the bps to 2400 as required.

41. **Answer: A.** In Interface Configuration mode, the `no shutdown` command re-enables the interface. B is incorrect; this command enters Privileged EXEC mode. C is incorrect because you don't need to specify the interface when you are in Line Configuration mode. D is incorrect; the `enable` command is not the proper command to achieve this goal.

42. **Answer: D.** If both the interface and line protocol are down, there is a cable or interface problem. A is incorrect because the interface and line protocol are functioning fine. B is incorrect because if the interface is down, the line protocol cannot be up. C is incorrect; this indicates a clocking or framing problem.

43. **Answer: C.** This situation indicates a clocking or framing problem. A is incorrect because the interface and line protocol are functioning fine. B is incorrect; if the interface is down, the line protocol cannot be up. D is incorrect because if both the interface and line protocol are down, there is a cable or interface problem.

44. **Answer: A.** The administrator has issued the `shutdown` command. B is incorrect because if the interface is down, the line protocol cannot be up. C is incorrect, as this indicates a clocking or framing problem. D is correct because if both the interface and line protocol are down, there is a cable or interface problem.

45. **Answer: D.** The `show controller` command shows the type of cable connected to the interface. This information is gathered when the router starts up. A is incorrect; the command does not exist. B is incorrect; `show interface` does not show the type of cable connected. C is incorrect. The `running-configuration` command does not show the type of cable connected.

46. **Answer: A.** The `media-type` command specifies settings such as `aui`, `10base-t`, and `100base-t` and might need to be set if it is not autodetected. B, C, and D are invalid commands that result in errors.

47. **Answer: D.** The clock rate needs to be set on the DCE device. A is incorrect because only the DCE device should be set. B is incorrect, as the DCE device must be configured with a clock rate. C is incorrect; the DCE, not the DTE device, needs to have the clock rate set.

48. **Answer: D.** The `service password-encryption` command allows you to use encrypted passwords. A, B, and C are invalid commands that result in error messages when used in the command-line interface.

49. **Answer: B.** This is Interface Configuration mode, used to change settings for a specific interface, including the IP address assigned to a specific interface. A is incorrect; this is Global Configuration mode, used for router-wide settings. C is a fictitious router mode. D is Line Configuration mode, used to configure the console or Telnet sessions.

50. **Answer: A.** This is Global Configuration mode, used for router-wide settings, such as the hostname, or the message of the day. B is Interface Configuration mode, used to change settings for a specific interface. C is a fictitious router mode. D is Line Configuration mode, used to configure the console or Telnet sessions.

TCP/IP Addressing and Protocol

1. Your junior network administrator wants to know what the default subnet mask is for a Class C IP address. What do you tell him?

   ❏ A. 255.0.0.0
   ❏ B. 255.255.0.0
   ❏ C. 255.245.255.0
   ❏ D. 255.255.255.0
   ❏ E. 255.255.255.255

2. An application needs to have reliable, end-to-end connectivity. Which of the following protocols will give you reliable connectivity?

   ❏ A. TCP
   ❏ B. UDP
   ❏ C. IP
   ❏ D. ICMP

3. You are designing a network, which needs to support 55 users. You don't plan to extend the segment beyond the current number of users. Which subnet mask would best meet your needs?

   ❏ A. 255.255.0.0
   ❏ B. 255.255.255.0
   ❏ C. 255.255.255.192
   ❏ D. 255.255.255.160

4. You have added a new switch to your network. You want to manage it remotely, so you need to assign it an IP address. Your router that connects to the switch has an IP address of 172.16.12.33/27. Which of the following addresses can you assign to this switch?

- ❏ A. 172.16.12.33/28
- ❏ B. 172.16.12.32/27
- ❏ C. 172.16.12.33/27
- ❏ D. 172.16.12.34/27
- ❏ E. 172.16.12.35/28
- ❏ F. 172.16.12.38/28
- ❏ G. 172.16.12.63/27

Quick Answer: 31
Detailed Answer: 32

5. The address 172.16.208.16/20 is a host address in which of the following subnets?

- ❏ A. 172.16.176.0–255.255.240.0
- ❏ B. 172.16.192.0–255.255.240.0
- ❏ C. 172.16.208.0–255.255.240.0
- ❏ D. 172.16.224.0–255.255.240.0

Quick Answer: 31
Detailed Answer: 32

6. You are designing an IP address scheme for your brand new remote office. The vice president of IT calls to tell you that you will be in charge of the 192.168.1.64/26 subnetwork. This supplies you with a single subnetwork with 62 hosts. You need to have at least two subnets with 14 hosts in each subnet. What custom subnet mask should you use?

- ❏ A. 255.255.255.128
- ❏ B. 255.255.255.192
- ❏ C. 255.255.255.224
- ❏ D. 255.255.255.240
- ❏ E. 255.255.255.248

Quick Answer: 31
Detailed Answer: 32

7. You have subnetted the 210.106.14.0 network with a /24 mask. Your boss at Acme, Inc. wants to know how many usable subnetworks and usable host addresses per subnet this would provide. What should you tell her?

- ❏ A. One network with 254 hosts
- ❏ B. Two networks with 128 hosts
- ❏ C. Four networks with 64 hosts
- ❏ D. Six networks with 30 hosts

Quick Answer: 31
Detailed Answer: 32

8. Identify three valid host addresses in any subnet of the 201.168.27.0 network, assuming a fixed subnet mask of 255.255.255.240. (Choose three.)

- ❏ A. 201.168.27.33
- ❏ B. 201.168.27.112
- ❏ C. 201.168.27.119
- ❏ D. 201.168.27.126
- ❏ E. 201.168.27.175
- ❏ F. 201.168.27.208

9. What is the subnetwork address for a host with the IP address 201.100.5.68/28?

- ❏ A. 201.100.5.0
- ❏ B. 201.100.5.32
- ❏ C. 201.100.5.64
- ❏ D. 201.100.5.65
- ❏ E. 201.100.5.31
- ❏ F. 201.100.5.1

10. Which of the following protocols uses a three-way handshake mechanism to establish sessions?

- ❏ A. TCP
- ❏ B. IP
- ❏ C. UDP
- ❏ D. IPX
- ❏ E. Frame relay

11. Which of the following protocols is connection-oriented?

- ❏ A. TCP
- ❏ B. IP
- ❏ C. IPX
- ❏ D. Frame relay

12. You are using an application on your Windows 2000 client machines that provides error correction. You need a protocol to provide fast transport. Which protocol should your application use?

- ❏ A. TCP
- ❏ B. IP
- ❏ C. UDP
- ❏ D. SPX
- ❏ E. AppleTalk

13. When using TCP, after a session is open, the applications can adjust the number of segments they receive before sending an acknowledgment. This behavior is known as _____.

    ❑ A. MTU adjustment

    ❑ B. Windowing

    ❑ C. Flexible Send Path

    ❑ D. FCS

Quick Answer: **31**
Detailed Answer: **34**

14. If the destination did not receive a segment, how will the TCP host know to resend the information?

    ❑ A. The ACK received will not include the segment number that was not received.

    ❑ B. The ACK received will include the segment number that was not received.

    ❑ C. The sending host will send a PACK to verify segment receipt.

    ❑ D. The destination host will send a YACK message back to the sending host.

Quick Answer: **31**
Detailed Answer: **34**

15. You are planning on using a single network that supports 208 users. Which IP address class would you choose to be the most efficient?

    ❑ A. Class A

    ❑ B. Class B

    ❑ C. Class C

    ❑ D. Class D

    ❑ E. Class E

Quick Answer: **31**
Detailed Answer: **34**

16. RFC 1918 defines the private IP address ranges. Which of the following IP addresses are considered part of these ranges? (Choose three.)

    ❑ A. 10.23.45.67

    ❑ B. 126.21.34.56

    ❑ C. 172.16.32.1

    ❑ D. 172.31.234.55

    ❑ E. 192.169.4.5

Quick Answer: **31**
Detailed Answer: **34**

Quick Check

17. A new network is being designed for your company, Acme, Inc. If you use a Class C IP network, which subnet mask will provide one usable subnet per department while allowing enough usable host addresses for each department specified in the table?

Department	Number of Users
Corporate	7
Customer Support	15
Financial	13
HR	7
Engineering	16

❏ A. 255.255.255.0
❏ B. 255.255.255.192
❏ C. 255.255.255.224
❏ D. 255.255.255.240
❏ E. 255.255.255.248

Quick Answer: **31**
Detailed Answer: **34**

18. Which of these protocols provides data transport, relying on the error correction capabilities of the application itself?

❏ A. UDP
❏ B. TCP
❏ C. SNMP
❏ D. ICMP

Quick Answer: **31**
Detailed Answer: **34**

19. Which of the following are used by TCP to ensure reliable delivery of data? (Choose two.)

❏ A. MAC address resolution
❏ B. Sequence numbers
❏ C. Acknowledgments
❏ D. Ping
❏ E. Routing updates

Quick Answer: **31**
Detailed Answer: **35**

20. You discover that you are able to adjust the window size of the TCP segment. You increase the window size to test the results. What will you observe happening on your network?

❏ A. Increased throughput
❏ B. Decreased throughput
❏ C. Increased latency
❏ D. Decreased reliability

Quick Answer: **31**
Detailed Answer: **35**

21. Your organization is using the 192.168.1.0/24 address space. You need 28 subnets. What subnet mask would you use to create these subnets?

    ❑ A. 255.255.255.0
    ❑ B. 255.255.255.128
    ❑ C. 255.255.255.192
    ❑ D. 255.255.255.224
    ❑ E. 255.255.255.240
    ❑ F. 255.255.255.248

22. Which of the following protocols maps IP addresses to MAC addresses for connectivity to occur between two hosts?

    ❑ A. ARP
    ❑ B. RARP
    ❑ C. SLARP
    ❑ D. DHCP

23. Your junior network administrator cannot seem to ping a host in another network and asks you why it isn't working. Which of the following is not an answer that you would give him?

    ❑ A. The host's default gateway is down.
    ❑ B. The destination host is not powered on.
    ❑ C. The IP address of the router interface is incorrect.
    ❑ D. The IP address of the switch to which the destination host connects is incorrect.
    ❑ E. The host is in a different subnet.

24. Which of the following classes of IP addresses is utilized for multicasting?

    ❑ A. Class A
    ❑ B. Class B
    ❑ C. Class C
    ❑ D. Class D

25. You give your IT department a spreadsheet of IP addresses and their subnets. You receive a call from one of the junior techs asking what the /26 means next to the IP addresses. You tell her:

    ❑ A. It represents the number of hosts possible on that subnetwork.
    ❑ B. It represents the number of subnetworks that are being used.
    ❑ C. It represents the class of IP address being used.
    ❑ D. It represents the number of bits in the subnet mask that are 1.

26. You are given an IP network of 192.168.5.0 and told that you need to separate this network into subnetworks that can support a maximum of 16 hosts per subnet. This will help alleviate congestion on the network. What subnet mask can you use to create the subnets necessary to meet the given criteria?

- ❏ A. 255.0.0.0
- ❏ B. 255.255.0.0
- ❏ C. 255.255.255.0
- ❏ D. 255.255.255.224
- ❏ E. 255.255.255.240

Quick Answer: **31**
Detailed Answer: **36**

27. Which of the following would a Class A network be assigned to?

- ❏ A. Government agency
- ❏ B. Small-to-medium sized corporation
- ❏ C. SOHO
- ❏ D. An individual

Quick Answer: **31**
Detailed Answer: **36**

28. A client has the IP address 192.168.5.98/27. Which of the following addresses are on the same subnet as this host? (Choose two.)

- ❏ A. 192.168.5.95
- ❏ B. 192.168.5.100
- ❏ C. 192.168.5.128
- ❏ D. 192.168.5.110

Quick Answer: **31**
Detailed Answer: **36**

29. Which of the following IP addresses is not a public IP address that can be routed over the Internet?

- ❏ A. 2.3.4.5
- ❏ B. 11.12.13.14
- ❏ C. 165.23.224.2
- ❏ D. 172.31.45.34
- ❏ E. 203.33.45.22

Quick Answer: **31**
Detailed Answer: **36**

30. You are given a Class B network. What is the default subnet mask assigned to the Class B network?

- ❏ A. 255.255.255.255
- ❏ B. 255.255.0.0
- ❏ C. 255.224.0.0
- ❏ D. 0.0.0.0

Quick Answer: **31**
Detailed Answer: **36**

31. You are troubleshooting your router's interfaces. For some reason, the Ethernet interface will not accept the IP address of 192.168.5.95/27 that you've assigned. Which of the following explains the router's refusal to take the IP address?

    ❑ A. Class C addresses cannot be assigned to Ethernet interfaces.
    ❑ B. The /27 is an invalid mask.
    ❑ C. It is a broadcast address.
    ❑ D. It is a public IP address.
    ❑ E. It is a private IP address.

Quick Answer: **31**
Detailed Answer: **36**

32. You are a network technician at Acme, Inc. You are required to divide the 172.12.0.0 network into subnets. Each subnet must have the capacity of 458 IP addresses. Also, according to the requirements, you must provide the maximum number of subnets. Which subnet mask should you use?

    ❑ A. 255.255.255.254
    ❑ B. 255.255.254.0
    ❑ C. 255.255.240.254
    ❑ D. 255.255.0.0

Quick Answer: **31**
Detailed Answer: **37**

33. What is the subnetwork and broadcast IP address of 192.168.2.37 with the subnet mask of 255.255.255.248?

    ❑ A. 192.168.2.24/192.168.2.31
    ❑ B. 192.168.2.32/192.168.2.39
    ❑ C. 192.168.2.40/192.168.2.47
    ❑ D. 192.168.2.48/192.168.2.55
    ❑ E. 192.168.2.56/192.168.2.63

Quick Answer: **31**
Detailed Answer: **37**

34. One of your co-workers at Acme, Inc., needs to convert the binary number 11011010 into a decimal. What is the decimal equivalent?

    ❑ A. 218
    ❑ B. 219
    ❑ C. 220
    ❑ D. 221
    ❑ E. 222

Quick Answer: **31**
Detailed Answer: **37**

35. One of your co-workers at Acme, Inc., needs to convert the binary number 01011010 into a decimal. What is the decimal equivalent?

    ❑ A. 75
    ❑ B. 83
    ❑ C. 90
    ❑ D. 97

Quick Answer: **31**
Detailed Answer: **37**

36. One of your co-workers at Acme, Inc., needs to convert the binary number 11010110 into a decimal. What is the decimal equivalent?
    - ❏ A. 198
    - ❏ B. 214
    - ❏ C. 252
    - ❏ D. 255

Quick Answer: **31**
Detailed Answer: **37**

37. One of your co-workers at Acme, Inc., needs to convert the binary number 10110110 into a decimal. What is the decimal equivalent?
    - ❏ A. 182
    - ❏ B. 192
    - ❏ C. 202
    - ❏ D. 212

Quick Answer: **31**
Detailed Answer: **37**

38. You are configuring a subnet for the Acme, Inc., branch office in Beijing. You need to assign IP addresses to hosts in this subnet. You have been given the subnet mask of 255.255.255.224. Which of these IP addresses would be valid? (Choose three.)
    - ❏ A. 15.234.118.63
    - ❏ B. 92.11.178.93
    - ❏ C. 134.178.18.56
    - ❏ D. 192.168.16.87
    - ❏ E. 201.45.116.159
    - ❏ F. 217.63.12.192

Quick Answer: **31**
Detailed Answer: **37**

39. You are a network technician at Acme, Inc. You have subnetted the 208.98.112.0 network with a /28 mask. Your boss asks you how many usable subnetworks and usable host addresses per subnet this will provide. What should you tell her, assuming your router is using `ip subnet-zero`?
    - ❏ A. 62 networks and 2 hosts
    - ❏ B. 6 networks and 30 hosts
    - ❏ C. 8 networks and 32 hosts
    - ❏ D. 16 networks and 16 hosts
    - ❏ E. 16 networks and 14 hosts

Quick Answer: **31**
Detailed Answer: **37**

40. What is a disadvantage of using a connection-oriented protocol such as TCP?

    ❑ A. Packet acknowledgment might add overhead.

    ❑ B. Packets are not tagged with sequence numbers.

    ❑ C. Loss or duplication of data packets is more likely to occur.

    ❑ D. The application layer must assume responsibility for the correct sequencing of the data packets.

Quick Answer: **31**
Detailed Answer: **38**

41. You are a network technician at Acme, Inc. You have subnetted the 192.168.72.0 network with a /30 mask for connections between your routers. Your boss asks you how many usable subnetworks and usable host addresses per subnet this will provide. What should you tell her, assuming your router cannot use `ip subnet-zero`?

    ❑ A. 62 networks and 2 hosts

    ❑ B. 6 networks and 30 hosts

    ❑ C. 8 networks and 32 hosts

    ❑ D. 16 networks and 16 hosts

    ❑ E. 14 networks and 14 hosts

Quick Answer: **31**
Detailed Answer: **38**

42. Which of the following IP addresses are considered "network" addresses with a /26 prefix? (Choose two.)

    ❑ A. 165.203.2.0

    ❑ B. 165.203.5.192

    ❑ C. 165.203.6.63

    ❑ D. 165.203.6.191

    ❑ E. 165.203.8.255

Quick Answer: **31**
Detailed Answer: **38**

43. Identify three valid hosts in any subnet of 192.168.32.0, assuming the subnet mask used is 255.255.255.240. (Choose three.)

    ❑ A. 192.168.32.33

    ❑ B. 192.168.32.112

    ❑ C. 192.168.32.119

    ❑ D. 192.168.32.126

    ❑ E. 192.168.32.175

    ❑ F. 192.168.32.208

Quick Answer: **31**
Detailed Answer: **38**

Quick Check

44. A Class C network address has been subnetted with a /27 mask. Which of the following addresses is a broadcast address for one of the resulting subnets?

- ❏ A. 198.57.78.33
- ❏ B. 198.57.78.64
- ❏ C. 198.57.78.97
- ❏ D. 198.57.78.97
- ❏ E. 198.57.78.159
- ❏ F. 198.57.78.254

Quick Answer: **31**
Detailed Answer: **38**

45. What is the subnetwork address for a host with IP address 165.100.5.68/28?

- ❏ A. 165.100.5.0
- ❏ B. 165.100.5.32
- ❏ C. 165.100.5.64
- ❏ D. 165.100.5.65
- ❏ E. 165.100.5.31
- ❏ F. 165.100.5.1

Quick Answer: **31**
Detailed Answer: **39**

46. Your boss wants to know what TCP stands for. What do you tell him?

- ❏ A. Transmission Check Protocol
- ❏ B. Transport Check Protocol
- ❏ C. Transmission Control Protocol
- ❏ D. Transport Control Protocol

Quick Answer: **31**
Detailed Answer: **39**

47. Your boss wants to know what UDP stands for. What do you tell him?

- ❏ A. Unreliable Data Protocol
- ❏ B. Unreliable Data Program
- ❏ C. User-Defined Protocol
- ❏ D. User Datagram Protocol

Quick Answer: **31**
Detailed Answer: **39**

Quick Check

48. Which of the following statements accurately describes UDP?

Quick Answer: **31**
Detailed Answer: **39**

❑ A. UDP copies files between a computer and a system running rshd, the remote shell service (daemon).

❑ B. UDP is a member of the TCP/IP suite of protocols that governs the exchange of electronic mail between message transfer agents.

❑ C. UDP is a member of the TCP/IP suite of protocols and is used to copy files between two computers on the Internet. Both computers must support their respective roles: one must be a client, and the other a server.

❑ D. UDP is a TCP complement that offers a connectionless datagram service guaranteeing neither delivery nor correct sequencing of delivered packets (much like IP).

49. Which of the following host addresses are members of networks that can be routed across the public Internet? (Choose three.)

Quick Answer: **31**
Detailed Answer: **39**

❑ A. 10.20.12.64
❑ B. 172.16.32.129
❑ C. 172.64.32.34
❑ D. 192.168.23.252
❑ E. 196.104.12.95
❑ F. 214.192.48.254

50. You are connecting your Serial 0/1 interface to the Internet. Which of the following need to be done for the connection to work? (Choose two.)

Quick Answer: **31**
Detailed Answer: **39**

❑ A. Assign a public IP address.
❑ B. Use the shutdown command.
❑ C. Use the no shutdown command.
❑ D. Make sure the interface is running in full-duplex.

Quick Check Answer Key

1. D	**26.** D
2. A	**27.** A
3. C	**28.** B, D
4. D	**29.** D
5. C	**30.** B
6. D	**31.** C
7. A	**32.** B
8. A, C, D	**33.** B
9. C	**34.** A
10. A	**35.** C
11. A	**36.** B
12. C	**37.** A
13. B	**38.** B, C, D
14. B	**39.** E
15. C	**40.** A
16. A, C, D	**41.** A
17. C	**42.** A, B
18. A	**43.** A, C, D
19. B, C	**44.** E
20. A	**45.** C
21. F	**46.** C
22. A	**47.** D
23. D	**48.** D
24. D	**49.** C, E, F
25. D	**50.** A, C

Answers and Explanations

1. **Answer: D.** The default subnet mask for Class C is 255.255.255.0. A is incorrect, as it is the default mask for Class A. B is incorrect, as it is the default mask for Class B. C is incorrect, as this is not a valid mask. Subnet masks must be consecutive ones. E is not correct, as it is the subnet mask of all ones.

2. **Answer: A.** Transmission Control Protocol (TCP) provides reliable end-to-end connectivity, along with error-detection capabilities. B is incorrect, as UDP does not provide any reliability. C is incorrect, as IP does not provide reliability. D is incorrect, as ICMP is used to help troubleshoot TCP/IP connections.

3. **Answer: C.** This particular subnet mask allows for up to 62 hosts per network. A is incorrect, as it allows for 65,534 hosts. B is incorrect, as it allows up to 254 hosts. D is incorrect, as it is not a valid subnet mask.

4. **Answer: D.** The next valid IP host address in the 172.16.12.32 network is 172.16.12.34. A is incorrect, as it is on a different subnetwork with a /28 mask. B is incorrect, as it is the network address for that particular subnetwork. C is incorrect, as it is the same IP address as the router interface. E and F are incorrect as well, as they are on different subnets than the router interface. Choice G is incorrect because it represents the broadcast address for the 172.16.12.32 subnetwork and cannot be used as a host address.

5. **Answer: C.** The network address for the IP address is 172.16.208.0–255.255.240.0. A, B, and D are incorrect, as they are different subnetworks.

6. **Answer: D.** This subnet mask gives you two additional subnets using VLSM, with up to 14 hosts per subnetwork. A is incorrect, as it is a higher subnet mask than your original /26, which is actually called *supernetting*. B is incorrect because it is your original subnet mask. C is incorrect, as it does not give you enough subnets. E is incorrect, as it gives you enough subnets (six), but you would have only six hosts.

7. **Answer: A.** You have actually not done any subnetting with a /24 mask; it is the default Class C subnet mask of 255.255.255.0. This gives you one network with 254 possible hosts. B, C, and D are incorrect because you have not borrowed any bits to create subnetworks.

8. **Answers: A, C, and D.** A subnet mask of 255.255.255.240 divides the fourth octet into subnet parts: the highest four bits and a host port (the lowest four bits). You simply check the fourth octet to ensure that all subnet and host parts are okay. The host bit portion cannot be 0000 or 1111. A, C, and D are correct because 33 in decimal is 00100001, 119 in decimal is 01110111, and 126 in decimal is 1111110. B is incorrect, as 112 in decimal is 1110000 in binary. This is not a valid host address in this network. All its host bits are zero. E is incorrect, as 175 in decimal is 10101111 in binary. All host bits are ones. This is the local broadcast address and cannot be used as a host address. F is incorrect, as 208 in decimal is 11010000 in binary. This is not a valid host address in this network, and all its host bits are zero.

9. **Answer: C.** The network address would be 201.100.5.64 with a subnet mask of 255.255.255.240. A is incorrect, as it is the network address of subnet zero. B is incorrect, as it is the network address of another subnetwork. D is incorrect, as it is a valid host address on the 201.100.5.64 subnetwork. E is incorrect, as it is a broadcast address on another subnetwork. F is incorrect, as it is a valid host address on another subnetwork.

10. **Answer: A.** TCP (Transmission Control Protocol) utilizes a three-way handshake to establish a session. B is incorrect, as IP (Internet Protocol) is used at Layer 3 of the OSI Model to provide logical addressing. C is incorrect, as UDP is not reliable and does not use a three-way handshake to establish a connection. D is incorrect, as IPX is not reliable and does not use a handshake method to provide a connection. E is incorrect, as frame relay does not provide any acknowledgment or error correction.

11. **Answer: A.** TCP provides reliable, connection-oriented sessions to ensure that data is transferred correctly. B is incorrect, as IP (Internet Protocol) is used at Layer 3 of the OSI Model to provide logical addressing. C is incorrect, as IPX is not reliable and does not use a handshake method to provide a connection. D is incorrect, as frame relay does not provide any acknowledgment or error correction, and thus is unreliable and connectionless.

12. **Answer: C.** UDP (User Datagram Protocol) relies on Layer 7 (Application) to handle error detection, correction, and control. Because of the low overhead, it is a very fast protocol. A is incorrect, as TCP contains significant overhead to handle the reliable delivery of data. B is incorrect, as IP (Internet Protocol) is used at Layer 3 of the OSI Model to provide logical addressing. D is incorrect, as SPX, Novell's proprietary connection-based protocol, provides reliable delivery and thus more latency. E is incorrect, as AppleTalk is a Layer 3 protocol that deals with logical addressing.

13. **Answer: B.** Applications and operating systems have the capability to adjust the window size of TCP. The window size is the amount of data that can be sent before TCP requires an acknowledgment, or ACK. A is incorrect because adjusting the Maximum Transmission Unit merely adjusts how big the packets are or how much data they can contain. C is incorrect, as it does not exist in the TCP/IP protocol stack. D is incorrect, as the Frame Check Sequence (FCS) is used at the Data-link layer of the OSI Model to check for corrupted frames.

14. **Answer: B.** When a host receiving information misses a segment from the TCP window, it sends an ACK message that shows the next segment number it is ready to receive. If this segment number is the same as a segment that was sent, the sending host knows to resend the information. A is incorrect, as the TCP segment number is included in the ACK sent. C and D are not valid acknowledgments and are thus incorrect.

15. **Answer: C.** A Class C network can support 254 hosts. A is incorrect, as a Class A network supports more than 16 million hosts. B is incorrect, as a Class B network supports more than 65 thousand hosts. D is incorrect, as a Class D network is for use by multicast applications. E is incorrect, as Class E addresses are experimental and used only by the government and research organizations.

16. **Answers: A, C, and D.** These addresses are all part of the private ranges of 10.x.x.x and 172.16.x.x–172.31.x.x. B is incorrect, as it does not fall into any of the RFC 1918-specified private ranges. Instead, it is a public IP address that is routable on the Internet. E is incorrect, as it is not a part of the private IP address range. It falls outside the 192.168.x.x range and thus is a public IP address.

17. **Answer: C.** The subnet mask 255.255.255.224 gives you six usable subnetworks, assuming you are not using ip subnet-zero, with up to 30 available hosts per subnet. This subnet mask meets the criteria you have been given and even allows a bit of future growth. A is incorrect, as it is the default Class C subnet mask. It provides one network with 254 hosts. B is incorrect, as it gives only two subnetworks, assuming you are not using ip subnet-zero. D is incorrect, as it gives enough subnetworks but not enough hosts for the Customer Support or Engineering departments. E is incorrect, as it gives enough subnetworks but not enough hosts for most of the departments.

18. **Answer: A.** User Datagram Protocol (UDP) relies on the applications to provide error correction or detection. B is incorrect, as TCP is reliable and provides connection-oriented sessions. C is incorrect, as SNMP is a management protocol used by devices to communicate information to a management system such as CiscoWorks or HP's OpenView. D is incorrect, as ICMP is used by such troubleshooting utilities as ping and traceroute.

19. **Answers: B and C.** TCP numbers the sequence of the segments sent out to ensure that all data arrives safely. The receiving side must send back acknowledgments that all segments were received. If it sends back negative acknowledgments, TCP resends the data. A is incorrect, as Address Resolution Protocol (ARP) or Inverse ARP provide MAC address resolution. D is incorrect, as ping is a utility that checks TCP/IP connectivity. E is incorrect, as routing updates are used by routing protocols such as RIP or OSPF to update information stored on another router's routing table.

20. **Answer: A.** By using windowing, you can increase the amount of data sent before an ACK is sent back by the receiving side. This increases throughput. B is incorrect, as increasing window size increases, not decreases, throughput. C is incorrect, as increasing window size decreases latency. D is incorrect, as the protocol still requires an ACK to be sent by the receiving side. This does not decrease reliability in the slightest.

21. **Answer: F.** The 255.255.255.248 subnet mask used on a Class C IP network produces 30 usable subnets. A is incorrect; it does not create any subnets, as it is the default Class C subnet mask. B is incorrect, as it creates only 2 subnets—that is, if the IOS recognizes IP subnet zero. C is incorrect, as 255.255.255.192 creates only 2 usable subnets. D is incorrect, as 255.255.255.224 creates only 6 usable subnets. E is incorrect, as 255.255.255.240 creates only 14 usable subnets.

22. **Answer: A.** Address Resolution Protocol (ARP) resolves IP addresses to MAC addresses. B is incorrect, as Reverse Address Resolution Protocol (RARP) resolves MAC addresses to IP addresses, thus the "reverse." C is incorrect, as Serial Line Address Resolution Protocol (SLARP) automatically assigns IP addresses to serial interfaces if AutoInstall is being used and HDLC is the protocol in use on that interface. D is incorrect, as DHCP automatically assigns IP addresses to interfaces.

23. **Answer: D.** The IP address of a Layer 2 switch is strictly for management purposes and doesn't affect Layer 3 connectivity. A, B, and C are incorrect, as they are valid reasons why a user cannot ping a remote host. E is incorrect because a remote host is in a different subnet by definition.

24. **Answer: D.** According to the IETF, the Class D IP address range is used for multicast group addresses. A is incorrect, as Class A addresses are used by large corporations and governments for unicast purposes. B is incorrect, as Class B addresses are used by large-to-medium corporations and service providers for unicast purposes. C is incorrect, as service providers, users, and small businesses use Class C addresses for unicast purposes. Unicast is based on one-to-one communication, whereas multicast is used for one-to-many communication.

25. **Answer: D.** Prefix notation, or / notation, shows the number of subnet mask bits that are turned to one, signifying a network portion of the address. A is incorrect, as it does not show the number of hosts on a subnetwork. B is incorrect, as it does not show the number of subnetworks in use. C is incorrect because, even though you can figure out whether it is a Class A, B, or C address based on the prefixes of /8, /16, or /24, it does not necessarily show the class of the address.

26. **Answer: D.** The custom subnet mask of 255.255.255.224 gives you 30 hosts. Even though this number exceeds the requested 16, if you borrow an additional bit, you have only 14 available hosts. A, B, and C do not give you any subnets at all, and thus are incorrect. E is incorrect, as it gives you only 14 available hosts.

27. **Answer: A.** Class A networks have all been assigned to governments and extremely large corporations. B is incorrect, as small-to-medium size companies would receive only a Class C network. C and D are incorrect, as a small office/home office (SOHO) or individual would not receive a network—only a few IP addresses from a Class C network.

28. **Answers: B and D.** The address 192.168.5.98/27 has a decimal subnet mask of 255.255.255.224 and uses an increment of 32. This ends up making the network range 192.168.5.96–192.168.5.127. Answer A is incorrect because this is the broadcast address of the previous subnet. Answer C is incorrect because it is the network address of the following subnet.

29. **Answer: D.** The IP address 172.31.45.34 is part of the RFC 1918-defined private IP address range for a Class B network. A, B, C, and E are incorrect, as they are all public IP addresses that can be routed on the Internet.

30. **Answer: B.** The default Class B subnet mask is 255.255.0.0, or /16 in prefix notation. A is incorrect, as it shows a broadcast. C is incorrect, as it is a custom subnet mask, more than likely used for a Class A network. D is incorrect, as it is a special mask typically used for default routes.

31. **Answer: C.** It is not a valid host address; 192.168.5.95/27 is a directed broadcast address for the 192.168.5.64 network. A is incorrect, as you can certainly assign Class C addresses to any type of interface. B is incorrect, as the /27 mask is the 255.255.255.224 subnet mask, which is perfectly valid. D is incorrect because it is a private IP address. E is incorrect, as the fact that it is a private IP address will not cause it to be refused by an interface.

32. **Answer: B.** This gives you 126 subnets, assuming you are not using `ip subnet-zero`, with 510 hosts per subnet. A is incorrect, as it does not provide you with enough hosts to meet the criteria. C is incorrect, as it is an invalid subnet mask. Subnet masks must have contiguous ones. D is incorrect, as it is the default Class B subnet mask, and as such, you would not have any subnets.

33. **Answer: B.** The address 192.168.2.37 is a valid host address on the 192.168.2.32 network, which has a directed broadcast address of 192.168.2.39. A, C, and D are incorrect, as 192.168.2.37 does not fall on any of those subnetworks with the given subnet mask.

34. **Answer: A.** The number 11011010 = 218 in decimal. B is incorrect, as 11011011 = 219. C is incorrect, as 11011100 = 220. D is incorrect, as 11011101 = 221.

35. **Answer: C.** The number 01011010 = 90 in decimal. A is incorrect, as 01001011 = 75. B is incorrect, as 01010011 = 83. D is incorrect, as 01100001 = 97.

36. **Answer: B.** The number 11010110 = 214 in decimal. A is incorrect, as 11000110 = 198. C is incorrect, as 11111100 = 252. D is incorrect, as 11111111 = 255.

37. **Answer: A.** The number 10110110 = 182 in decimal. B is incorrect, as 11000000 = 192. C is incorrect, as 11001010 = 202. D is incorrect, as 11010100 = 212.

38. **Answers: B, C, and D.** They are valid host addresses when using a 255.255.255.224 subnet mask against the address. A is incorrect, as it is a broadcast address on the 16.234.118.32 network. E is incorrect, as it is a broadcast address on the 210.45.116.128 network. F is incorrect, as it is the network address for 237.63.12.192.

39. **Answer: E.** The 255.255.255.248, or /28 subnet mask, gives you 16 subnetworks and 14 usable hosts, using the 2^n formula for subnets and $(2^n - 2)$ formula for usable hosts, where n equals the number of bits borrowed for the subnet, or number of bits left for the hosts. You are able to use the first and last subnetworks because of the `ip subnet-zero` command on your router. A is incorrect, as it would be a /30 mask. B is incorrect, as it would be a /27 mask. C is incorrect, as there would never be 32 hosts per subnet; you always have to subtract 2 from the 2^n formula because of the network ID and the directed broadcast address on each subnetwork. D is incorrect, as you would never have 16 hosts per subnet; you always have to subtract 2 from the 2^n formula because of the network ID and the directed broadcast address on each subnetwork.

40. **Answer: A.** TCP adds overhead with acknowledgments and session hand-shakes. B is incorrect, as TCP tags with sequence numbers. C is incorrect, as TCP is reliable and ensures data delivery. D is incorrect, as TCP has built-in mechanisms to handle sequencing and delivery and does not require the appli-cation's assistance.

41. **Answer: A.** The mask /30 gives you 62 subnetworks and two available hosts per subnet using the (2^n [ms] 2) formula, where n equals the number of bits borrowed for the subnet, or number of bits left for the hosts. Because the router is not using `ip subnet-zero`, you cannot use the first or last subnet, which is why you subtract 2 from both the subnetworks and hosts. B is incor-rect, as that would be a /27 mask. C is incorrect, as there would never be 32 hosts per subnet; you always have to subtract 2 from the 2^n formula because of the network ID and the directed broadcast address on each subnetwork. D is incorrect, as you would never have 16 hosts per subnet; you always have to sub-tract 2 from the 2^n formula because of the network ID and the directed broadcast address on each subnetwork. E is incorrect, as the /28 subnet mask gives you 14 subnetworks and 14 possible hosts.

42. **Answers: A and B.** They are considered network ID addresses. They have all zeros in the host portion of the IP address with the subnet mask given. C, D, and E are incorrect, as they are all directed Broadcast Addresses on subnets.

43. **Answers: A, C, and D.** A subnet mask of 255.255.255.240 divides the fourth octet into subnet parts: the highest four bits and a host port (the lowest four bits). You simply check the fourth octet to ensure that all subnet and host parts are okay. The host bit portion cannot be 0000 or 1111. A, C, and D are correct because 33 in decimal is 00100001, 119 in decimal is 01110111, and 126 in decimal is 1111110. B is incorrect, as 112 in decimal is 1110000 in binary, which is not a valid host address in this network—all host bits are zero. E is incorrect, as 175 in decimal is 10101111 in binary—all host bits are ones. This is the local broadcast address and cannot be used as a host address. F is incor-rect, as 208 in decimal is 11010000 in binary. This is not a valid host address in this network, as it has all host bits of zero.

44. **Answer: E.** The fourth byte in the IP address is 159, the binary value of which is 1011111. So, this is the broadcast address for 198.57.78.0/27 network. A is incorrect, as the binary value for 33 is 00100001. B is incorrect, as the binary value for 64 is 01000000. C and D are incorrect, as the binary value for 97 is 01100001. F is incorrect, as the binary value for 254 is 11111110. These are not broadcast addresses for the 198.57.78.0/27 network.

45. **Answer: C.** If you use the subnet mask prefix value /28, 4 bits are left for the host portion. The total number of hosts is 16 (2 are reserved for network and broadcast in each subnetwork). The 165.100.5.68 host resides in subnetwork 165.100.5.64. Valid hosts in this network are 165.100.5.65–165.100.5.79. A is incorrect, as it is the network address for the first subnet, also known as subnet 0. B is incorrect, as it is the network address for 165.100.5.32. Valid hosts are 165.100.5.33–165.100.5.46. D is incorrect, as it is one of the valid hosts in subnetwork 165.100.5.64. E is incorrect, as it is the broadcast address. F is incorrect, as it is a valid host in subnetwork 165.100.5.0.

46. **Answer: C.** TCP stands for Transmission Control Protocol. A, B, and D are incorrect, as they are nonexisting protocols.

47. **Answer: D.** UDP stands for User Datagram Protocol. It is part of the TCP/IP protocol suite and operates at Layer 4 of the OSI Model. A, B, and C name nonexistent protocols or programs.

48. **Answer: D.** UDP relies on applications to provide error correction and reliability of transmission. A is incorrect, as it describes Remote Copy Protocol (RCP). B is incorrect, as it describes Simple Mail Transfer Protocol (SMTP). C is incorrect, as it describes File Transfer Protocol (FTP).

49. **Answers: C, E, and F.** These addresses are not private addresses defined by RFC 1918. These addresses can be routed across the public Internet. A is incorrect, as it is part of the private range of 10.x.x.x. B is incorrect, as it is part of the private range of 172.16.x.x–172.16.31.x.x. D is incorrect, as it is part of the private range of 192.168.x.x.

50. **Answers: A and C.** A is correct because you must have a public IP address assigned to your interface to be able to communicate across the Internet. C is correct, as you must turn on the interface by using the no shutdown command. B is incorrect, as you must turn on the interface, not disable it with the shutdown command. D is incorrect, as duplex settings are not valid on serial interfaces, only on Ethernet interfaces.

Basic IOS Configuration and Basic Serial WAN Connectivity

Quick Check

1. In which of the following modes in Cisco's IOS can you issue show commands? (Choose two.)

   ❑ A. User
   ❑ B. Privileged
   ❑ C. Line Configuration
   ❑ D. Global Configuration

Quick Answer: **55**
Detailed Answer: **56**

2. You are the network administrator for a large corporation. You want to be able to store all your configurations in a centralized location. Which of these servers will allow you to do so? (Choose two.)

   ❑ A. FTP
   ❑ B. TFTP
   ❑ C. SQL
   ❑ D. Oracle

Quick Answer: **55**
Detailed Answer: **56**

3. You need to troubleshoot your network IP connectivity. Which of the following commands would you use to find the IP address on your Ethernet 0 interface?

   ❑ A. ping
   ❑ B. IPConfig
   ❑ C. traceroute
   ❑ D. Show interface Ethernet 0

Quick Answer: **55**
Detailed Answer: **56**

4. Which command would you use at the CLI in User mode to enter Privileged EXEC mode?

   ❑ A. Privilege
   ❑ B. Admin
   ❑ C. Enable
   ❑ D. Disable

Quick Answer: **55**
Detailed Answer: **56**

5. You have just received 14 Catalyst switches for your network. You would like to install these switches into your production network to provide separate collision domains for each of the connected devices. What configuration is required to provide this functionality?

   ❑ A. No configuration is required.
   ❑ B. You must set up an IP address on the switch.
   ❑ C. You must configure unique VLANs on the switches.
   ❑ D. You must install the Cisco IOS.

Quick Answer: **55**
Detailed Answer: **56**

6. Which of the following prompts indicates your router is in Privileged EXEC mode?

   ❑ A. `Router>`
   ❑ B. `Router#`
   ❑ C. `Router&`
   ❑ D. `Router$`

Quick Answer: **55**
Detailed Answer: **56**

7. You have made a console connection to your Cisco Catalyst switch and you see the > symbol in HyperTerminal. What does it mean?

   ❑ A. You are in Privileged EXEC mode.
   ❑ B. You are in User EXEC mode.
   ❑ C. The switch has not been configured.
   ❑ D. The switch is in need of repairs.

Quick Answer: **55**
Detailed Answer: **56**

8. You would like to assign a meaningful name to your Catalyst switch. What command should you use?

   ❑ A. `enable`
   ❑ B. `host name`
   ❑ C. `hostname`
   ❑ D. `name`

Quick Answer: **55**
Detailed Answer: **56**

9. You need to assign an IP address to your Catalyst 2950 switch. You are at the `HQ_SW1>` prompt. What is the correct series of commands? (cr = carriage return)

   ❑ A. `enable <cr> ip address 10.1.1.1`
   ❑ B. `enable <cr> ip address 10.1.1.1 255.255.255.0`
   ❑ C. `enable <cr> configure terminal <cr> ip address 10.1.1.1 255.255.255.0`
   ❑ D. `enable <cr> configure terminal <cr> interface vlan 1 <cr> ip address 10.1.1.1 255.255.255.0`

Quick Answer: **55**
Detailed Answer: **57**

10. Which of the following commands displays the syntax for the clock command?

Quick Answer: **55**
Detailed Answer: **57**

   ❏   A. cl?
   ❏   B. clock?
   ❏   C. clock ?
   ❏   D. cl ?

11. Which of the following commands allows you to configure a welcoming message whenever you log in to a router?

Quick Answer: **55**
Detailed Answer: **57**

   ❏   A. Router(config)# banner message
   ❏   B. Router(config)# banner motd &
   ❏   C. Router# banner motd #
   ❏   D. Router# banner message !

12. You need to connect to your 2621XM router to configure an interface. Which of the following methods allows you to connect to and issue commands on the router? (Choose three.)

Quick Answer: **55**
Detailed Answer: **57**

   ❏   A. Telnet
   ❏   B. FTP
   ❏   C. Console connection
   ❏   D. AUX connection

13. You want to prevent unauthorized users from plugging their laptops into the router. What type of password helps prevent this issue?

Quick Answer: **55**
Detailed Answer: **57**

   ❏   A. vty
   ❏   B. Interface
   ❏   C. Console
   ❏   D. Enable

14. You have connected to the console port and are running HyperTerminal. You see only scrambled characters and symbols. What is the most likely solution to this problem?

Quick Answer: **55**
Detailed Answer: **57**

   ❏   A. Change the connectors.
   ❏   B. Use a different Terminal program.
   ❏   C. Reset the router.
   ❏   D. Adjust the baud rate of your COM port.

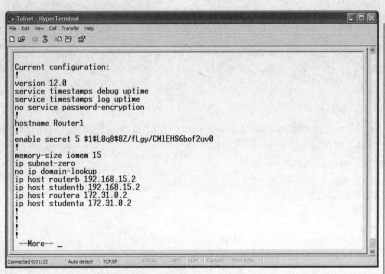

15. Which of the following commands would you type to receive this output shown in the figure above?

 ❑ A. Show running-config

 ❑ B. Show startup-config

 ❑ C. Show ip route

 ❑ D. Show version

Quick Answer: **55**
Detailed Answer: **57**

16. You are configuring a router named East for authentication with a router named West using CHAP. What username should you configure on East to allow the routers to communicate?

 ❑ A. East

 ❑ B. West

 ❑ C. South

 ❑ D. North

Quick Answer: **55**
Detailed Answer: **58**

17. What is the default point-to-point encapsulation protocol used on a Cisco router?

 ❑ A. PPP

 ❑ B. SLIP

 ❑ C. HDLC

 ❑ D. ATM

Quick Answer: **55**
Detailed Answer: **58**

18. What type of handshake occurs with CHAP authentication?

   ❏ A. One-way

   ❏ B. Two-way

   ❏ C. Three-way

   ❏ D. Mutual

Quick Answer: **55**
Detailed Answer: **58**

19. You have connected to your Cisco router through a Telnet connection. To test one of your connections, you use a `debug ip packet` command. Even though you are sure traffic is passing through your router, nothing is reported in your terminal window. What is the most likely cause of this problem?

   ❏ A. There is no `debug ip packet` command.

   ❏ B. You need to type in the `terminal monitor` command to see debug output from a Telnet session.

   ❏ C. This command displays information only if the interface experiences trouble. No output indicates that the interface is fine.

   ❏ D. Cisco routers do not allow you to enable `debug` commands remotely due to security restrictions.

Quick Answer: **55**
Detailed Answer: **58**

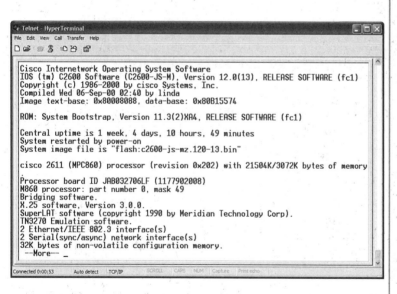

Quick Check

20. Which of the following commands would you type to see this output on your Cisco router shown in the previous figure?

❑ A. Show version

❑ B. Show running-config

❑ C. Show startup-config

❑ D. Show router setup

Quick Answer: **55**

Detailed Answer: **58**

```
Telnet - HyperTerminal
File  Edit  View  Call  Transfer  Help

Interface        IP-Address      OK? Method Status        Protocol
Ethernet0/0      1.1.1.1         YES NVRAM  up            down
Serial0/0        172.31.0.1      YES NVRAM  up            up
Ethernet0/1      172.16.0.10     YES NVRAM  up            up
Serial0/1        192.168.15.1    YES NVRAM  up            up
Loopback10       unassigned      YES unset  up            up
Loopback674      unassigned      YES unset  up            up
Central#
Central#
Central#
Central#
Central#
Central#
Central#
Central#
Central#
Central#_

Connected 0:06:03   Auto detect   TCP/IP        SCROLL   CAPS   NUM   Capture   Print echo
```

21. Which of the following commands would you type to see this output shown in the figure above?

❑ A. Show interface Ethernet 0/0

❑ B. Show ip interface detail

❑ C. Show interface Serial 0/1

❑ D. Show ip interface brief

Quick Answer: **55**

Detailed Answer: **58**

Quick Check

```
Serial0/1 is up, line protocol is Down
  Hardware is PowerQUICC Serial
  Description: connected to StudentB
  Internet address is 10.0.0.2/8
  MTU 1500 bytes, BW 1544 Kbit, DLY 20000 usec, rely 255/255, load 1/255
  Encapsulation HDLC, loopback not set, keepalive set (10 sec)
  Last input 00:00:06, output 00:00:06, output hang never
  Last clearing of "show interface" counters never
  Input queue: 0/75/0 (size/max/drops); Total output drops: 0
  Queueing strategy: weighted fair
  Output queue: 0/1000/64/0 (size/max total/threshold/drops)
     Conversations  0/1/256 (active/max active/max total)
     Reserved Conversations 0/0 (allocated/max allocated)
  5 minute input rate 0 bits/sec, 0 packets/sec
  5 minute output rate 0 bits/sec, 0 packets/sec
     116459 packets input, 7366332 bytes, 0 no buffer
     Received 115397 broadcasts, 0 runts, 0 giants, 0 throttles
     1 input errors, 0 CRC, 1 frame, 0 overrun, 0 ignored, 0 abort
     116606 packets output, 7375122 bytes, 0 underruns
     0 output errors, 0 collisions, 2 interface resets
     0 output buffer failures, 0 output buffers swapped out
     2 carrier transitions
     DCD=up  DSR=up  DTR=up  RTS=up  CTS=up
--More-- _
```

```
Serial0/1 is up, line protocol is down
  Hardware is PowerQUICC Serial
  Description: connected to Student
  Internet address is 10.0.0.1/8
  MTU 1500 bytes, BW 1544 Kbit, DLY 20000 usec, rely 255/255, load 1/255
  Encapsulation PPP, loopback not set, keepalive set (10 sec)
  LCP REQsent
  Closed: IPCP, CDPCP
  Last input 00:00:04, output 00:00:00, output hang never
  Last clearing of "show interface" counters never
  Input queue: 0/75/0 (size/max/drops); Total output drops: 0
  Queueing strategy: weighted fair
  Output queue: 0/1000/64/0 (size/max total/threshold/drops)
     Conversations  0/1/256 (active/max active/max total)
     Reserved Conversations 0/0 (allocated/max allocated)
  5 minute input rate 0 bits/sec, 0 packets/sec
  5 minute output rate 0 bits/sec, 0 packets/sec
     116775 packets input, 7382936 bytes, 0 no buffer
     Received 115454 broadcasts, 0 runts, 0 giants, 0 throttles
     10 input errors, 0 CRC, 10 frame, 0 overrun, 0 ignored, 0 abort
     116596 packets output, 7372890 bytes, 0 underruns
     0 output errors, 0 collisions, 17 interface resets
     0 output buffer failures, 0 output buffers swapped out
--More--
```

22. Your routers at ACME, Inc., are having some connectivity issues. You issue show commands for each connecting router's interface. Why are they unable to communicate (see figures above)?

❑ A. Incorrect IP address
❑ B. Wrong routing protocol
❑ C. Bad cable
❑ D. Encapsulation mismatch

Quick Answer: 55
Detailed Answer: 59

23. You need to back up the configurations you just made, but no TFTP servers are available. Which of the following commands are options to back up your currently running configuration? (Choose two.)

   ❑ A. `Router1#copy running-config startup-config`

   ❑ B. `Router1#copy running-config flash`

   ❑ C. `Router1#copy startup-config running-config`

   ❑ D. `Router1#copy running-config http`

24. You are consulting a small business that is establishing its first WAN link. The client wants to know what encapsulation you will be using on the link. Which of the following are valid encapsulations for WAN links? (Choose three.)

   ❑ A. Frame relay

   ❑ B. Ethernet

   ❑ C. Token ring

   ❑ D. PPP

   ❑ E. HDLC

25. Your boss is concerned about security on your network. She wants to make sure that no one can identify passwords if he or she happens to view a configuration on your router. What command encrypts all passwords on your router?

   ❑ A. `Router1#service password-encryption`

   ❑ B. `Router1(config)#service password-encryption`

   ❑ C. `Router1#enable secret password`

   ❑ D. `Router1(config)#enable secret password`

26. You need to set up a password that will prevent unauthorized users from telnetting into your router. What series of commands would you use?

   ❑ A. `Acme1(config)# line console 0`

       `Acme1(config-line)# password acme`

       `Acme1(config-line)# login`

   ❑ B. `Acme1(config)# line vty 0`

       `Acme1(config-line)# enable password acme`

   ❑ C. `Acme1(config)# line vty 0`

       `Acme1(config-line)# enable secret acme`

       `Acme1(config-line)# login`

   ❑ D. `Acme1(config)# line vty 0`

       `Acme1(config-line)# password acme`

       `Acme1(config-line)# login`

27. When you are setting up your serial interfaces, what does the clockrate command do for your connection?

    ❏   A. Establishes the timing at which you send data
    ❏   B. Establishes keepalives
    ❏   C. Establishes the advertised bandwidth
    ❏   D. Establishes the time on the router

28. You need to set up passwords on all your default Telnet lines. What command would you start with?

    ❏   A. `Router1(config)#telnet configuration`
    ❏   B. `Router1(config)#interface Ethernet 0/1`
    ❏   C. `Router1(config)#line vty 1 5`
    ❏   D. `Router1(config)#line vty 0 4`

29. You can execute show commands at which prompt? (Choose two.)

    ❏   A. `Router1#`
    ❏   B. `Router1(config)#`
    ❏   C. `Router1(config-router)#`
    ❏   D. `Router1>`
    ❏   E. `romon1>`

30. You are configuring your router and type in an Enable password and an Enable Secret password. Your fellow network technician asks you why you have two passwords set when you need only one. What do you tell him?

    ❏   A. The Enable password is used by low-level applications.
    ❏   B. If you reverted to an older version of the IOS, it would not understand the Secret password.
    ❏   C. Both passwords are treated the same.
    ❏   D. It is a failsafe method of ensuring that people need to type two passwords instead of just one.

31. You need to get back to Privileged EXEC mode from Interface Configuration mode. What is the quickest method?

    ❏   A. Ctrl+Shift+6; then press X
    ❏   B. Ctrl+Esc
    ❏   C. Ctrl+Z
    ❏   D. Type exit

Quick Check

32. When you are establishing a PPP link, which of the following would be negotiated? (Choose three.)

    ❏ A. IPCP
    ❏ B. CHAP
    ❏ C. UDP
    ❏ D. Q.931
    ❏ E. Multilink Protocol

Quick Answer: **55**
Detailed Answer: **60**

33. Which of the following commands returns your router to a previously saved configuration?

    ❏ A. `Router1#setup`
    ❏ B. `Router1#copy running-config startup-config`
    ❏ C. `Router1#copy startup-config running-config`
    ❏ D. `Router1#reload`

Quick Answer: **55**
Detailed Answer: **60**

34. You are in Interface Configuration mode and would like to recall the last command you typed, move your cursor to the beginning of the command line, and type no before the recalled command. You notice your up- and down-arrow keys do not function because you are using an older terminal program. What command combinations could you use to recall the previous command and move your cursor to the beginning of the line?

    ❏ Press Ctrl+P to recall the previous command and Ctrl+A to move to the beginning of the command line.
    ❏ Press Ctrl+L to recall the previous command and Ctrl+B to move to the beginning of the command line.
    ❏ Press Ctrl+D to recall the previous command and Ctrl+A to move to the beginning of the command line.
    ❏ Press Ctrl+E to recall the previous command and Ctrl+A to move to the beginning of the command line.

Quick Answer: **55**
Detailed Answer: **61**

35. What is the baud rate setting for your terminal emulation program so that you can communicate through your console port?

    ❏ A. 2400
    ❏ B. 9600
    ❏ C. 14400
    ❏ D. 36300

Quick Answer: **55**
Detailed Answer: **61**

Quick Check

36. What must be configured on a Cisco device to enable Telnet functionality?

   ❑ A. A management IP address
   ❑ B. SNMP
   ❑ C. CDP
   ❑ D. vty ports

Quick Answer: **55**
Detailed Answer: **61**

37. You are configuring your Cisco router and need to go back to User EXEC mode. What command takes you back to User EXEC mode?

   ❑ A. Router1#enable
   ❑ B. Router1#exit
   ❑ C. Router1#configure terminal
   ❑ D. Router1#disable

Quick Answer: **55**
Detailed Answer: **61**

38. Which of the following commands places an IP address on your Catalyst switch?

   ❑ A. Switch1#ip address 10.2.2.2 255.255.255.0
   ❑ B. Switch1(config)#Set IP 10.2.2.2 255.255.255.0
   ❑ C. Switch1(config-vlan)#ip address 10.2.2.2
   ❑ D. Switch1(config-vlan)#ip address 10.2.2.2 255.255.255.0

Quick Answer: **55**
Detailed Answer: **61**

```
System flash directory:
File  Length   Name/status
  1   6295616  c2600-js-mz.120-13.bin
  2   1602     central-confg
  3   942      studenta-confg
  4   924      studentb-confg
  5   58       network-confg
  6   2414     blah
[6301948 bytes used, 2086660 available, 8388608 total]
8192K bytes of processor board System flash (Read/Write)

Central#_
```

39. Which of the following commands would you enter to receive this output shown in the figure above?

   ❑ A. Router1#show NVRAM
   ❑ B. Router1#show Flash
   ❑ C. Router1#show Flash-Mem
   ❑ D. Router1#show Version

Quick Answer: **55**
Detailed Answer: **61**

Quick Check

40. Your senior network administrator is unable to telnet to a Catalyst switch because she forgot the IP address. You have physical access and are able to console in. Which of the following commands is the best to get the IP address on the switch?

Quick Answer: 55
Detailed Answer: 61

❑ A. `Switch1#show ip`
❑ B. `Switch1#show vlan 1`
❑ C. `Switch1#show ip route`
❑ D. `Switch1#show interface vlan1`

```
        --- System Configuration Dialog ---
Continue with configuration dialog? [yes/no]: yes

At any point you may enter a question mark '?' for help.
Use ctrl-c to abort configuration dialog at any prompt.
Default settings are in square brackets '[]'.

Basic management setup configures only enough connectivity
for management of the system, extended setup will ask you
to configure each interface on the system

Would you like to enter basic management setup? [yes/no]: _
```

41. You have powered up your Cisco 3640 router. The first thing you see is this output. Which of the following statements about this screen is accurate (see figure above)?

Quick Answer: 55
Detailed Answer: 62

❑ A. Your IOS is corrupt and unable to load.
❑ B. Your configuration is missing parameters.
❑ C. You do not have a configuration saved in NVRAM.
❑ D. You have typed setup in the Privileged mode.

42. You type in a command and are shown the following output:

`% Ambiguous command: "show con"`

Quick Answer: 55
Detailed Answer: 62

What does this mean?

❑ A. You did not enter enough characters for your device to recognize the command.
❑ B. You did not enter all the keywords or values required by this command.
❑ C. You entered the command incorrectly.
❑ D. Context-sensitive help is unable to help you with this command.

43. You are typing a command into the Cisco IOS. It is more than one terminal line long. What will the IOS do?

 ❑ A. The router automatically moves the cursor to the next line and uses a caret (^) to indicate the line break.

 ❑ B. The router truncates the command because commands longer than one line are not allowed.

 ❑ C. The router automatically scrolls the line to the left and uses a dollar sign ($) to indicate that there is text to the left of the $.

 ❑ D. The router shortens all the commands to squeeze the command on to the screen.

44. You want to change the size of the command history buffer. Which of the following commands will set it permanently to 100?

 ❑ A. `Router1#terminal history 100`

 ❑ B. `Router1#history size 100`

 ❑ C. `Router1(config)#terminal history 100`

 ❑ D. `Router1(config-line)#history size 100`

45. You have configured a description on your serial interfaces. Which of the following commands displays the description? (Choose two.)

 ❑ A. `Show running-config`

 ❑ B. `Show flash`

 ❑ C. `Show interfaces`

 ❑ D. `Show ip protocols`

46. You are typing commands into your Cisco IOS on your 3640 router. However, your typing is consistently interrupted by console messages, forcing you to retype. Which of the following commands forces the IOS to retype your original input after it displays the console message?

 ❑ A. `Exec-timeout`

 ❑ B. `Logging synchronous`

 ❑ C. `Line console`

 ❑ D. `Exec message readout`

47. You are configuring a router and issue the command `inter-face ethernet 1/0/0`. What do the numbers represent?

 ❑ A. Slot/port/interface

 ❑ B. Slot/interface/port

 ❑ C. Port/slot/port number

 ❑ D. Slot/port adapter/port number

48. Which of the following commands correctly sets the physical speed of a serial interface to 64Kbps?

   ❏ A. `Router1(config-if)#bandwidth 64`
   ❏ B. `Router1(config-if)#bandwidth 64000`
   ❏ C. `Router1(config-if)#clockrate 64`
   ❏ D. `Router1(config-if)#clockrate 64000`

Quick Answer: **55**
Detailed Answer: **62**

49. In what mode do you use the `encapsulation` command?

   ❏ A. Interface Configuration mode
   ❏ B. Sub-interface Configuration mode
   ❏ C. User mode
   ❏ D. Privileged mode

Quick Answer: **55**
Detailed Answer: **63**

50. You are configuring your router, and your boss happens to look over your shoulder as you type a `show running-config` command. She sees one of the lines that says `password 7 14361F009A056E7D` and asks what this means. What do you tell her?

   ❏ A. It is the actual password.
   ❏ B. It is the result of a service password-encryption command.
   ❏ C. The console output made a mistake.
   ❏ D. It is the result of an `enable secret` command.

Quick Answer: **55**
Detailed Answer: **63**

Quick Check Answer Key

1. A, B
2. A, B
3. D
4. C
5. A
6. B
7. B
8. C
9. D
10. C
11. B
12. A, C, D
13. C
14. D
15. A
16. B
17. C
18. C
19. B
20. A
21. D
22. D
23. A, B
24. A, D, E
25. B

26. D
27. A
28. D
29. A, D
30. B
31. C
32. A, B, E
33. D
34. A
35. B
36. A
37. D
38. D
39. B
40. D
41. C
42. A
43. C
44. D
45. A, C
46. B
47. D
48. D
49. A
50. B

Answers and Explanations

1. **Answers: A and B.** You can issue show or debug commands in either User EXEC or Privileged mode. C is incorrect, as you cannot use show commands while in Line Configuration mode. D is incorrect, as you cannot use show commands while in Global Configuration mode.

2. **Answers: A and B.** You can store Cisco device configurations on FTP and TFTP servers. TFTP is preferred because of its lower overhead. C is incorrect, as SQL databases do not store Cisco device configurations. D is incorrect, as Oracle databases are not used to store Cisco device configurations.

3. **Answer: D.** The show interface command gives you all the physical and logical configuration information about a particular interface. A is incorrect, as ping is a TCP/IP utility that allows you to "ping" a connection to see whether there is connectivity. B is incorrect, as this is the command you use on a Microsoft Windows PC to find your IP address. C is incorrect, as the traceroute command allows you to track the packet's path to its destination.

4. **Answer: C.** You type enable to enter Privileged EXEC mode. A is incorrect, as it is not a valid command. B is incorrect, as it is not a valid command. D is incorrect, as this command takes you out of Privileged EXEC mode.

5. **Answer: A.** The Catalyst switches have default configurations set up so that they can perform their basic switching roles (which provides separate collision domains for the attached devices) without any further configurations. B is incorrect, as setting up an IP address assists you in remote management via Telnet, but isn't required. C is incorrect because VLANs create separate broadcast domains, not collision domains. D is incorrect, as the Cisco IOS is not required for switches to function. In fact, some low-end Catalyst switches do not have the IOS running.

6. **Answer: B.** The prompt Router# indicates the router is in Privileged EXEC mode. A is incorrect, as this prompt indicates that you are in User EXEC mode. C is incorrect, as this is not a valid prompt. D is incorrect, as this is not a valid prompt.

7. **Answer: B.** The > tells you that you are in User EXEC mode. A is incorrect, as you are not in Privileged EXEC mode. C is incorrect, as you can have the User EXEC mode prompt without configuring anything. D is incorrect, as the > prompt does not indicate any hardware failures.

8. **Answer: C.** The hostname command assigns a name to your device. A is incorrect, as enable gets you into Privileged EXEC mode on the switch. B is incorrect, as the hostname command is one word, not two. D is incorrect, as this is not a valid command.

9. **Answer: D.** You must place the Management IP address on the Management VLAN, which is VLAN 1, by default. A and B are incorrect because you cannot configure IP address settings while in Privileged mode. Answer C is incorrect. Although this syntax was used to assign an IP address to a Catalyst 1900 switch, this series of switch has long since been discontinued from Cisco's product line.

10. **Answer: C.** The command `clock ?` gives you all the parameters (syntax) that follow after the `Clock` main command. A is incorrect, as `cl?` simply tells you what commands start with `cl`. B is incorrect, as the IOS attempts to clarify all commands that start with `clock`, which is the actual command here. D is incorrect because you get an `invalid command` error message.

11. **Answer: B.** The command `banner motd [delimiting character]` is what sets up a displayed message when you log in to a router. In this case, you use the command `banner motd &`, indicating that you will use the `&` sign to signal the end of your logon banner. A is incorrect, as the command is `banner motd`. C is incorrect, as you must issue the command in Global Configuration mode, not Privileged mode. D is incorrect, as that is an invalid command.

12. **Answers: A, C, and D.** You can telnet into a Cisco router if you know the IP address of one of the interfaces or the name of the router with DNS running. You can connect with a rollover cable to the Console port. You can also dial in via modem through an AUX port. B is incorrect, as FTP merely allows you to download a configuration.

13. **Answer: C.** The console password requires anyone who attempts to plug a rollover serial cable into the console port to provide a password to log on. A is incorrect, as a vty is a virtual port or Telnet port. B is incorrect, as there are no interface passwords. D is incorrect, as the `Enable` password prevents unauthorized users from entering privileged mode.

14. **Answer: D.** You probably have the baud rate set too low or too high. The baud rate for your PC's COM port needs to be configured at 9600bps. A is incorrect, as you must use an RJ-45 rollover cable. You cannot change the connectors. B is incorrect, as you will more than likely encounter the same issue with any other terminal program. C is incorrect, as you rarely, if ever, need to restart the router to fix a problem.

15. **Answer: A.** The `show running-config` command shows you all currently running configurations in RAM. B is incorrect, as you would see similar output; however, this shows the `Current` configuration. C is incorrect, as that command shows you the routing table on your router. D is incorrect, as the `show version` command gives you the up-to-date information on which IOS you are running, as well as the configuration register settings.

16. **Answer: B.** You give the East router the username of the router to which you want to authenticate. In this case, it would be West. A is incorrect, as East would be the hostname of the router, not the username. C and D are incorrect, as neither one of these routers is mentioned as a possible connection. If there were routers named North and South, the East router would need usernames for both of them.

17. **Answer: C.** High-level Data Link Control (HDLC) is the default serial encapsulation on Cisco routers. A is incorrect, as you must configure your Cisco router for PPP. B is incorrect, as you must specify SLIP as an encapsulation. D is incorrect, as ATM is ordered through a service provider and is not the default encapsulation.

18. **Answer: C.** Challenge Handshake Authentication Protocol (CHAP) requires a three-way handshake. It requires a challenge, reply, and Accept/Reject response. A is incorrect, as there are no one-way authentications. B is incorrect, as CHAP has three-way, and Password Authentication Protocol (PAP) uses a two-way handshake. D is incorrect, as all authentication protocols need mutual agreement.

19. **Answer: B.** Cisco routers do not display any console messages or debug output to the vty ports (Telnet sessions) by default. To enable this feature, you need to type terminal monitor from the standard Privileged EXEC mode prompt. Answer A is incorrect because there is a debug ip packet command. Answer C is incorrect because the debug command shows every single packet going through your router, not just the troubled interfaces. D is incorrect, as you can enable debug commands through any access method that allows you to reach a Privileged EXEC mode prompt.

20. **Answer: A.** This output is generated by the show version command. It gives you the current version of the IOS that is running, as well as other information about the router. B is incorrect, as this does not show the currently running configuration. C is incorrect, as this does not show the configuration that is saved in NVRAM. D is incorrect, as there is no such command.

21. **Answer: D.** The show ip interface brief command gives you a summary of all interfaces on the router. This is a good command to use to identify any issues with your interface's connectivity. A is incorrect, as this gives you detailed information on interface Ethernet 0/0. B is incorrect, as this is not a valid command. C is incorrect, as this command gives you detailed information about serial interface 0/1.

22. **Answer: D.** Notice that one router is running HDLC while the other is running PPP. They are not able to communicate. A is incorrect, as both have addresses that are on the appropriate network. B is incorrect, as routers that are directly connected do not need a routing protocol to communicate. C is incorrect, as you notice that on both routers, the lines are "up," which means that there is electrical connectivity (Layer 1).

23. **Answers: A and B.** You can copy your `running-config` to NVRAM (`startup-config`) and to the flash memory (if there is room). C is incorrect, as correct syntax for a `copy` command is `source` to `destination`. Because you are copying from your `running-config`, that is the source, not the destination. D is incorrect, as the Cisco router does not allow you to transfer your configuration using the HTTP protocol.

24. **Answers: A, D, and E.** Frame relay, Point-to-Point Protocol (PPP), and HDLC are all WAN encapsulation protocols. B is incorrect, as Ethernet is a LAN encapsulation. C is incorrect, as token ring is a LAN encapsulation, as well.

25. **Answer: B.** The command `service password-encryption` encrypts all of the system passwords that are set. A is incorrect, as you cannot issue this command at the Privileged EXEC mode prompt. It must be done in Global Configuration mode. C is incorrect, as this command does not work in Privileged EXEC mode and does not encrypt all of the passwords. D is incorrect, as this command gives you only an encrypted Privileged EXEC mode password, not all of the system passwords.

26. **Answer: D.** You must first go to the `vty` line where you want to put the password and then use the `password` command. You finish by specifying that users must log in with the password by using the `login` command. A is incorrect, as it is the correct method to configure a password on the console interface, not Telnet. B is incorrect, as the second command typed is invalid. C is incorrect, as the command for the password is incorrect. You do not use the `enable secret` command here.

27. **Answer: A.** The `clockrate` command sets the *clocking*, or physical speed of the interface. It establishes the DCE side of a serial connection. It acts as sort of a metronome that specifies the timing of sending data. Because the service provider is typically the clock rate source, this command is primarily used in lab environments to emulate a service provider connection. B is incorrect, as keepalives are sent on Ethernet interfaces. C is incorrect, as the advertised bandwidth of an interface is set with the `bandwidth` command. D is incorrect, as you use the `clock` command to set the time on your router, or you can have it set to receive its time from an NNTP server.

28. **Answer: D.** There are five vty (Telnet) lines established by default on a Cisco router. They start at vty 0. A is incorrect, as this is an invalid command. B is incorrect, as this allows you to configure your Ethernet interface, not Telnet lines. C is incorrect, as the numbering of the vty lines starts at 0, not 1.

29. **Answers: A and D.** You can issue show commands from User EXEC mode (>) or Privileged EXEC mode (#). B is incorrect, as you cannot issue show commands from Global Configuration mode. C is incorrect, as you cannot issue show commands from Route Protocol mode. E is incorrect, as ROMON mode, or RomMonitor, is a low-level maintenance utility that helps bring back a corrupted router's IOS image.

30. **Answer: B.** Older versions of the IOS do not support encrypted Privileged EXEC mode passwords. By placing an Enable password, you still have a way to keep people out of Privileged EXEC mode if reverting to an older IOS. A is incorrect, as applications do not use Privileged EXEC mode passwords to access a Cisco router. C is incorrect, as the router ignores the Enable password after the Enable Secret password is configured. D is incorrect, as you type the Enable Secret password only to access Privileged EXEC mode.

31. **Answer: C.** The keyboard shortcut Ctrl+Z brings you back to Privileged EXEC mode. A is incorrect, as this is the method to suspend a Telnet session. B is incorrect, as this is one of the ways to stop a process from running. D is incorrect, as this merely moves you back one mode. In this case, you merely go back to Global Configuration mode.

32. **Answers: A, B, and E.** The Network Control Protocols (NCPs) are negotiated for the Layer 3 protocols in use on the WAN, such as IPXCP for IPX/SPX, IPCP for TCP/IP, and other Layer 3 protocols. CHAP authentication and Multilink Protocol are options that can also be negotiated during the LCP portion. C is incorrect, as UDP is a Layer 4 protocol, and PPP does not work at Layer 4. D is incorrect, as Q.931 is a signaling standard used by ISDN.

33. **Answer: D.** Reloading the router forces the router to reboot and load the configuration in the router's NVRAM. A is incorrect, as this places you into the router configuration setup script. B is incorrect, as this copies your currently running configuration into NVRAM. C is incorrect, as this merely "merges" the saved configuration with the currently running configuration. If changes made to the running configuration were not addressed in your saved configuration, they remain and are not overwritten.

34. **Answer: A.** Ctrl+P is used in place of the up arrow on the keyboard for older terminal programs. Ctrl+A is used to move to the beginning of the command line. Answer B is incorrect, as there is no Ctrl+L command and Ctrl+B moves back a character. Answer C is incorrect because Ctrl+D deletes the character under the curser. Ctrl+E moves the cursor to the end of the command line, making D incorrect.

35. **Answer: B.** The correct baud rate is 9600; thus, B is the correct answer. A, C, and D are incorrect baud rate settings and cause your screen to incorrectly display information from your console port.

36. **Answer: A.** You must have an IP address configured on an interface for a router or on a Management VLAN for a Catalyst switch. B is incorrect, as Simple Network Management Protocol (SNMP) is not required for Telnet. C is incorrect, as Cisco Discovery Protocol (CDP) is not required for Telnet to work. D is incorrect, as Cisco Devices have five vty ports configured by default.

37. **Answer: D.** The `disable` command takes you from Privileged EXEC mode back to User EXEC mode. A is incorrect, as this is the command that takes you from User EXEC mode to Privileged EXEC mode. B is incorrect, as this logs you out of your connection. C is incorrect, as this command places you in Global Configuration mode.

38. **Answer: D.** You must be in vlan configuration mode for VLAN1. A is incorrect because you cannot configure IP addresses in Privileged EXEC mode. B is incorrect because that is not a correct command. C is incorrect because you must specify the subnet mask when performing this command.

39. **Answer: B.** The `show flash` command gives you the contents of the flash memory, as well as the amount of remaining memory. A is incorrect, as this command shows all the configurations stored in NVRAM. C is incorrect, as this is not a valid command. D is incorrect, as `show version` gives you the currently running IOS image and information about the router, such as uptime and configuration register settings.

40. **Answer: D.** You use the `show interface vlan` command to verify the IP address on that switch. A is incorrect because the `show ip` command is no longer used on the Catalyst switch series. B is incorrect because this merely gives you information on what ports belong to a VLAN. C is incorrect because this command shows you the routing table on the switch, if the switch has Layer 3 capabilities.

41. **Answer: C.** You are taken to the System Configuration dialog if there are no configurations saved in NVRAM. A is incorrect, as you are taken to ROMON mode if the IOS is corrupted. B is incorrect, as missing parameters do not start the System Configuration dialog. D is incorrect, as the question stated that you saw the output after powering up the router. You can get this text if you issue that command, but that would have happened after you had logged in.

42. **Answer: A.** The command show con does not have enough characters for the IOS to finish it. B is incorrect, as you see the incomplete command output. C is incorrect, as this produces the unknown command output. D is incorrect, as context-sensitive help requires the use of the ?.

43. **Answer: C.** The dollar sign ($) indicates that there is text to the left of the symbol. A is incorrect, as the (^) symbol typically indicates where a command has erred. B is incorrect, as commands longer than one line are allowed. D is incorrect, as the router does not shorten any commands unless you have typed in a shortened version, such as config t for configure terminal.

44. **Answer: D.** The history size command permanently alters the command history buffer. A is incorrect, as this command adjusts the buffer only for the current session. B is incorrect, as you cannot issue the history size command from Privileged EXEC mode. C is incorrect, as you do not issue the terminal history command from Global Configuration mode, and it is the wrong command as well.

45. **Answers: A and C.** You can view the descriptions placed on the interfaces with the show interfaces command or show running-config. B is incorrect, as the show flash command shows the IOS images and any configurations saved to flash memory. D is incorrect, as this command gives you all the running routing protocols, such as RIP or IGRP.

46. **Answer: B.** The logging synchronous command enables the IOS to retype your input after displaying a console message. This does not interrupt your command. A is incorrect, as exec-timeout sets how long a session can remain idle without logging off the user. C is incorrect, as this command merely brings you to Line Configuration mode. D is incorrect, as this is an invalid command.

47 **Answer: D.** This is the command issued on a 7000 or 7500 Cisco router with a VIP card. It has a slot, port adapter, and port number. A, B, and C are incorrect definitions.

48. **Answer: D.** You issue the clockrate command in Interface Configuration mode, and it must be set in bits per second. A and B are incorrect, as the bandwidth command is good only for the advertised bandwidth. C is incorrect, as you must specify the speed in bits per second, not Kbps.

49. **Answer: A.** You use the `encapsulation` command in Interface Configuration mode—for example, `router1(config-if)#encapsulation frame-relay`. B is incorrect, as you issue the command in Interface Configuration mode. C is incorrect, as you can issue limited `show` commands only in User mode. D is incorrect, as you can enter configuration modes and perform router maintenance.

50. **Answer: B.** All your passwords are shown in encrypted form after issuing the `service password-encryption` command. The passwords encrypted are identified as password type 7. A is incorrect, as the encrypted passwords are shown in a hashed format. C is incorrect, as the rest of the output looks correct. D is incorrect, as the `enable secret` command gives you an encrypted Privileged EXEC mode password, which is identified as password type 5.

Network Management

Quick Check

1. Which protocol is proprietary to Cisco, providing administrators with information regarding directly connected devices?
   - ❏ A. UDP
   - ❏ B. TCP
   - ❏ C. CDP
   - ❏ D. SNMP

Quick Answer: 75
Detailed Answer: 76

2. At which layer of the OSI Model does CDP operate?
   - ❏ A. Physical layer
   - ❏ B. Data-link layer
   - ❏ C. Network layer
   - ❏ D. Transport layer

Quick Answer: 75
Detailed Answer: 76

3. Which of the following items can CDP provide a neighboring device? (Choose five.)
   - ❏ A. Platform
   - ❏ B. Capabilities
   - ❏ C. Address list
   - ❏ D. Open ports
   - ❏ E. IOS version
   - ❏ F. Device identifier

Quick Answer: 75
Detailed Answer: 76

4. You've just set up a Cisco router and want to enable CDP on the device. What do you need to do?
   - ❏ A. Do nothing; it's enabled by default.
   - ❏ B. Turn it on in Global Configuration mode.
   - ❏ C. Turn it on in Interface Configuration mode.
   - ❏ D. Do nothing; it's always on and cannot be turned off.

Quick Answer: 75
Detailed Answer: 76

5. CDP is not enabled on one of your routers, but you would like to enable it for the entire router. Which of the following commands must you enter?

   ❑ A. `router(config-if)#cdp enable`
   ❑ B. `router(config)#cdp enable`
   ❑ C. `router(config-if)#cdp run`
   ❑ D. `router(config)#cdp run`

6. You need to disable CDP on your Cisco router. Which of the following commands must you enter?

   ❑ A. `cdp disable`
   ❑ B. `no cdp run`
   ❑ C. `no cdp enable`
   ❑ D. `cdp off`

7. What tool is used to remotely manage a Cisco device from any TCP/IP host?

   ❑ A. Telnet
   ❑ B. FTP
   ❑ C. TFTP
   ❑ D. CDP

8. You have a console connection to your Catalyst 2950 switch. You want to telnet to a router named Router1. What command could be entered at the command prompt? (Choose three.)

   ❑ A. `Router1`
   ❑ B. `telnet router1`
   ❑ C. `telnet Router1`
   ❑ D. `Router2`

9. You want to view the current Telnet connections initiated from your router. What command should you enter?

   ❑ A. `show telnet`
   ❑ B. `show connections`
   ❑ C. `show sessions`
   ❑ D. `show users`

10. You want to view the current Telnet connections connecting to your router. What command should you enter?

    ❑ A. `show telnet`
    ❑ B. `show connections`
    ❑ C. `show sessions`
    ❑ D. `show users`

Quick Answer: **75**
Detailed Answer: **77**

11. When you are viewing multiple sessions with the `show sessions` command, which symbol indicates your last session?

    ❑ A. #
    ❑ B. %
    ❑ C. ^
    ❑ D. *

Quick Answer: **75**
Detailed Answer: **77**

12. Which key sequence allows you to resume your last session after viewing the `show sessions` output?

    ❑ A. Tab
    ❑ B. Ctrl+Shift+x
    ❑ C. Enter
    ❑ D. Ctrl+Esc

Quick Answer: **75**
Detailed Answer: **77**

13. You need to suspend your current Telnet session. What key sequence allows you to do this?

    ❑ A. Ctrl+Shift+6, followed by x
    ❑ B. Ctrl+Shift+x
    ❑ C. Ctrl+Esc
    ❑ D. This cannot be done.

Quick Answer: **75**
Detailed Answer: **77**

14. What IOS command allows you to continue a suspended session? (Choose three.)

    ❑ A. Pressing the Enter key
    ❑ B. `resume`
    ❑ C. `resume <session number>`
    ❑ D. `continue session`

Quick Answer: **75**
Detailed Answer: **77**

15. You have noticed several sessions connected to your router, and they have long idle times. You would like to close these sessions. What is the proper IOS syntax?

    ❑ A. `clear line <linenumber>`
    ❑ B. `close session <session number>`
    ❑ C. `end session <session number>`
    ❑ D. `end telnet <session number>`

Quick Answer: **75**
Detailed Answer: **77**

16. You need to verify connectivity to a remote host. You want as little traffic as possible generated to confirm connectivity. What network utility will quickly provide you this information?

   ❏ A. ping
   ❏ B. trace
   ❏ C. telnet
   ❏ D. tftp

Quick Answer: **75**
Detailed Answer: **77**

17. You have noticed intermittent connectivity to a remote host. You want to determine the route traffic is taking to help narrow down the problem. Which of the following commands shows you the actual routes of packets between devices?

   ❏ A. ping
   ❏ B. trace
   ❏ C. telnet
   ❏ D. tftp

Quick Answer: **75**
Detailed Answer: **77**

18. Which internal router component contains the software and data structures that allow the router to function, including the IOS?

   ❏ A. RAM
   ❏ B. ROM
   ❏ C. Flash
   ❏ D. NVRAM
   ❏ E. Configuration register

Quick Answer: **75**
Detailed Answer: **77**

19. Which internal router component contains microcode for basic functions to start and maintain the router, including bootstrap and POST?

   ❏ A. RAM
   ❏ B. ROM
   ❏ C. Flash
   ❏ D. NVRAM
   ❏ E. Configuration register

Quick Answer: **75**
Detailed Answer: **78**

20. Which internal router component is nonvolatile and primarily used to store the Cisco IOS software image?

   ❏ A. RAM
   ❏ B. ROM
   ❏ C. Flash
   ❏ D. NVRAM
   ❏ E. Configuration register

Quick Answer: **75**
Detailed Answer: **78**

21. Which of the following internal router components is mainly used to store the saved configuration file named startup-config?

Quick Answer: **75**
Detailed Answer: **78**

- ❏ A. RAM
- ❏ B. ROM
- ❏ C. Flash
- ❏ D. NVRAM
- ❏ E. Configuration register

22. Which internal router component controls how the router boots up and is part of NVRAM?

Quick Answer: **75**
Detailed Answer: **78**

- ❏ A. RAM
- ❏ B. ROM
- ❏ C. Flash
- ❏ D. Configuration register

23. Which of the following is a low-level operating system normally used for troubleshooting and password recovery?

Quick Answer: **75**
Detailed Answer: **78**

- ❏ A. Bootstrap code
- ❏ B. ROMMON
- ❏ C. POST
- ❏ D. "Mini" IOS software file

24. Which of the following is microcode used to test the basic functionality of the router hardware and determine the router hardware configuration?

Quick Answer: **75**
Detailed Answer: **79**

- ❏ A. Bootstrap code
- ❏ B. ROMMON
- ❏ C. POST
- ❏ D. "Mini" IOS software file

25. Which of the following is used to bring the router up during initialization and reads the configuration register to determine how to boot?

Quick Answer: **75**
Detailed Answer: **79**

- ❏ A. Bootstrap code
- ❏ B. ROMMON
- ❏ C. POST
- ❏ D. "Mini" IOS software file

26. Which of the following is capable of loading a new IOS image into flash and performing other maintenance operations?

    ❏ A. Bootstrap code

    ❏ B. ROMMON

    ❏ C. POST

    ❏ D. "Mini" IOS software file

Quick Answer: **75**
Detailed Answer: **79**

27. You want to view the IOS image that is currently stored in flash. What command displays the image?

    ❏ A. `show ios`

    ❏ B. `show flash`

    ❏ C. `ls flash`

    ❏ D. `list flash`

Quick Answer: **75**
Detailed Answer: **79**

28. What command displays information stored in RAM?

    ❏ A. `show ram`

    ❏ B. `show running-config`

    ❏ C. `show startup-config`

    ❏ D. `list ram`

Quick Answer: **75**
Detailed Answer: **79**

29. What command displays information stored in NVRAM?

    ❏ A. `show ram`

    ❏ B. `show running-config`

    ❏ C. `show startup-config`

    ❏ D. `list ram`

Quick Answer: **75**
Detailed Answer: **79**

30. Your configuration register boot field is set to 0x0. What is the effect on how the router boots?

    ❏ A. It uses ROM monitor mode.

    ❏ B. It automatically boots from ROM.

    ❏ C. It examines NVRAM for boot system commands.

    ❏ D. It automatically boots from RAM.

Quick Answer: **75**
Detailed Answer: **80**

31. Your configuration register boot field is set to 0x1. What is the effect on how the router boots?

    ❏ A. It uses ROM monitor mode.

    ❏ B. It automatically boots from ROM.

    ❏ C. It examines NVRAM for boot system commands.

    ❏ D. It automatically boots from RAM.

Quick Answer: **75**
Detailed Answer: **80**

Quick Check

32. Your configuration register boot field is set to 0x2. What is the effect on how the router boots?

- ❏ A. It uses ROM monitor mode.
- ❏ B. It automatically boots from ROM.
- ❏ C. It examines NVRAM for boot system commands.
- ❏ D. It automatically boots from RAM.

Quick Answer: **75**
Detailed Answer: **80**

33. You need to confirm the value set in your configuration register before you restart your router. What command should you issue?

- ❏ A. show running-config
- ❏ B. show startup-config
- ❏ C. show reg
- ❏ D. show version

Quick Answer: **75**
Detailed Answer: **80**

34. What command should you enter to modify the value of the configuration register?

- ❏ A. config register
- ❏ B. configure register
- ❏ C. config-register
- ❏ D. conf-register

Quick Answer: **75**
Detailed Answer: **80**

35. What functions are controlled by the bits of the configuration register? (Choose two.)

- ❏ A. Enable IP
- ❏ B. Set baud rate
- ❏ C. Use NVRAM config
- ❏ D. Enable AUX port

Quick Answer: **75**
Detailed Answer: **80**

36. Which of the following are URL prefixes used in the Cisco IOS filesystem? (Choose four.)

- ❏ A. bootflash:
- ❏ B. flh:
- ❏ C. flash:
- ❏ D. nvram:
- ❏ E. ram:
- ❏ F. rom:

Quick Answer: **75**
Detailed Answer: **80**

37. You've executed the show flash command and see the file
    c2500-js-1_120-3.bin is stored there. What does the js represent?

    ❑ A. The platform
    ❑ B. Special capabilities
    ❑ C. Where the image runs
    ❑ D. The version number

38. What does CDP stand for?

    ❑ A. Cisco Detection Protocol
    ❑ B. Cisco Discovery Protocol
    ❑ C. Connection Discovery Protocol
    ❑ D. Connection Detection Protocol

39. You need to create a backup image file of your IOS. Which of
    the following commands accomplishes this task?

    ❑ A. copy startup-config running-config
    ❑ B. copy running-config startup-config
    ❑ C. copy flash tftp
    ❑ D. copy tftp flash

40. You want to clear out the current startup-config stored in
    NVRAM on your router. What is the appropriate IOS command?

    ❑ A. erase startup-config
    ❑ B. delete startup-config
    ❑ C. clear nvram
    ❑ D. delete nvram

41. Your debug information doesn't include information that lets
    you know the time when the information was recorded. What
    command should you issue to remedy this situation?

    ❑ A. log timing
    ❑ B. enable time
    ❑ C. service timestamps
    ❑ D. log timestamps

Quick Check

42. After enabling debugging on your router, you want to ensure that maximum resources are freed up by disabling all debugging. What command should you enter?

- ❏ A. disable debug
- ❏ B. no debugging
- ❏ C. no debug all
- ❏ D. debug off

Quick Answer: **75**
Detailed Answer: **81**

43. Which of the following commands should not be entered, as it may cause a system crash?

- ❏ A. write mem
- ❏ B. copy starting-config running-config
- ❏ C. debug all
- ❏ D. erase starting-config

Quick Answer: **75**
Detailed Answer: **81**

44. Before you load a new IOS image, you want to make sure you have enough flash memory to support the image. What command should you run to check how much total flash memory is installed?

- ❏ A. show memory
- ❏ B. show flash
- ❏ C. show startup-config
- ❏ D. show nvram

Quick Answer: **75**
Detailed Answer: **81**

45. You are attempting to troubleshoot a remote router via a Telnet session. You want to view console messages on the current terminal line. What command is appropriate?

- ❏ A. telnet debug console
- ❏ B. telnet console
- ❏ C. terminal monitor
- ❏ D. terminal debug monitor

Quick Answer: **75**
Detailed Answer: **81**

46. You are troubleshooting your router's performance, and you want to use the debug command. However, you are concerned about debug further degrading the router's performance. What command can help you determine whether you should run debug?

- ❏ A. service timestamps
- ❏ B. debug minimal
- ❏ C. show processes
- ❏ D. debug test

Quick Answer: **75**
Detailed Answer: **81**

47. You need to make many alterations to the configuration your router is currently using. You want to be sure you are able to revert to this configuration when you are done, in case problems arise. What command should you run?

Quick Answer: **75**
Detailed Answer: **81**

- ❑ A. `copy running-config tftp`
- ❑ B. `copy startup-config tftp`
- ❑ C. `copy tftp running-config`
- ❑ D. `copy tftp startup-config`

48. You are copying a configuration from the TFTP server into the configuration in RAM. What will happen with the two configurations?

Quick Answer: **75**
Detailed Answer: **82**

- ❑ A. The RAM configuration is backed up.
- ❑ B. The RAM configuration is lost.
- ❑ C. The two configurations merge.
- ❑ D. An error message is returned.

49. You are copying a configuration from the RAM into the configuration in NVRAM. What will happen with the two configurations?

Quick Answer: **75**
Detailed Answer: **82**

- ❑ A. The NVRAM configuration is backed up.
- ❑ B. The NVRAM configuration is lost.
- ❑ C. The two configurations merge.
- ❑ D. An error message is returned.

50. You have loaded the wrong IOS image, and the router will not boot. What is your first step?

Quick Answer: **75**
Detailed Answer: **82**

- ❑ A. Enter ROMMON mode.
- ❑ B. `erase flash`
- ❑ C. `erase ram`
- ❑ D. `erase nvram`

Quick Check Answer Key

1. C	26. D
2. B	27. B
3. A, B, C, E, F	28. B
4. A	29. C
5. D	30. A
6. B	31. B
7. A	32. C
8. A, B, C	33. D
9. C	34. C
10. D	35. B, C
11. D	36. A, B, C, D
12. C	37. B
13. A	38. B
14. A, B, C	39. C
15. A	40. A
16. A	41. C
17. B	42. C
18. A	43. C
19. B	44. B
20. C	45. C
21. D	46. C
22. D	47. A
23. B	48. C
24. C	49. B
25. A	50. A

Answers and Explanations

1. **Answer: C.** The Cisco Discovery Protocol is proprietary to Cisco and can give an administrator's address and other information regarding directly connected devices. A is incorrect, as UDP is a fast, connectionless, and nonproprietary protocol. B is incorrect, as TCP is a nonproprietary, connection-oriented, and reliable protocol used in network communication. D is incorrect because SNMP is used for network management and is not proprietary to Cisco.

2. **Answer: B.** CDP runs at the Data-link layer, allowing it to be network layer protocol-independent, working with both IP- and IPX-based networks. A is incorrect, as CDP does not operate at the Physical layer, and D is incorrect because CDP does not operate at the Transport layer. C is incorrect because IP and IPX are network-based protocols, but CDP is not.

3. **Answers: A, B, C, E, and F.** CDP can provide the device hardware platform, a list of supported features such as source-route bridge, the network layer address, IOS version, and a device identifier such as the device's hostname. D is incorrect as CDP doesn't display open ports on the neighboring device.

4. **Answer: A.** CDP is enabled by default. B and C are incorrect because even though CDP can be controlled in Global Configuration mode, it is enabled by default. D is incorrect because CDP can be turned on or off as necessary.

5. **Answer: D.** You must enter the cdp run command from Global Configuration mode. A is incorrect because the cdp enable command is used in interface configuration mode and enables CDP on a particular interface. B is incorrect because the cdp enable command does not work in Global Configuration mode. C is incorrect; the command is right but must be in Global Configuration mode, not Interface Configuration mode.

6. **Answer: B.** The proper syntax on Cisco routers is no cdp run. A is incorrect; cdp disable is not a valid command. C is incorrect; the syntax is proper for older Catalyst Switches only, and is not valid today. D is incorrect; this is an invalid command resulting in an error message.

7. **Answer: A.** Telnet can be used to gather information about remote devices. B is incorrect; FTP is used to transfer files and can include authentication. C is incorrect; TFTP uses no authentication. D is incorrect, as CDP can gather information about neighboring devices only. If you telnet to a remote device, CDP may show information about the remote device's neighbors. However, without Telnet, CDP has no capability to display remote device information.

8. **Answer: A, B, and C.** Each of these commands attempts a Telnet session with Router1. D is incorrect, as you want to telnet to Router1, not Router2.

9. **Answer: C.** The `show sessions` command verifies your Telnet connectivity and displays a list of hosts to which you have established a connection. A and B are incorrect because they are not valid IOS commands. D is incorrect; the `show users` command displays remote users who have initiated a session to your router.

10. **Answer: D.** The `show users` command displays remote users who have initiated a session to your router. A and B are not valid IOS commands. C is incorrect; `show sessions` verifies your Telnet connectivity and displays a list of hosts to which you have established a connection.

11. **Answer: D.** The asterisk indicates your last session in the `show session's` output. A is incorrect; this symbol is most closely associated with Privileged EXEC mode. B is incorrect; this symbol does not indicate the most recent session. C is incorrect; the caret indicates where an error begins in a mistyped command.

12. **Answer: C.** Simply pressing Enter resumes the last session. A is incorrect; pressing Tab completes partially entered commands. B and D are incorrect; these sequences do not perform the desired function.

13. **Answer: A.** The correct key sequence to perform this task is Ctrl+Shift+6, followed by pressing x. B, C, and D are incorrect, as all other key sequences do not perform the correct task.

14. **Answers: A, B, and C.** These are all valid ways to continue a suspended session. D is incorrect; `continue session` is not a valid IOS command.

15. **Answer: A.** The `clear line` command, accompanied by the line number, clears the session. B is incorrect; this syntax is not supported. C and D are invalid IOS commands.

16. **Answer: A.** `ping` uses ICMP and generates information regarding connectivity to the remote host. B is incorrect; although `trace` can determine connectivity, it generates more traffic than `ping`. C is incorrect; telnetting to the remote host can confirm connectivity, but it generates more traffic to do so. D is incorrect; `tftp` cannot be used to test connectivity to a remote router.

17. **Answer: B.** `trace` can determine connectivity, and it shows the path the traffic takes to the destination. A is incorrect, as `ping` uses ICMP and generates information regarding connectivity to the remote host but does not show the path. C is incorrect because telnetting to the remote host can confirm connectivity, but it doesn't provide path information. D is incorrect because `tftp` cannot be used to test connectivity to a remote router; it is used for transferring files.

18. **Answer: A.** RAM contains the software and data structures that allow the router to function, so A is the correct response. IOS and the running configuration are part of RAM. B is incorrect, as ROM contains the microcode for

functions such as bootstrap and POST, and also contains ROMMON. C is incorrect; flash memory contains the Cisco IOS software image and is non-volatile. D is incorrect because NVRAM is nonvolatile and is used to store the startup-config. E is incorrect; the configuration register controls how the router boots up.

19. **Answer: B.** ROM contains the microcode for functions such as bootstrap and POST, and also contains ROMMON. A is incorrect because RAM contains the software and data structures that allow the router to function. IOS and the running configuration are part of RAM. C is incorrect; Flash memory contains the Cisco IOS software image and is nonvolatile. D is incorrect, as NVRAM is nonvolatile and is used to store the startup-config. E is incorrect because the configuration register controls how the router boots up.

20. **Answer: C.** Flash memory contains the Cisco IOS software image and is non-volatile. A is incorrect because RAM contains the software and data structures that allow the router to function, and IOS and the running configuration are part of RAM. B is incorrect; ROM contains the microcode for functions such as bootstrap and POST, and also contains ROMMON. D is incorrect because while NVRAM is nonvolatile, it is used to store the startup-config, not the IOS software image itself. E is incorrect; the configuration register controls how the router boots up.

21. **Answer: D.** NVRAM is nonvolatile and is used to store the startup-config. A is incorrect, as RAM contains the software and data structures that allow the router to function, and IOS and the running configuration are part of RAM. B is incorrect because ROM contains the microcode for functions such as boot-strap and POST, and also contains ROMMON. C is incorrect because flash memory contains the Cisco IOS software image and is nonvolatile. E is incorrect; the configuration register controls how the router boots up.

22. **Answer: D.** The configuration register controls how the router boots up, so D is the correct answer. A is incorrect, as RAM contains the software and data structures that allow the router to function, and IOS and the running configuration are part of RAM. B is incorrect because ROM contains the microcode for functions such as bootstrap and POST, and also contains ROMMON. C is incorrect; Flash memory contains the Cisco IOS software image and is non-volatile.

23. **Answer: B.** ROMMON is a low-level operating system used for password recovery and troubleshooting; it has no routing or IP capabilities. A is incorrect; bootstrap code is used to bring the router up during initialization and to read the configuration register to determine how to boot. C is incorrect; POST is the microcode used to determine the router's hardware configuration. D is

incorrect, as the mini-IOS software file is a subset of the Cisco IOS for loading a new IOS image into flash and performing other maintenance operations.

24. **Answer: C.** POST is the microcode used to determine the router's hardware configuration. A is incorrect because bootstrap code is used to bring the router up during initialization and to read the configuration register to determine how to boot. B is incorrect; ROMMON is a low-level operating system used for password recovery and troubleshooting, and it has no routing or IP capabilities. D is incorrect because the mini-IOS software file is a subset of the Cisco IOS for loading a new IOS image into flash and performing other maintenance operations.

25. **Answer: A.** Bootstrap code is used to bring the router up during initialization and to read the configuration register to determine how to boot. B is incorrect because POST is the microcode used to determine the router's hardware configuration. C is incorrect, as ROMMON is a low-level operating system used for password recovery and troubleshooting; it has no routing or IP capabilities. D is incorrect, as the mini-IOS software file is a subset of the Cisco IOS for loading a new IOS image into flash and performing other maintenance operations.

26. **Answer: D.** The mini-IOS software file is a subset of the Cisco IOS for loading a new IOS image into flash and performing other maintenance operations. A is incorrect because bootstrap code is used to bring the router up during initialization and to read the configuration register to determine how to boot. B is incorrect; POST is the microcode used to determine the router's hardware configuration. C is incorrect; ROMMON is a low-level operating system used for password recovery and troubleshooting, and it has no routing or IP capabilities.

27. **Answer: B.** The show flash command lists the contents of flash memory, including the IOS image file stored there. A is incorrect; show ios is an invalid command. C is incorrect; ls works in Unix, but it is not a Cisco IOS command. D is incorrect because list flash is not a valid IOS command.

28. **Answer: B.** The show running-config command displays the current running configuration of the router, which is kept in RAM. C is incorrect; show startup-config lists the contents of NVRAM and the configuration used on startup. A and D are incorrect because they are invalid IOS commands.

29. **Answer: C.** The show startup-config command lists the contents of NVRAM and the configuration used on startup. B is incorrect because show running-config displays the current running configuration of the router, which is kept in RAM. A and D are invalid IOS commands.

30. **Answer: A.** A configuration register value of 0x0 in the boot field causes the router to use ROM monitor mode, so A is the correct response. B is incorrect because a configuration register value of 0x1 in the boot field causes the router to automatically boot from ROM. C is incorrect, as a configuration register value of 0x2 in the boot field causes the router to examine NVRAM for boot system commands. D is incorrect because a configuration register value to automatically boot from RAM is not defined.

31. **Answer: B.** A configuration register value of 0x1 in the boot field causes the router to automatically boot from ROM. A is incorrect because a configuration register value of 0x0 in the boot field causes the router to use ROM monitor mode. C is incorrect because a configuration register value of 0x2 in the boot field causes the router to examine NVRAM for boot system commands. D is incorrect, as a configuration register value to automatically boot from RAM is not defined.

32. **Answer: C.** A configuration register value of 0x2 in the boot field causes the router to examine NVRAM for boot system commands. A is incorrect because a configuration register value of 0x0 in the boot field causes the router to use ROM monitor mode. B is incorrect because a configuration register value of 0x1 in the boot field causes the router to automatically boot from ROM. D is incorrect, as a configuration register value to automatically boot from RAM is not defined.

33. **Answer: D.** The show version command displays the configuration register setting. A is incorrect, as show running-config does not display the configuration register. B is incorrect, as the command show startup-config does not display the configuration register value. C is an invalid IOS command.

34. **Answer: C.** The config-register command followed by the register setting is the correct syntax to use for setting the configuration register. B is incorrect because this is not the proper syntax to set the configuration register. A and D are not valid IOS commands.

35. **Answers: B and C.** The bits of the configuration register can also set the baud rate and have the router use the configuration saved in NVRAM. A is incorrect; the configuration register does not enable IP. D is incorrect; the configuration register cannot enable the AUX port.

36. **Answers: A, B, C, and D.** The prefix bootflash: refers to bootflash memory, flh: refers to flash load helper log files, flash: refers to flash memory, and nvram: refers to NVRAM. E and F are incorrect, as ram: and rom: are not valid IFS prefixes.

37. **Answer: B.** Special capabilities are represented by the second portion (js). A is incorrect; the platform is represented by the first portion (c2500). C is

incorrect; where the image runs is indicated by the third portion ("1"). D is incorrect; the last portion (120-3) is the version number.

38. **Answer: B.** CDP stands for Cisco Discovery Protocol, which is used to help manage and monitor Cisco devices. A, B, and D are incorrect, as they are not valid protocols.

39. **Answer: C.** The copy flash tftp command copies the contents located in flash to TFTP. A is incorrect, as this merges your starting configuration into your running configuration. B is incorrect; this overwrites your starting configuration with your active, running configuration. D is incorrect, as this copies data from the TFTP server into flash.

40. **Answer: A.** The erase startup-config command deletes the information stored in NVRAM. B, C, and D are invalid IOS commands.

41. **Answer: C.** The service timestamps command records a time stamp with logged information, so C is the correct response. A, B, and D are invalid IOS commands.

42. **Answer: C.** The no debug all command disables all debugging on the router. The other responses are all invalid IOS commands.

43. **Answer: C.** The debug all command is extremely resource-intensive and should not be used. A is incorrect; this command can be used, even though it is an older form of copy running-config startup-config. B is incorrect because this command does not cause a system crash; it merges your starting configuration into your running configuration. D is an invalid IOS command.

44. **Answer: B.** The show flash command displays the current amount of flash memory installed on the system. A is incorrect; show memory shows detailed information about the RAM on the router. C is incorrect because the startup configuration does not include memory information. D is an invalid IOS command.

45. **Answer: C.** The terminal monitor command displays console messages to your Telnet session and is useful for remote troubleshooting. The other responses are all invalid IOS commands.

46. **Answer: C.** The show processes command displays information regarding the CPU utilization on the router, so C is correct. If the CPU is heavily taxed, debugging may cause extreme performance degradation. A is incorrect; this command enables time stamps with logging information. B and D are invalid IOS commands.

47. **Answer: A.** This command copies the configuration currently in use (running-config) to your TFTP server. B is incorrect; this command copies the starting

configuration to your TFTP server. The starting configuration is not the currently running configuration, but the configuration used when the router boots. C is incorrect; this command copies from the TFTP server to the running configuration. D is incorrect, as this command copies from the TFTP server to the starting configuration.

48. **Answer: C.** When you copy from any location into RAM, a merge occurs. Nonconflicting settings are kept and added, and conflicting settings are overwritten. A is incorrect; you should perform a backup when making this operation, but one is not performed automatically. B is incorrect; the running configuration is not lost. D is incorrect; no error message is returned.

49. **Answer: B.** When you copy the running configuration from RAM into the startup configuration, the startup configuration is lost, replaced by the running configuration. A is incorrect; a backup is created only if you manually create one. C is incorrect; merges occur only when you are copying from anywhere into RAM. D is incorrect, as no error message is returned.

50. **Answer: A.** This problem can be fixed in ROMMON mode, and this is the first step you must take. B is incorrect because you must enter ROMMON mode first. C is incorrect; the problem does not lie in RAM, and you must enter ROMMON mode first, regardless. D is incorrect; the problem is not in NVRAM, and you must enter ROMMON mode first.

Catalyst Switches and End-User Connectivity

1. In today's networks, more and more corporations are replacing hubs with switches. Which of the following is a reason for switching to a Catalyst switch from a hub?

   ❑ A. Catalyst switches take less time to process frames than hubs take.

   ❑ B. Catalyst switches decrease the amount of bandwidth available to hosts.

   ❑ C. Catalyst switches increase the number of collision domains in the network.

   ❑ D. Catalyst switches do not forward broadcasts.

2. Which of the following statements are true regarding half-duplex Ethernet? (Choose two.)

   ❑ A. Half-duplex Ethernet typically operates in a shared collision domain.

   ❑ B. Half-duplex Ethernet typically operates in a private collision domain.

   ❑ C. Half-duplex Ethernet has higher effective throughput.

   ❑ D. Half-duplex Ethernet has lower effective throughput.

   ❑ E. Half-duplex Ethernet operates in a private broadcast domain.

3. Which of the following commands places an IP address on your Catalyst switch?

   ❑ A. `HQ_SW1#ip address 10.2.2.2 255.255.255.0`

   ❑ B. `HQ_SW1(config)#Set IP 10.2.2.2 255.255.255.0`

   ❑ C. `HQ_SW1(config-vlan)#ip address 10.2.2.2`

   ❑ D. `HQ_SW1(config-vlan)#ip address 10.2.2.2 255.255.255.0`

4. Which of the following transmission methods checks the entire frame before sending it out an interface on a Catalyst switch?

Quick Answer: **94**
Detailed Answer: **95**

   ❑ A. Store-and-forward
   ❑ B. Buffered
   ❑ C. Cut-through
   ❑ D. Fragment-free

5. What are the default configuration settings on a Catalyst switch? (Choose three.)

Quick Answer: **94**
Detailed Answer: **95**

   ❑ A. CDP Enabled
   ❑ B. CDP Disabled
   ❑ C. Ports at 100Mbps/Full Duplex
   ❑ D. Ports Auto-Negotiate
   ❑ E. Spanning-Tree Protocol Enabled
   ❑ F. Spanning-Tree Protocol Disabled

6. Which of the following are valid MAC addresses? (Choose two.)

Quick Answer: **94**
Detailed Answer: **95**

   ❑ A. 2222-3333-3333-2222-9999
   ❑ B. 2222-3333-9999
   ❑ C. 2222-AAAA-GGGG
   ❑ D. 2222-AAAA-FFFF
   ❑ E. 2222-BBBB-GGGG

7. Your friend is new to the networking world and asks you to brief him on the differences and similarities between bridges and switches. What should you tell him? (Choose two.)

Quick Answer: **94**
Detailed Answer: **95**

   ❑ A. Switches are slower than bridges because they have fewer ports.
   ❑ B. A switch is a multiport bridge.
   ❑ C. Bridges and switches learn MAC addresses by examining the source MAC address of each frame received.
   ❑ D. A bridge forwards a broadcast, but a switch does not.

8. Layer 2 switches create multiple collision domains for each of their interfaces. Which of the following terms describes this behavior?

Quick Answer: **94**
Detailed Answer: **96**

   ❑ A. Virtual connectivity
   ❑ B. Multiplicity
   ❑ C. Microsegmentation
   ❑ D. Virtual segmentation

9. Which of the following is an advantage of store-and-forward switching in comparison to cut-through switching?

   ❑ A. Store-and-forward switching is faster.
   ❑ B. Store-and-forward switching requires less memory on the switch.
   ❑ C. Store-and-forward switching is compatible with third-party devices.
   ❑ D. Store-and-forward switching can check frame integrity before forwarding the frame.

Quick Answer: **94**
Detailed Answer: **96**

10. You are configuring a switch for remote access. What command must be issued in Global Configuration mode to allow the switch to be accessed from a subnet other than its own?

    ❑ A. `ip-default gateway`
    ❑ B. `router ip`
    ❑ C. `router rip`
    ❑ D. `routing enabled`

Quick Answer: **94**
Detailed Answer: **96**

11. Your boss asks you what Spanning-Tree Protocol does. What do you tell her?

    ❑ A. STP stops routing loops in your network.
    ❑ B. STP stops broadcasts in your network.
    ❑ C. STP allows routing loops in your network.
    ❑ D. STP monitors and contains loops in your switched network.

Quick Answer: **94**
Detailed Answer: **96**

12. Which of the following STP modes allows MAC addresses to be placed into the CAM table but does not forward frames?

    ❑ A. Blocking
    ❑ B. Listening
    ❑ C. Learning
    ❑ D. Forwarding

Quick Answer: **94**
Detailed Answer: **96**

13. Which of the following STP modes occurs when a port becomes a designated port?

    ❑ A. Blocking
    ❑ B. Listening
    ❑ C. Learning
    ❑ D. Forwarding

Quick Answer: **94**
Detailed Answer: **96**

14. A switch in your network is unplugged. Assuming that the default convergence parameters have not been altered, how soon will the other switches react and converge when running 802.1d STP?

    ❑ A. 30 seconds
    ❑ B. 40 seconds
    ❑ C. 50 seconds
    ❑ D. 60 seconds

Quick Answer: **94**
Detailed Answer: **96**

15. What is the effective throughput for each of 24 PCs connecting to a Catalyst switch's FastEthernet ports operating in half-duplex mode?

    ❑ A. 1Mbps
    ❑ B. 10Mbps
    ❑ C. 100Mbps
    ❑ D. 2400Mbps

Quick Answer: **94**
Detailed Answer: **96**

16. You want to disable CDP on all the interfaces on your switch. What command do you type to accomplish this?

    ❑ A. `no cdp run`
    ❑ B. `no cdp enable`
    ❑ C. `no cdp allow`
    ❑ D. `cdp limited`

Quick Answer: **94**
Detailed Answer: **97**

17. You want to disable CDP advertisements from going out one of your trunk ports. Which command disables CDP on that interface without affecting the others?

    ❑ A. `no cdp run`
    ❑ B. `no cdp enable`
    ❑ C. `cdp disable`
    ❑ D. `cdp interface disable`

Quick Answer: **94**
Detailed Answer: **97**

18. Which of the following are advertisements used in Spanning-Tree Protocol?

    ❑ A. Packets
    ❑ B. Frames
    ❑ C. BPDUs
    ❑ D. VTP

Quick Answer: **94**
Detailed Answer: **97**

Quick Check

19. Which portion of the Bridge Protocol Data Unit is used to choose the root bridge in Spanning-Tree Protocol?
    - ❏ A. Root ID
    - ❏ B. Bridge ID
    - ❏ C. STP ID
    - ❏ D. MAC address

Quick Answer: **94**
Detailed Answer: **97**

20. Which of the following is true about Ethernet full-duplex operation? (Choose two.)
    - ❏ A. It requires point-to-point links.
    - ❏ B. Full-duplex provides for collision-free operation.
    - ❏ C. It provides ways to schedule retransmissions.
    - ❏ D. It provides two wires to both transmit and receive.

Quick Answer: **94**
Detailed Answer: **97**

21. You are configuring a Cisco Catalyst switch for connectivity to a user workstation. In which mode do you apply the speed and duplex configuration commands?
    - ❏ A. User EXEC mode
    - ❏ B. Privileged EXEC mode
    - ❏ C. Global Configuration mode
    - ❏ D. Interface Configuration mode

Quick Answer: **94**
Detailed Answer: **97**

22. You are adding a brand-new switch to your environment and want to make sure it is the root bridge. What do you do to ensure that it receives this role?
    - ❏ A. Change the MAC address
    - ❏ B. Increase the bridge priority
    - ❏ C. Decrease the bridge priority
    - ❏ D. Change the router ID

Quick Answer: **94**
Detailed Answer: **97**

23. Which of the following frame transmission methods check only the first 64 bytes before forwarding the frame? (Choose two.)
    - ❏ A. Store-and-forward
    - ❏ B. Cut-through
    - ❏ C. Frame-check
    - ❏ D. Modified cut-through
    - ❏ E. Fragment-free

Quick Answer: **94**
Detailed Answer: **97**

Quick Check

24. You want to configure the FastEthernet 0/20 port on your Catalyst switch for port security. If anyone other than the MAC address 0001.3232.AABB connects to the port, it should immediately shut down. Which of the following configurations accomplishes this objective?

Quick Answer: **94**
Detailed Answer: **97**

❑ A. `interface fa0/20`
   `switchport mode access`
   `switchport port-security`
   `switchport port-security mac-address 0001.3232.AABB`
   `switchport port-security violation shutdown`

❑ B. `interface fa0/20`
   `switchport mode access`
   `mac-address 0001.3232.AABB`
   `port-security violation shutdown`

❑ C. `interface fa0/20`
   `switchport mode access`
   `port-security`
   `mac-address 0001.3232.AABB`
   `port-security violation shutdown`

❑ D. `interface fa0/20`
   `switchport mode access`
   `switchport port-security`
   `mac-address 0001.3232.AABB`
   `switchport port-security violation shutdown`

25. What command allows you to verify your port security configuration on interface FastEthernet 0/20?

Quick Answer: **94**
Detailed Answer: **98**

❑ A. `show interface fa0/20`
❑ B. `show ip interface fa0/20`
❑ C. `show interface fa0/20 switchport`
❑ D. `show port-security interface fa0/20`

26. Which of the following is the IEEE standard for Ethernet? (The original Ethernet specification, developed by Xerox, and jointly specified by DEC, Intel, and Xerox is somewhat different from this standard.)

Quick Answer: **94**
Detailed Answer: **98**

❑ A. 802.1
❑ B. 802.2
❑ C. 802.3
❑ D. 802.5

27. Which of the following connections allows for full-duplex connectivity?

    Quick Answer: **94**
    Detailed Answer: **98**

    ❏ A. A switch connecting to another switch
    ❏ B. A switch connecting to a hub
    ❏ C. A hub connecting to another hub
    ❏ D. A router connecting to another hub

28. What command changes the duplex setting for an individual interface on a Catalyst switch?

    Quick Answer: **94**
    Detailed Answer: **98**

    ❏ A. `SW1#duplex full`
    ❏ B. `SW1#set duplex full`
    ❏ C. `SW1(config)#duplex full`
    ❏ D. `SW1(config)#set duplex full`
    ❏ E. `SW1(config-if)#duplex full`
    ❏ F. `SW1(config-if)#set duplex full`

29. Which of the following contribute to congestion on an Ethernet network? (Choose two.)

    Quick Answer: **94**
    Detailed Answer: **98**

    ❏ A. Creation of a new collision domain
    ❏ B. Creation of a new VLAN
    ❏ C. Addition of a hub to the network
    ❏ D. Use of switches in the network
    ❏ E. Amount of ARP or IPX SAP traffic

30. Which of the following are required for a switch to be managed remotely via Telnet from another IP subnet? (Choose two.)

    Quick Answer: **94**
    Detailed Answer: **98**

    ❏ A. An IP address on the switch
    ❏ B. A routing protocol
    ❏ C. Full-duplex connections
    ❏ D. A default gateway on the switch
    ❏ E. A static route from the switch to a router

31. One of the switches in your network fails, but you have redundant UTP cabling to another switch in place. Assuming that the default convergence parameters have not been altered, how long before your backup switch will be able to forward frames on all segments?

    Quick Answer: **94**
    Detailed Answer: **99**

    ❏ A. Immediately
    ❏ B. 10 seconds
    ❏ C. 40 seconds
    ❏ D. 50 seconds

32. In Spanning-Tree Protocol, what describes the state at which the root bridge has been elected and all ports are either in their blocked or forwarding state?

    ❑ A. Stable
    ❑ B. Blocking
    ❑ C. Converged
    ❑ D. Static

Quick Answer: **94**
Detailed Answer: **99**

33. Which of the following PDUs does a Layer 2 switch process?

    ❑ A. Bits
    ❑ B. Frames
    ❑ C. Packets
    ❑ D. Segments

Quick Answer: **94**
Detailed Answer: **99**

34. Which of the following statements are true regarding full-duplex communication? (Choose two.)

    ❑ A. Full-duplex provides greater bandwidth than half-duplex.
    ❑ B. Full-duplex is faster than half-duplex token ring.
    ❑ C. Full-duplex has more collisions than half-duplex.
    ❑ D. Full-duplex requires point-to-point connections.

Quick Answer: **94**
Detailed Answer: **99**

35. You have noticed that the amount of broadcast traffic has increased in your environment. A junior network administrator suggests that the company purchase switches with greater port density. Will this solution solve the problem?

    ❑ A. Yes, with more ports, the number of broadcasts will decrease.
    ❑ B. Yes, with more ports, the switch will be able to forward broadcasts more efficiently.
    ❑ C. No, with more ports, you will add to the amount of broadcast traffic.
    ❑ D. No, with more ports, you will forward broadcasts only to switches, causing CPU utilization to increase on the switches.

Quick Answer: **94**
Detailed Answer: **99**

36. You want to adjust the likelihood of your switch becoming the root bridge in your Spanning-Tree network. What command accomplishes this?

    ❑ A. `Switch(config)# spanning-tree root`
    ❑ B. `Switch(config)# spanning-tree mac-address 0000.0000.0001`
    ❑ C. `Switch(config)# spanning-tree priority 65000`
    ❑ D. `Switch(config)# spanning-tree vlan 1 priority 4096`

Quick Answer: **94**
Detailed Answer: **99**

37. What command changes the duplex setting for an individual interface on a Catalyst switch?

   ❑ A. `ExamCram2#duplex full`
   ❑ B. `ExamCram2#set duplex full`
   ❑ C. `ExamCram2 (config)#duplex full`
   ❑ D. `ExamCram2 (config)#set duplex full`
   ❑ E. `ExamCram2 (config-if)#duplex full`
   ❑ F. `ExamCram2 (config-if)#set duplex full`

Quick Answer: **94**
Detailed Answer: **100**

38. What are the three duplex settings available on a Catalyst switch? (Choose three.)

   ❑ A. Full
   ❑ B. Auto
   ❑ C. Half
   ❑ D. Control

Quick Answer: **94**
Detailed Answer: **100**

39. Which of the following are valid MAC addresses? (Choose two.)

   ❑ A. 1111-3333-3333-2222-9999
   ❑ B. 1111-3333-9999
   ❑ C. 1111-AAAA-XXXX
   ❑ D. 1111-AAAA-FFFF
   ❑ E. 1111-BBBB-XXXX

Quick Answer: **94**
Detailed Answer: **100**

40. What type of address does a Layer 2 switch utilize?

   ❑ A. Media Access Control
   ❑ B. Burned Access Address
   ❑ C. Internet Protocol
   ❑ D. Internet Packet Exchange

Quick Answer: **94**
Detailed Answer: **100**

41. Which of the following devices provides microsegmentation to reduce Ethernet collision domains?

   ❑ A. Hub
   ❑ B. Repeater
   ❑ C. Switch
   ❑ D. Terminal adapter

Quick Answer: **94**
Detailed Answer: **100**

42. A switch typically operates at Layer 2 of the OSI Model. What Layer 3 functionality can it utilize to help create broadcast domains?

   ❑ A. CDP
   ❑ B. RIP
   ❑ C. VLANs
   ❑ D. Full-duplex
   ❑ E. Half-duplex

Quick Answer: **94**
Detailed Answer: **100**

43. Which of the following commands shows you the MAC address table that has been learned on a switch?

   ❑ A. `show ip interface`
   ❑ B. `show dynamic mac`
   ❑ C. `show mac-address-table`
   ❑ D. `show mac interface`

Quick Answer: **94**
Detailed Answer: **100**

44. Which of the following contributes to congestion on an Ethernet network?

   ❑ A. Use of full-duplex mode
   ❑ B. Creation of new collision domain
   ❑ C. Creation of new broadcast domain
   ❑ D. Addition of a hub to the network

Quick Answer: **94**
Detailed Answer: **100**

45. Which of the following frame transmission methods has the most latency?

   ❑ A. Store-and-forward
   ❑ B. Cut-through
   ❑ C. Modified cut-through
   ❑ D. Fragment-free

Quick Answer: **94**
Detailed Answer: **100**

46. Which of the following hexadecimal values represents the decimal value of 215?

   ❑ A. 0xBA
   ❑ B. 0x9F
   ❑ C. 0xAA
   ❑ D. 0xD7

Quick Answer: **94**
Detailed Answer: **101**

47. Which of the following hexadecimal values represents the decimal value of 105?

- ❏ A. 0x69
- ❏ B. 0x23
- ❏ C. 0xAA
- ❏ D. 0xD7

Quick Answer: **94**
Detailed Answer: **101**

48. Which of the following binary values represents 0xB2?

- ❏ A. 10110010
- ❏ B. 10110101
- ❏ C. 11001100
- ❏ D. 11010100

Quick Answer: **94**
Detailed Answer: **101**

49. Your boss asks you to explain why you purchased switches instead of the "cheaper" hubs, because they do the same thing. What do you tell him to justify the purchase of the switches?

- ❏ A. Hubs do not extend the length of an Ethernet segment.
- ❏ B. Hubs do not offer half-duplex connections.
- ❏ C. Hubs do not give dedicated bandwidth to each end user.
- ❏ D. Hubs do not accept 100Mbps connections.

Quick Answer: **94**
Detailed Answer: **101**

50. What is the maximum number of switch hops that the 802.1d Spanning-Tree Protocol can monitor?

- ❏ A. 4
- ❏ B. 5
- ❏ C. 6
- ❏ D. 7
- ❏ E. 8

Quick Answer: **94**
Detailed Answer: **101**

Quick Check Answer Key

1. C	**26.** C
2. A, D	**27.** A
3. D	**28.** E
4. A	**29.** C, E
5. A, D, E	**30.** A, D
6. B, D	**31.** D
7. B, C	**32.** C
8. C	**33.** B
9. D	**34.** A, D
10. A	**35.** C
11. D	**36.** D
12. C	**37.** E
13. D	**38.** A, B, C
14. C	**39.** B, D
15. C	**40.** A
16. A	**41.** C
17. B	**42.** C
18. C	**43.** C
19. B	**44.** D
20. A, B	**45.** A
21. D	**46.** D
22. C	**47.** A
23. D, E	**48.** A
24. A	**49.** C
25. D	**50.** D

Answers and Explanations

1. **Answer: C.** Switches provide a separate circuit for each interface, and thus provide a separate collision domain for each interface. A is incorrect because hubs do not process frames. B is incorrect because hubs suffer from collisions that decrease bandwidth. D is incorrect, as switches flood received broadcasts.

2. **Answers: A and D.** Half-duplex Ethernet typically operates in a shared collision domain. This allows only one device to send or receive data at a time. If any additional devices attempt to transmit, a collision results. Network hubs operate in this manner. Because of this limitation, half-duplex has lower effective throughput than full-duplex, so D is correct as well. B is incorrect, as full-duplex connections typically operate in a private collision domain. C is incorrect because full-duplex has a higher effective throughput. E is incorrect, as Ethernet has no control over broadcasts.

3. **Answer: D.** You must be in VLAN Configuration mode for VLAN1. A is incorrect because you cannot configure IP addresses in Privileged EXEC mode. B is incorrect because that is not a valid command. C is incorrect because you must specify the subnet mask when performing this command.

4. **Answer: A.** Store-and-forward transmission checks the entire length of the frame before sending it out the appropriate interface or interfaces. B is incorrect, as there is no such method. C is incorrect, as cut-through transmission sends the frame through as soon as the destination MAC address is read. D is incorrect, as fragment-free transmission checks the first 64 bytes before sending the frame.

5. **Answers: A, D, and E.** By default, a switch boots up with the following configuration:

No IP address

CDP Enabled

Ports Auto-Negotiate

Spanning-Tree Enabled

No Console Password

6. **Answers: B and D.** MAC addresses are 48-bit hexadecimal numbers that are often shown as 12 digits. The allowable values in hexadecimal are 0–9 and A–F. Answer A has too many digits, and C and E include the letter G.

7. **Answers: B and C.** Bridges build the bridge table by listening to incoming frames and examining the source MAC address in the frame. Switches are multiport bridges that allow you to create multiple collision domains. A is incorrect, as bridges are software-based, and switches have hardware that assist

in speeding up transactions. D is incorrect, as both bridges and switches forward broadcasts.

8. **Answer: C.** Cisco and other networking companies refer to the addition of segments on a network as *microsegmentation*. Answers A, B, and D are not real terms.

9. **Answer: D.** As the frame check sequence (FCS) is located in the frame trailer, only store-and-forward switching, which buffers the whole frame before sending it, is able to perform such checks. A is incorrect, as store-and-forward is the slowest of all transmission types. B is incorrect, as the switch uses more memory to store the incoming frames. C is incorrect, as store-and-forward and cut-through are nonproprietary.

10. **Answer: A.** By issuing the `ip-default gateway` command, you are specifying a router that the switch can send frames to if they are sent outside the network segment. This is necessary whenever you want to telnet to a switch from a remote network. B is a nonexistent command on a switch. C is used only on routers. D is a nonexistent command.

11. **Answer: D.** Spanning-Tree Protocol was developed by DEC and updated by the IEEE 802.1d standard. It dynamically monitors your switched environment and blocks ports to stop loops from happening in your switched environment. A and C are incorrect, as they do not contain or create routing loops. B is incorrect because STP does not stop broadcasts.

12. **Answer: C.** When a port is in Learning mode, it learns MAC addresses and places them into the Content Addressable Memory (CAM) table, but it does not forward data frames. This allows the switch to know the MAC address(es) connected to the port before the port begins forwarding. A and B are incorrect, as both of those modes do not learn MAC addresses. D is incorrect because the port learns MAC addresses as well as forwards frames.

13. **Answer: D.** Designated ports on a network segment are placed into a forwarding state. A is incorrect, as nondesignated ports are placed into a blocked state. While designated ports transition through the listening and learning states, they do not remain there; thus, B and C are incorrect.

14. **Answer: C.** The convergence time of 802.1d STP is approximately 50 seconds. Thus A, B, and D are incorrect.

15. **Answer: C.** The 24 FastEthernet Ports operate at 100Mbps in either full- or half-duplex mode. In half-duplex mode, they have 100Mbps to send or receive traffic. If changed to full-duplex mode, the hosts have 100Mbps to send and 100Mbps to receive (theoretically doubling the amount of bandwidth). Answers A, B, and D are incorrect values.

16. **Answer: A.** If you issue the command no cdp run, the switch does not allow CDP frames to be sent out of any interface on the switch. This command is given in Global Configuration mode. B is incorrect, as it disables CDP only on a particular interface. C and D are not valid commands, and thus are incorrect.

17. **Answer: B.** If you issue the command no cdp enable, the switch disables CDP advertisements on a particular interface. A is incorrect, as no cdp run disables all interfaces. C and D are not valid commands, and thus are incorrect.

18. **Answer: C.** Bridge Protocol Data Units are used by STP to monitor the switched environment and perform root bridge elections. A is incorrect, as packets are Layer 3 data units, whereas Spanning-Tree is Layer 2. B is incorrect, as data frames are not affected by STP. D is incorrect because VTP is used to advertise VLAN information to other switches.

19. **Answer: B.** Bridge ID is made up of the bridge priority and MAC address of a particular port. The lowest bridge ID for a switch on a network segment becomes the root bridge. A and C are incorrect, as a BPDU does not have these items. D is incorrect, as the MAC address by itself is not enough to choose the root bridge; rather, it is combined with the bridge priority field to create the bridge ID.

20. **Answers: A and B.** Full-duplex requires point-to-point links and provides collision-free operation, as it has a separate pair of wires for transmitting and receiving. C is incorrect, as it has no need to reschedule transmissions. D is incorrect, as two pairs of wires for transmitting and receiving are necessary for full-duplex.

21. **Answer: D.** You make the speed and duplex settings in Interface Configuration mode. A, B, and C are incorrect, as those modes do not allow you to make speed and duplex changes.

22. **Answer: C.** When you decrease the default bridge priority of 32768, you ensure that the switch will have the lowest bridge ID. A is incorrect, as the MAC address is a burned-in address on the interfaces. B is incorrect, as the lowest bridge ID decides the root bridge, not the highest. D is incorrect, as the router ID is used in OSPF, which is not a Layer 2 switch ability.

23. **Answers: D and E.** Modified cut-through transmission (also known as *fragment-free*) checks the first 64 bytes of a frame before forwarding it out. A is incorrect, as store-and-forward transmission waits until the entire frame is checked before sending it out. B is incorrect, as cut-through transmission checks the destination address only before forwarding. C is not a valid frame transmission method.

24. **Answer: A.** When you are configuring port security, all commands begin with the switchport port-security syntax. In addition, the port must be configured

as an access port before the port-security features will function (by typing `switchport mode access`). The `switchport port-security` command enables the port-security feature. You must then add your MAC addresses using the `switchport port-security mac-address` command. Finally, using the `switchport port-security violation shutdown` command instructs the port to shut down when it sees a bad MAC address. All other answers are missing one or more critical pieces of this syntax.

25. **Answer: D.** The `show port-security interface fa0/20` command allows you to see any port security features you have enabled on an interface. A is incorrect because the `show interface` command just shows you port statistics such as the number of packets and bytes sent and received. B is incorrect because this command shows you Layer 3 statistics for the interface, and is typically used for routed interfaces. Answer C is incorrect because this command displays the access or trunking characteristics of the port.

26. **Answer: C.** The 802.3 protocol specifies Ethernet. A is incorrect; 802.1 standards specify general networking recommendations and requirements, which are media- and vendor-neutral. The 802.1 protocol also specifies bridging/switching standards. B is incorrect, as 802.2 protocols specify the Logical Link Control sublayer of the Data Link layer. D is incorrect, as 802.5 specifies token ring technologies.

27. **Answer: A.** Full-duplex requires a point-to-point connection, and a switch connecting to another switch provides it. B, C, and D are incorrect because any device connecting to a hub is not considered a point-to-point connection.

28. **Answer: E.** You make this configuration setting on a particular interface, thus the need to be in Interface Configuration mode. A and C are incorrect because the commands are given in the wrong configuration mode. B, D, and F are incorrect commands.

29. **Answers: C and E.** Hubs work on half-duplex mode. If more devices connect to a hub and are sending simultaneously, collisions occur. ARP and IPX SAP traffic is broadcast-based and also creates congestion in the network. A is incorrect, as the creation of a new collision domain means connecting a switch instead of a hub. This does not contribute to congestion. B is incorrect, as the creation of VLANs in a switch isolates a broadcast domain. D is incorrect, as switches help contain congestion.

30. **Answers: A and D.** For an administrator to remotely manage a switch, an IP address must be assigned, and a default gateway must be set for return traffic. B is incorrect, as a routing protocol is not mandatory; static routes can be used. C is incorrect, as some routers and switches can use half-duplex to communicate. E is incorrect, as you do not need a route from the router to the switch; that's what the default gateway accomplishes.

31. **Answer: D.** Spanning-Tree Protocol (STP) ensures that there are no loops in your redundant switched network. When a port or switch fails, STP converges through four stages, taking approximately 50 seconds to do so. A, B, and C are incorrect times of convergence, even when using STP modifications such as PortFast, BackboneFast, and UplinkFast.

32. **Answer: C.** When STP is merely monitoring the switched network and all ports are in their appropriate blocking or forwarding state, it is known as a *converged network*. A is incorrect; although you might describe a converged network as stable, it is not the correct definition. B is incorrect, as blocking is a port state. D is incorrect, as STP dynamically monitors the switched network for any changes because of failed switches or disabled ports.

33. **Answer: B.** The Protocol Data Units (PDUs) that operate at Layer 2 of the OSI Model are called *frames*. A is incorrect, as bits are at Layer 1. C is incorrect, as packets are at Layer 3. D is incorrect, as segments are at Layer 4.

34. **Answers: A and D.** Full-duplex provides separate transmit and receive circuits, thus effectively doubling the total bandwidth. Because of this behavior, it requires point-to-point connections. B is incorrect, as full- and half-duplex are Ethernet behaviors, not token ring, which relies on token passing. C is incorrect, as full-duplex, with its separate transmit and receive circuits, does not have collisions.

35. **Answer: C.** By default, Layer 2 switches cannot stop broadcasts, and floods them out all ports except the port on which the broadcast was received. A is incorrect as it reads, because adding more ports means adding more end-user broadcasts. B is incorrect, as switches are not efficient with forwarding broadcasts: They flood broadcasts out all ports by default. Only by using VLANs are they able to control broadcasts. D is incorrect, as switches do not "process" broadcasts; they merely flood them out all other ports. However, CPU utilization increases on PCs.

36. **Answer: D.** Adjusting your spanning-tree priority to a lower number reduces the switch Bridge ID. This makes it more likely to become the root of the spanning-tree network. The lower the switch Bridge ID, the more likely the chance of becoming the root. Answer A is incorrect because there is no `spanning-tree root` command. You could use the `spanning-tree vlan 1 root primary` command, which automatically lowers the Bridge Priority to 4096. Answer B is incorrect, as you are not able to change the MAC address your switch uses for STP in this way. Answer C is incorrect because you need to dictate which VLAN the STP priority is changed for (because Cisco switches run an instance of STP per VLAN). In addition, adjusting the priority to a higher number makes it less likely to become the root.

37. **Answer: E.** You make this configuration setting on a particular interface, thus the need to be in Interface Configuration mode. A and C are incorrect, as the commands are given in the wrong configuration mode. B, D, and F are incorrect commands.

38. **Answers: A, B, and C.** The correct command is `duplex [full/half/auto]`. D is incorrect, as `control` is not a duplex setting on a Catalyst switch.

39. **Answers: B and D.** MAC addresses are 48-bit hexadecimal numbers that are often shown as 12 digits. The allowable values in hexadecimal are 0–9 and A–F. A is incorrect because it has too many digits. C and E are incorrect because they include the letter *X*.

40. **Answer: A.** A media access control (MAC) address is a unique physical address that is "burned" into a network interface. It operates at Layer 2 of the OSI Model. B is incorrect because there is no such thing. C is incorrect, as an IP address is a logical address that can be assigned or changed, and it operates at Layer 3 of the OSI Model. D is incorrect, as IPX is a Novell proprietary protocol that operates at Layer 3 of the OSI Model.

41. **Answer: C.** A switch helps provide more collision domains, thus keeping collisions from occurring. A and B are incorrect, as hubs and repeaters cannot segment your network; they merely retransmit whatever comes in. D is incorrect, as a terminal adapter is used to connect a non–ISDN-ready device to a NT1.

42. **Answer: C.** Virtual local area networks (VLANs) allow a switch to separate ports into different network segments or broadcast domains. A is incorrect, as CDP is used by Cisco devices to share management information. B is incorrect because RIP is a routing protocol that is not used by Layer 2 switches. D and E are incorrect, as duplex settings do not help set up broadcast domains.

43. **Answer: C.** The `show mac-address-table` command reports all static and dynamically learned MAC addresses to the terminal. A is incorrect, as the `show ip interface` command is used to verify routed interfaces on a router or L3 switch. B and D are incorrect, as there are no such commands.

44. **Answer: D.** Hubs are notorious for allowing collisions in a network, as they operate on a shared-wire technology. A is incorrect, as full-duplex does not allow collisions. B is incorrect, as creating collision domains lessens collisions and congestion. C is incorrect, as creating a broadcast domain decreases the number of broadcasts (which cause congestion) in your network.

45. **Answer: A.** Store-and-forward transmission buffers the entire contents of the frame before sending it out. B is incorrect, as cut-through transmission sends the frame through as soon as the destination MAC address is read. C and D are

incorrect, as modified cut-through and fragment-free transmission check the first 64 bytes before sending the frame.

46. **Answer: D.** The hexadecimal value of 215 is 0xAA, which equals 11010111 in binary. A, B, and C equal 186, 159, 170, respectively.

47. **Answer: A.** The hexadecimal value of 105 is 0x69, which equals 1101001 in binary. B, C, and D equal 35, 170, and 215, respectively.

48. **Answer: A.** The binary 10110010 is the equivalent of the hexadecimal 0xB2. B, C, and D equal 0xB5, 0xCC, and 0xD4, respectively.

49. **Answer: C.** Hubs do not separate each port into a separate collision domain. Separate collision domains grant dedicated bandwidth to each port, and thus each end user plugged into that port. A is not correct, as hubs can extend the length of an Ethernet segment. Hubs are also known as *multiport repeaters*. B is incorrect, as hubs do offer half-duplex connections. D is incorrect, as there are hubs that support FastEthernet connections.

50. **Answer: D.** The 802.1d STP can listen to up to seven consecutive *hops*, or switches chained together, before it is unable to monitor the topology. This is sometimes known as the *STP radius*. A, B, and C are incorrect, as STP can handle up to seven hops, and the question asks for the maximum. E is incorrect, as it exceeds the maximum of seven.

VLANs

1. You are creating a report recommending the use of VLANs in your network. Which of the following features are provided by VLANs? (Choose three.)
   - ❏ A. Segmentation
   - ❏ B. Flexibility
   - ❏ C. Logging
   - ❏ D. Security

2. Which of the following statements regarding VLANs is true?
   - ❏ A. A VLAN is a physical broadcast domain spanning multiple logical subnets.
   - ❏ B. A VLAN is a logical broadcast domain spanning multiple physical subnets.
   - ❏ C. A VLAN is a logical broadcast domain spanning multiple logical subnets.
   - ❏ D. A VLAN is a physical broadcast domain spanning multiple physical subnets.

3. On which of the following devices can you implement VLANs?
   - ❏ A. Bridges
   - ❏ B. Routers
   - ❏ C. Hubs
   - ❏ D. Switches

4. Which of the following allows a port to carry traffic for multiple VLANs?
   - ❏ A. Port spanning
   - ❏ B. A trunk
   - ❏ C. Fast Ethernet
   - ❏ D. Split horizon

Quick Check

5. Which of the following are membership modes supported by VLANs? (Choose two.)

Quick Answer: **113**
Detailed Answer: **114**

- ❑ A. Public
- ❑ B. Private
- ❑ C. Static
- ❑ D. Dynamic

6. You need to configure a VLAN Management Policy Server. Which of the following switches can fill this role? (Choose two.)

Quick Answer: **113**
Detailed Answer: **114**

- ❑ A. Catalyst 1924
- ❑ B. Catalyst 2950
- ❑ C. Catalyst 5000
- ❑ D. Catalyst 6509

7. Which piece of information is used by a VLAN Management Policy Server to dynamically assign a port to a VLAN?

Quick Answer: **113**
Detailed Answer: **114**

- ❑ A. Source IP address
- ❑ B. Source hostname
- ❑ C. Source MAC address
- ❑ D. Source port

8. Which of the following statements about VLAN Membership modes are correct? (Choose two.)

Quick Answer: **113**
Detailed Answer: **114**

- ❑ A. A dynamic port can belong to multiple VLANs at once.
- ❑ B. Multiple hosts from different VLANs can be active on a dynamic port.
- ❑ C. The Catalyst switch queries a VMPS when a frame arrives on a dynamic port.
- ❑ D. The VMPS contains a database mapping MAC address to VLAN membership.

9. Which of the following technologies are methods to implement trunking? (Choose two.)

Quick Answer: **113**
Detailed Answer: **115**

- ❑ A. 802.1Q
- ❑ B. WEP
- ❑ C. ISL
- ❑ D. IEEE 1394

10. In 802.1Q trunking, what is the default native VLAN ID?

    ❑ A. VLAN 0

    ❑ B. VLAN 1

    ❑ C. VLAN A

    ❑ D. There is no default VLAN ID.

Quick Answer: **113**
Detailed Answer: **115**

11. Which of the following statements about 802.1Q frame tagging are correct? (Choose two.)

    ❑ A. The 802.1Q protocol tags frames for the native VLAN.

    ❑ B. The 802.1Q protocol doesn't tag frames for the native VLAN.

    ❑ C. Tagged frames can be read by ordinary stations.

    ❑ D. Tagged frames cannot be read by ordinary stations.

Quick Answer: **113**
Detailed Answer: **115**

12. Adding a tag recomputes which portion of the 802.1Q frame?

    ❑ A. Destination

    ❑ B. Source

    ❑ C. Data

    ❑ D. FCS

Quick Answer: **113**
Detailed Answer: **115**

13. Which of the following are characteristics of ISL? (Choose three.)

    ❑ A. Vendor interoperability

    ❑ B. Supports full-duplex

    ❑ C. Supports half-duplex

    ❑ D. Trunking

    ❑ E. Encryption

    ❑ F. Authentication

Quick Answer: **113**
Detailed Answer: **115**

14. ISL functions at which layer of the OSI Model?

    ❑ A. Physical layer

    ❑ B. Data-link layer

    ❑ C. Network layer

    ❑ D. Session layer

Quick Answer: **113**
Detailed Answer: **115**

15. What does ISL use to confirm that a frame has not been damaged during transit?

    ❑ A. CRC

    ❑ B. Digital signature

    ❑ C. Data integrity

    ❑ D. BPDU

Quick Answer: **113**
Detailed Answer: **115**

16. The VTP functions at which layer of the OSI Model?

   ❏ A. Physical layer
   ❏ B. Data-link layer
   ❏ C. Network layer
   ❏ D. Session layer

Quick Answer: **113**
Detailed Answer: **115**

17. Which of the following is the primary function of VTP?

   ❏ A. Encryption
   ❏ B. Authentication
   ❏ C. Pruning
   ❏ D. Messaging

Quick Answer: **113**
Detailed Answer: **115**

18. How many VTP domains can a switch be configured in?

   ❏ A. 1
   ❏ B. 64
   ❏ C. 255
   ❏ D. Unlimited

Quick Answer: **113**
Detailed Answer: **116**

19. Which of the following are modes under which VTP operates? (Choose three.)

   ❏ A. Server
   ❏ B. Client
   ❏ C. Peer
   ❏ D. Transparent
   ❏ E. Static
   ❏ F. Dynamic

Quick Answer: **113**
Detailed Answer: **116**

20. You have installed a Catalyst switch in your network. Which VTP mode is it operating in by default?

   ❏ A. Server
   ❏ B. Client
   ❏ C. Peer
   ❏ D. Transparent
   ❏ E. Static
   ❏ F. Dynamic

Quick Answer: **113**
Detailed Answer: **116**

21. Where are VLAN configurations stored?

   ❏ A. RAM
   ❏ B. NVRAM
   ❏ C. Flash
   ❏ D. They are not stored.

Quick Answer: **113**
Detailed Answer: **116**

22. Which of the following is a VTP mode and does not save configuration information?

   ❑ A. Server

   ❑ B. Client

   ❑ C. Peer

   ❑ D. Transparent

   ❑ E. Static

   ❑ F. Dynamic

Quick Answer: **113**
Detailed Answer: **116**

23. Which of the following are VTP modes with the capability to create, modify, and delete VLANs? (Choose two.)

   ❑ A. Server

   ❑ B. Client

   ❑ C. Peer

   ❑ D. Transparent

   ❑ E. Static

   ❑ F. Dynamic

Quick Answer: **113**
Detailed Answer: **116**

24. Which of the following VTP modes forward advertisements? (Choose three.)

   ❑ A. Server

   ❑ B. Client

   ❑ C. Peer

   ❑ D. Transparent

   ❑ E. Static

   ❑ F. Dynamic

Quick Answer: **113**
Detailed Answer: **116**

25. Which of the following VTP modes does not synchronize its information?

   ❑ A. Server

   ❑ B. Client

   ❑ C. Peer

   ❑ D. Transparent

   ❑ E. Static

   ❑ F. Dynamic

Quick Answer: **113**
Detailed Answer: **116**

26. By default, how often are VTP advertisements sent?

   ❑ A. 30 seconds

   ❑ B. 1 minute

   ❑ C. 5 minutes

   ❑ D. 10 minutes

Quick Answer: **113**
Detailed Answer: **117**

Quick Check

27. Which transmission method does VTP use to send advertisements?

Quick Answer: **113**
Detailed Answer: **117**

- ❑ A. Broadcast
- ❑ B. Unicast
- ❑ C. Multicast
- ❑ D. Groupcast

28. Which of the following commands resets the configuration revision number on a Catalyst switch?

Quick Answer: **113**
Detailed Answer: **117**

- ❑ A. `vtp reset`
- ❑ B. `vtp server reset`
- ❑ C. `delete vtp`
- ❑ D. `vtp revision 0`

29. When a switch receives advertisements containing conflicting VLAN configuration information, how is the conflict resolved?

Quick Answer: **113**
Detailed Answer: **117**

- ❑ A. The first advertisement received is processed.
- ❑ B. The last advertisement received is processed.
- ❑ C. The latest time stamp is kept.
- ❑ D. The highest revision number is kept.

30. Which process uses VLAN advertisements to determine when a trunk connection is unnecessarily flooding traffic?

Quick Answer: **113**
Detailed Answer: **117**

- ❑ A. Flood detection
- ❑ B. Broadcast quenching
- ❑ C. Flood quenching
- ❑ D. VTP pruning

31. Which of the following VTP modes supports the enabling of VTP pruning?

Quick Answer: **113**
Detailed Answer: **117**

- ❑ A. Server
- ❑ B. Client
- ❑ C. Peer
- ❑ D. Transparent
- ❑ E. Static
- ❑ F. Dynamic

32. On a Catalyst 2950, what is the default VTP domain name?

Quick Answer: **113**
Detailed Answer: **117**

- ❑ A. VLAN1
- ❑ B. VLAN0
- ❑ C. VTP 0
- ❑ D. None

33. Which mode must you be in to configure a VTP domain for a Catalyst 2950 switch? (Choose the best answer.)

    ❏ A. Privileged EXEC mode
    ❏ B. Global Configuration mode
    ❏ C. VLAN Configuration mode
    ❏ D. User EXEC mode

Quick Answer: **113**
Detailed Answer: **117**

34. You want to configure a trunk port on a Catalyst 5000 series switch to use desirable negotiation. What command must you enter?

    ❏ A. `trunk desirable`
    ❏ B. `trunk negotiation desirable`
    ❏ C. `set trunk desirable`
    ❏ D. `negotiation desirable`

Quick Answer: **113**
Detailed Answer: **117**

35. You need to assign a port as the trunk port. What configuration mode must you be in?

    ❏ A. Privileged EXEC mode
    ❏ B. Global Configuration mode
    ❏ C. Interface Configuration mode
    ❏ D. User EXEC mode

Quick Answer: **113**
Detailed Answer: **118**

36. What command enables pruning on a Catalyst 2950 switch?

    ❏ A. `vtp pruning on`
    ❏ B. `pruning on`
    ❏ C. `vtp pruning enable`
    ❏ D. `pruning enable`

Quick Answer: **113**
Detailed Answer: **118**

37. Which of the following commands defines `cisco01` for your VTP domain name?

    ❏ A. `vtp name cisco01`
    ❏ B. `vtp domain cisco01`
    ❏ C. `vtp domain name cisco01`
    ❏ D. `domain cisco01`

Quick Answer: **113**
Detailed Answer: **118**

38. You are configuring a trunk on your Catalyst 2950 switch. Which command is appropriate?

    ❏ A. `switchport trunk`
    ❏ B. `port trunk`
    ❏ C. `switchport mode trunk`
    ❏ D. `port mode trunk`

Quick Answer: **113**
Detailed Answer: **118**

39. Which of the following are considered true trunking protocols? (Choose two.)

    ❏ A. ISL
    ❏ B. VTP
    ❏ C. 802.1q
    ❏ D. 802.1d

Quick Answer: **113**
Detailed Answer: **118**

40. Which mode must you be in to configure an ISL trunk port?

    ❏ A. Interface Configuration mode
    ❏ B. Port Configuration mode
    ❏ C. Global Configuration mode
    ❏ D. Line Configuration mode

Quick Answer: **113**
Detailed Answer: **118**

41. You are trying to create VLANs that will be automatically propagated out to all other switches. You create the VLANs, but they are not propagated to other switches. You type the show vtp status command and receive the following output. What is wrong?

Quick Answer: **113**
Detailed Answer: **118**

```
VLANSwitch> show vtp status
VTP Version                  : 2
Configuration Revision       : 0
Maximum VLANs supported locally : 250
Number of existing VLANs     : 18
VTP Operating Mode           : Transparent
VTP Domain Name              :
VTP Pruning Mode             : Enabled
VTP V2 Mode                  : Disabled
VTP Traps Generation         : Disabled
MD5 digest                   : 0xBF 0x84 0x94 0x33
0xFC 0xAF 0xB5 0x70
Configuration last modified by 0.0.0.0 at 0-0-00
00:00:00
```

    ❏ A. You must first disable VTP pruning to allow the revisions to propagate.
    ❏ B. The VTP version number is wrong.
    ❏ C. You need to change the VTP mode to Client mode.
    ❏ D. You need to change the VTP mode to Server mode.

Quick Check

42. What is the maximum number of VLANs that can be configured on a switch?

- ❑ A. 8
- ❑ B. 128
- ❑ C. 255
- ❑ D. Switch-dependent

Quick Answer: 113
Detailed Answer: 118

43. You have hired a new salesperson. All sales associates are
placed in VLAN5. You are adding a port on your Catalyst
2950 switch to VLAN 5. Which commands accomplish this
goal?

- ❑ A. `wg_sw1(config-if)#switchport access vlan 5`
- ❑ B. `wg_sw1(config)#vlan-membership port vlan 5`
- ❑ C. `wg_sw1(config-if)#vlan-membership static 5`
- ❑ D. `wg_sw1(config) #port membership vlan 5`

Quick Answer: 113
Detailed Answer: 118

44. Which statement is accurate when describing the role of a
VLAN in a corporate network?

- ❑ A. It can be used to reduce the segments in a network.
- ❑ B. It can be used to reduce broadcasts/multicasts in a network.
- ❑ C. It reduces the security capability of a network.
- ❑ D. It does not allow Quality of Service to be deployed.

Quick Answer: 113
Detailed Answer: 119

45. You want to view VLAN information for your Catalyst 2950,
including when the configuration was last modified. What
command should you enter?

- ❑ A. `show vlan`
- ❑ B. `show vtp`
- ❑ C. `show vtp status`
- ❑ D. `show ports`

Quick Answer: 113
Detailed Answer: 119

46. You want to quickly view the VLANs running STP, the number of ports in each VLAN, and the ports on the switch that
are blocking. Which command should you enter?

- ❑ A. `show spantree`
- ❑ B. `show stp`
- ❑ C. `show vlan`
- ❑ D. `show vtp`

Quick Answer: 113
Detailed Answer: 119

47. A VLAN you created previously is now no longer needed, and you want to remove it. The VLAN is named VLAN4. Which command should you enter?

Quick Answer: **113**
Detailed Answer: **119**

❏ A. `vlan VLAN4 delete`
❏ B. `no vlan VLAN4`
❏ C. `delete vlan VLAN4`
❏ D. `vlan VLAN4 disable`

48. On a Catalyst 2950, which mode must you be in to delete a VLAN?

Quick Answer: **113**
Detailed Answer: **119**

❏ A. VLAN Configuration mode
❏ B. Global Configuration mode
❏ C. Interface Configuration mode
❏ D. Privileged EXEC mode

49. For traffic to pass from one VLAN to another, a _____ is required that can understand trunking protocols.

Quick Answer: **113**
Detailed Answer: **119**

❏ A. Router
❏ B. Switch
❏ C. Hub
❏ D. Trunking bridge

50. You want to verify VLAN membership on a Catalyst 2950. You want to display VLAN assignment and membership type for all switch ports; however, you do not want to view any extra information. Which command best displays this information?

Quick Answer: **113**
Detailed Answer: **119**

❏ A. `show vlan short`
❏ B. `show vlan brief`
❏ C. `display vtp brief`
❏ D. `display vtp short`

Quick Check Answer Key

1. A, B, D
2. B
3. D
4. B
5. C, D
6. C, D
7. C
8. C, D
9. A, C
10. B
11. B, D
12. D
13. B, C, D
14. B
15. A
16. B
17. D
18. A
19. A, B, D
20. A
21. B
22. B
23. A, D
24. A, B, D
25. D
26. C
27. C
28. C
29. D
30. D
31. A
32. D
33. C
34. C
35. C
36. C
37. B
38. C
39. A, C
40. A
41. D
42. D
43. A
44. B
45. C
46. A
47. B
48. A
49. A
50. B

Answers and Explanations

1. **Answers: A, B, and D.** A is correct because VLANs can segment stations logically by function or team. B is correct because flexibility is added; users can be grouped by department, cross-functional product teams, or other grouping definitions you choose. D is correct; security is provided because members of one VLAN do not see the traffic on another VLAN. C is incorrect; there is no logging inherent to VLANs.

2. **Answer: B.** VLANs are logical broadcast domains, defined by the administrator, and can span multiple physical subnets. A is incorrect because VLANs are logical broadcast domains, not physical. C is incorrect because VLANs span multiple physical subnets, not logical subnets. D is incorrect because VLANs create logical broadcast domains, not physical domains.

3. **Answer: D.** VLANs are supported on switches. A is incorrect, as bridges do not support VLANs. B is incorrect because VLANs are not implemented on routers. C is incorrect, as hubs do not provide support for VLANs.

4. **Answer: B.** A trunk provides capability for a VLAN to span across multiple switches because it can carry traffic for multiple VLANs. A is incorrect because port spanning is not the technology used to carry traffic for multiple VLANs. C is incorrect because fast Ethernet is a version of Ethernet that can operate at 100Mbps. D is incorrect because split horizon helps prevent routing loops by not sending route information out the interface that received it.

5. **Answers: C and D.** C is correct because static mode refers to port assignments configured manually by an administrator. D is correct because dynamic port configuration is supported as well, when using a VLAN Management Policy Server. A is incorrect; there is no public membership mode. B is incorrect, as there is no private VLAN membership mode.

6. **Answers: C and D.** The Catalyst 5000 series can be configured as a VMPS, and the 6509 can be configured as a VMPS. A is incorrect, as the Catalyst 1924 does not support configuration as a VMPS. B is incorrect, as the Catalyst 2950 also does not support configuration as a VMPS.

7. **Answer: C.** The source MAC address of the sending station is used to assign a port to a specific VLAN. A is incorrect because the source IP address is irrelevant to the server. B is incorrect, as the hostname of the source device is not used to assign VLANs. D is incorrect because the source port of the traffic is not a consideration when assigning VLANs.

8. **Answers: C and D.** When a Catalyst switch receives a frame on a dynamic port, it queries the VMPS. The VMPS then checks its database, which contains mappings of MAC addresses to VLANs. A is incorrect because a dynamic port

can belong to only one VLAN at a time. B is incorrect because multiple hosts from different VLANs cannot all be active on a dynamic port.

9. **Answers: A and C.** The 802.1Q protocol is an IEEE standard, nonproprietary method to implement trunking, and ISL is a proprietary Cisco protocol for implementing trunking. B is incorrect, as WEP is used to secure wireless networks. D is incorrect because IEEE 1394 (also known as FireWire) is a PC communications port.

10. **Answer: B.** In 802.1Q trunking, the identifier value of the native VLAN is VLAN 1. A is incorrect because VLAN 1 is the default VLAN, not VLAN 0. C is incorrect because the default VLAN identifier is numerical. D is incorrect, as there is a default VLAN ID (VLAN 1).

11. **Answers: B and D.** The 802.1Q protocol doesn't tag native VLAN frames, and tagged frames cannot be read by ordinary stations. A is incorrect because native VLAN frames are not tagged. C is incorrect because the information added when a frame is tagged renders it unreadable by ordinary stations.

12. **Answer: D.** Adding a tag recomputes the frame check sequence. A is incorrect because the destination of the frame remains unchanged. B is incorrect, as the source of the frame does not change. C is incorrect because the data remains unchanged.

13. **Answers: B, C, and D.** ISL supports full-duplex and half-duplex, and trunking is supported to allow VLAN information among different switches. A is incorrect because ISL is proprietary to Cisco. E is incorrect because ISL does not provide encryption. F is incorrect because ISL does not provide authentication.

14. **Answer: B.** ISL functions at Layer 2, the Data-link layer of the OSI Model. A, C, and D are incorrect because ISL does not function at those layers of the OSI Model.

15. **Answer: A.** The CRC ensures the frame has not been damaged in transit. B is incorrect because a digital signature is not used by ISL. C is not correct, because even though the idea of data integrity is to ensure that data is not modified, it does not specifically address the question. D is incorrect; Bridge Protocol Data Units indicate whether the frame is a spanning-tree BPDU.

16. **Answer: B.** VTP functions at Layer 2, the Data-link layer of the OSI Model. A, C, and D are incorrect because VTP does not function at those layers of the OSI Model.

17. **Answer: D.** The primary function of VTP is messaging, to ensure VLAN configuration consistency and the management of additions, deletions, and name changes. C is incorrect. VTP does manage deletions; however, it is not the sole, primary function of VTP. A and B are incorrect because encryption and authentication are not features of VTP.

18. **Answer: A.** A switch can be in only a single VTP domain. B, C, and D are incorrect, as a switch cannot belong to 64, 255, or an unlimited number of domains.

19. **Answers: A, B, and D.** Server mode is one of three VTP modes of operation; Client mode is a VTP mode of operation that does not allow creation, modification, or deletion of VLANs; and although Transparent mode acts much like Server mode, it does not synchronize information. C, E, and F are incorrect because Peer, Static, and Dynamic are not VTP modes.

20. **Answer: A.** Server mode is one of three VTP modes of operation, and is the default. B is incorrect, because although Client mode is a VTP mode of operation that doesn't allow the creation, modification, or deletion of VLANs, it is not the default. D is incorrect, because although Transparent mode acts much like Server mode, it does not synchronize information and is not the default. C, E, and F are not VTP modes.

21. **Answer: B.** NVRAM is used to store VLAN configurations, not RAM or flash memory. D is incorrect; configurations are stored in NVRAM in case of a power failure.

22. **Answer: B.** Client mode forwards advertisements and synchronizes information. It does not save information in NVRAM. A is incorrect, as Server mode is a VTP mode that creates, modifies, and deletes VLANs. It forwards advertisements it receives, synchronizes information, and saves configuration information in NVRAM. D is incorrect, as Transparent mode creates, modifies, and deletes VLANs, and it forwards advertisements and saves configurations in NVRAM, but it does not synchronize. C, E, and F are not VTP modes.

23. **Answers: A and D.** Server mode is a VTP mode that creates, modifies, and deletes VLANs. It forwards advertisements it receives, synchronizes information, and saves configuration information in NVRAM. D is correct because Transparent mode creates, modifies, and deletes VLANs. B is incorrect; Client mode forwards advertisements and synchronizes information, but it does not save information in NVRAM. C, E, and F are not VTP modes.

24. **Answers: A, B, and D.** Server mode is a VTP mode that creates, modifies, and deletes VLANs. It forwards advertisements it receives and synchronizes information. It saves configuration information in NVRAM. Client mode forwards advertisements and synchronizes information. It does not save information in NVRAM. Finally, Transparent mode creates, modifies, and deletes VLANs. C, E, and F are incorrect because they are not VTP modes.

25. **Answer: D.** Transparent mode creates, modifies, and deletes VLANs. It forwards advertisements and saves configurations in NVRAM. It does not synchronize, however. A is incorrect because Server mode is a VTP mode that

creates, modifies, and deletes VLANs, forwards advertisements it receives, synchronizes information, and saves configuration information in NVRAM. B is incorrect because Client mode forwards advertisements and synchronizes information but does not save information in NVRAM. C, E, and F are not VTP modes.

26. **Answer: C.** VTP advertisements are flooded through the management domain every five minutes by default. Answers A, B, and D are not the default settings.

27. **Answer: C.** VTP uses multicast to send advertisements in the management domain. A is incorrect because broadcasts are not used for the propagation of advertisements. B is incorrect because unicasts are not as efficient for sending advertisements as multicast. D is incorrect, as there is no such method in VTP.

28. **Answer: C.** The `delete VTP` command resets the configuration revision number. A, B, and D are invalid commands.

29. **Answer: D.** Conflicts are resolved through revision numbers, and the higher revision number is processed. A is incorrect because order of reception is not a controlling factor. B is incorrect; the last advertisement is processed only if it has a higher revision number. C is incorrect because time stamps are not used.

30. **Answer: D.** VTP pruning is the process of reducing unnecessary flooded traffic. A is incorrect because flood detection is not a valid method. B and C are incorrect, as broadcast quenching and flood quenching are not valid processes.

31. **Answer: A.** Server mode is one of three VTP modes of operation, and is the default. It supports VTP pruning. B is incorrect, as Client mode is a VTP mode of operation that does not allow the creation, modification, or deletion of VLANs, and it doesn't support pruning. D is incorrect, because although Transparent mode acts much like Server mode, it does not synchronize information, and it doesn't support pruning. C, E, and F are not VTP modes.

32. **Answer: D.** There is no default VTP domain set. A is incorrect because VLAN1 is simply the management VLAN. B and C are invalid.

33 **Answer: C.** VTP domains on a Catalyst 2950 are created in VLAN Configuration mode. A is incorrect, because even as Privileged EXEC mode is required, you must enter the VLAN database command to get to VLAN Configuration mode. B is incorrect because this is valid only for Catalyst 1900 switches, which are now end of life. D is incorrect because no configuration changes can be made in User EXEC mode.

34. **Answer: C.** The correct syntax on a Catalyst 5000 switch is `set trunk desirable`. A is incorrect, as this is the improper syntax for this switch; however, it is correct for a Catalyst 1900 series switch. B is incorrect, as this command does not achieve the desired effect. D is incorrect, as this command results in an error.

35. **Answer: C.** Trunk ports are defined in Interface Configuration mode. A is incorrect, because even though Privileged EXEC mode is required, you must then enter Interface Configuration mode. B is incorrect; from Global Configuration mode, you must enter Interface Configuration mode. D is incorrect because no configuration changes are made in User EXEC mode.

36. **Answer: C.** The vtp pruning enable command enables pruning on the switch. A and D are incorrect, as these commands result in an error message. B is incorrect because this is an invalid IOS command.

37. **Answer: B.** The correct syntax is vtp domain name—in this case, vtp domain cisco01. A and C are incorrect because they are invalid syntax. D is incorrect, as this command is invalid.

38. **Answer: C.** The switchport mode trunk command sets the port as a trunk port for 802.1Q traffic. This command is used in Interface Configuration mode. A is incorrect because this command results in an error message. B and D are not valid IOS commands.

39. **Answers: A and C.** Interswitch Link and IEEE 802.1q are protocols that help define VLAN traffic over a single link. B is incorrect because VTP is merely a management protocol that helps to propagate VLANs to switches that belong to the same domain. D is incorrect because 802.1d is the IEEE standard for Spanning-Tree Protocol.

40. **Answer: A.** You are configuring a port interface, so Interface Configuration mode is required. B is incorrect because there is no such Interface Configuration mode. C is incorrect because this is an interface, not a global setting; thus, Global Configuration mode is not appropriate. D is incorrect because Line Configuration mode is not the correct mode.

41. **Answer: D.** A switch must be in VTP Server mode to propagate VLAN information to other switches. A is incorrect, as VTP pruning doesn't stop VTP revisions from propagating; it merely stops broadcasts from going to switches that do not have ports belonging to the VLANs that have the broadcasts. B is incorrect, as the VTP version number doesn't affect the propagation of advertisements. C is incorrect, as clients are unable to create VLANs.

42. **Answer: D.** The exact maximum number of VLANs supported is switch-dependent. A, B, and C are incorrect because they are fixed numbers and not switch-dependent.

43. **Answer: A.** You go to the particular interface/port you want to assign to VLAN 5 and enter the command switchport access vlan (vlan#). B is incorrect because it is an invalid command. C is incorrect because this assigns a port to a VLAN on a 1900 series switch, not the 2950. D is incorrect because it is an invalid command.

44. **Answer: B.** A VLAN is considered its own broadcast domain. It helps contain broadcasts in a networked environment. A is incorrect because a VLAN actually segments the network even more. C is incorrect because VLANs are separate subnets that allow for Access-Lists to be applied, providing greater security. D is incorrect because Quality of Service can harness the power of VLANs to increase its functionality.

45. **Answer: C.** The show vtp status command displays the requested information. A is incorrect; this command is valid but does not show the requested information. B is incorrect, as this command is valid for a 1900 series switch. D is incorrect because show ports is an invalid command.

46. **Answer: A.** The show spantree command displays the requested information most effectively. B is incorrect because this command is not valid. C and D are valid commands but do not show the requested information.

47. **Answer: B.** The no vlan command followed by the VLAN ID is the proper syntax. A is incorrect because this is an invalid IOS command. C is incorrect, and this command results in an error. D is incorrect, as this is not the proper syntax for the requested task.

48. **Answer: A.** VLAN Configuration mode is used on Catalyst 2950 switches. B is incorrect; this command is entered in Global Configuration mode on a 1900 series switch. C and D are incorrect, as they are not the proper configuration modes.

49. **Answer: A.** The router can route between the different subnets for the VLANs. It also can run ISL or 802.1q. B is incorrect because a Layer 2 switch has no Layer 3 comprehension. C is incorrect because a Hub is merely a multi-port repeater with no capabilities to pass traffic between subnets. D is incorrect because there is no such device.

50. **Answer: B.** The show vlan brief command displays the required information. A, C, and D are incorrect, as these are invalid IOS commands.

Routing and Routing Protocols

Quick Check

1. You are setting up OSPF on your network and your junior administrator asks you about the router ID. She wants to know what sets the router ID for OSPF on your router. Your network is made up of ten 2611 routers with two serial, two Ethernet, and two loopback interfaces. What do you tell her?

Quick Answer: **136**
Detailed Answer: **137**

   ❑ A. It's the lowest IP address on your physical interfaces.
   ❑ B. It's the highest IP address on your physical interfaces.
   ❑ C. It's the highest IP address on your logical interfaces.
   ❑ D. It's the lowest IP address on your logical interfaces.
   ❑ E. It's the lowest IP address on any interface, physical or logical.

2. Your boss asks you to explain the difference between a routed protocol and a routing protocol. Which of the following statements best describe the difference? (Choose two.)

Quick Answer: **136**
Detailed Answer: **137**

   ❑ A. Routed protocols cannot cross routers.
   ❑ B. Routing protocols can identify data.
   ❑ C. Routed protocols help transport data between network segments.
   ❑ D. Routing protocols are used by routers to communicate routing information.

3. You have placed a static route on your router to get to Network A. You also have RIPv1 and OSPF running on your router. The router receives updates from RIP and OSPF on how to get to Network A. Which of the routes does the router use to get to Network A?

Quick Answer: **136**
Detailed Answer: **137**

   ❑ A. The static route
   ❑ B. The RIP route
   ❑ C. The OSPF route
   ❑ D. None of the above, as they will cancel each other out

Quick Check

Quick Answer: **136**
Detailed Answer: **137**

4. You issue the following command:

```
StudentA#show ip route

Codes: C - connected, S - static, I - IGRP, R - RIP, M - mobile,
➡ B - BGP D - EIGRP, EX - EIGRP external, O - OSPF, IA - OSPF
➡ inter area N1 - OSPF NSSA external type 1, N2 - OSPF NSSA
➡ external type 2 E1 - OSPF external type 1, E2 - OSPF external
➡ type 2, E - EGP i - IS-IS, L1 - IS-IS level-1, L2 - IS-IS
➡ level-2, * - candidate default U - per-user static route, o -
➡ ODR
Gateway of last resort is 172.31.0.1 to network 0.0.0.0
D 192.168.15.0/24 [90/2681856] via 10.0.0.2, 3w2d, Serial0/1
R 172.16.0.0/16 [120/1] via 172.31.0.1, 00:00:05, Serial0/0
  172.31.0.0/16 is variably subnetted, 2 subnets, 2 masks
D 172.31.0.0/16 is a summary, 3w2d, Null0
C 172.31.0.0/24 is directly connected, Serial0/0
C 192.168.250.0/24 is directly connected, Serial0/1.1
C 10.0.0.0/8 is directly connected, Serial0/1
  150.1.0.0/16 is variably subnetted, 2 subnets, 2 masks
C 150.1.3.0/24 is directly connected, Ethernet0/0
D 150.1.0.0/16 is a summary, 3w2d, Null0
S* 0.0.0.0/0 [1/0] via 172.31.0.1
```

What is the meaning of the [90/2681856] in the output following the command?

- ❏ A. It's the port number and hop count of the RIP routing protocol.
- ❏ B. It's the administrative distance and hop count of the EIGRP routing protocol.
- ❏ C. It's the port number and metric of the EIGRP routing protocol.
- ❏ D. It's the administrative distance and metric of the route learned through EIGRP.

5. On an OSPF router, you use the following command in Router Configuration mode for OSPF:

Quick Answer: **136**
Detailed Answer: **137**

```
network 0.0.0.0 255.255.255.255 area 0
```

What is the effect of this command?

- ❏ A. This command instructs OSPF to send an update to Area 0.
- ❏ B. This command configures the OSPF router with a router ID.
- ❏ C. This command includes all the connected interfaces and networks in the OSPF routing process.
- ❏ D. This command is invalid and is not accepted.

Quick Check

6. Which of the following is a link-state protocol that uses a complex database to choose the best route for each network?

❑ A. RIP

❑ B. OSPF

❑ C. IGRP

❑ D. BGP

Quick Answer: **136**
Detailed Answer: **138**

7. Which of the following commands enable IGRP routing on the ExamCram 4 router? (Choose three.)

❑ A. `ExamCram4(config)#router igrp`

❑ B. `ExamCram4(config)#router igrp 100`

❑ C. `ExamCram4(config-router)#network 192.168.0.0`

❑ D. `ExamCram4(config-router)#network 192.168.2.0`

❑ E. `ExamCram4(config-router)#network all`

❑ F. `ExamCram4(config-router)#network 192.168.3.0`

Quick Answer: **136**
Detailed Answer: **138**

8. When dealing with distance-vector routing protocols, you encounter the term *split-horizon*. Which of the following statements describes this feature?

❑ A. It allows routers to split up networks.

❑ B. All distance-vector protocols require fallback routers that might cause momentary loops as the topology changes.

❑ C. Convergence is achieved if all information about routers is sent out on all active interfaces.

❑ D. Information about a route should not be sent back in the direction from which the original update came.

Quick Answer: **136**
Detailed Answer: **138**

9. You are using RIP as your routing protocol. Your WAN service provider asks you to use the `passive-interface` command for the serial interface that is attached to the service provider. What does this command accomplish?

❑ A. It puts the interface in shutdown.

❑ B. It tells a router to send routing updates out the interface but not to listen to any routing updates.

❑ C. It allows an interface to remain up despite the fact that the service provider does not provide keepalives.

❑ D. It tells a router to receive routing updates on an interface but not to send updates via that interface.

Quick Answer: **136**
Detailed Answer: **138**

Quick Check

10. You need to configure a static route to reach the 10.20.0.0 network. Which of the following is an example of the correct syntax you should use?

   ❑ A. `ip route 10.20.0.0 255.255.0.0 10.10.0.1`
   ❑ B. `ip route 10.20.0.0 0.0.255.255 10.10.0.1`
   ❑ C. `route 10.20.0.0 255.255.0.0 serial 0 100`
   ❑ D. `route 10.20.0.0 255.255.0.0 10.10.0.1`

Quick Answer: **136**
Detailed Answer: **138**

11. What class of routing protocol combines aspects of the link-state and distance-vector algorithms?

   ❑ A. Mix
   ❑ B. Hybrid
   ❑ C. Link-distance
   ❑ D. Distance-link

Quick Answer: **136**
Detailed Answer: **138**

12. Which of the following routing protocols has a default administrative distance of 120 on Cisco routers?

   ❑ A. RIP
   ❑ B. IGRP
   ❑ C. OSPF
   ❑ D. EIGRP

Quick Answer: **136**
Detailed Answer: **138**

13. When a router sets the metric for a network that has gone down to the maximum value, what is it doing?

   ❑ A. Applying split-horizon
   ❑ B. Putting the route in hold-down
   ❑ C. Poisoning the route
   ❑ D. Sending a triggered update

Quick Answer: **136**
Detailed Answer: **139**

14. Which of these statements is true regarding distance-vector routing protocols?

   ❑ A. They send the entire routing table to directly connected neighbors.
   ❑ B. They send the entire routing table to every router in the network.
   ❑ C. They send the changes to the routing table to directly connected neighbors.
   ❑ D. They send the changes to the routing table to every router in the network.

Quick Answer: **136**
Detailed Answer: **139**

15. To prevent routing loops, distance-vector routing protocols use a maximum metric. What is the maximum reachable metric for RIP?

   ❑ A. 10
   ❑ B. 15
   ❑ C. 16
   ❑ D. 60
   ❑ E. 100
   ❑ F. 255

16. What routing loop solution prevents a router from sending information back to the neighbor that originally sent the information?

   ❑ A. Split-horizon
   ❑ B. Hold-down timer
   ❑ C. Maximum hop count
   ❑ D. Route poisoning
   ❑ E. Counting to infinity

17. After typing the command show ip route, you see a list of IP addresses with [120/8] next to them. What does the [120/8] mean?

   ❑ A. Cost/Metric
   ❑ B. Administrative Distance/Metric
   ❑ C. Metric/Distance
   ❑ D. Cost/Hop Count

18. You type show ip route on Router A to find out what entries are in your RIP routing table. Which of the following routes would not be found on a separate router receiving an RIP update from Router A?

   ❑ A. R 172.16.0.0/16 [120/4]
   ❑ B. R 192.168.9.0/24 [120/2]
   ❑ C. C 192.168.4.0/24
   ❑ D. R 192.168.7.0/24 [120/15]
   ❑ E. R 192.168.8.0/24 [120/8]

Quick Check

Quick Answer: **136**

Detailed Answer: **140**

19. You have configured the routers shown in the figure below using the EIGRP protocol. The relevant configuration is as follows:

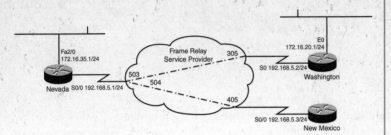

Routers using EIGRP Protocol.

Washington Router:

```
Wash(config)#router eigrp 100
Wash(config-router)#network 172.16.0.0
Wash(config-router)#network 192.168.5.0
Wash(config-router)#no auto-summary
```

Nevada Router:

```
Nev(config)#router eigrp 100
Nev(config-router)#network 172.16.0.0
Nev(config-router)#network 192.168.5.0
Nev(config-router)#no auto-summary
```

New Mexico Router:

```
NewM(config)#router eigrp 100
NewM(config-router)#network 172.16.0.0
NewM(config-router)#network 192.168.5.0
NewM(config-router)#no auto-summary
```

Users in Washington and New Mexico are complaining about connectivity issues; however, users in Nevada seem to be working just fine. What is the most likely cause of the problem?

❏ A. The EIGRP protocol is not to be used on frame relay networks. Cisco recommends using either OSPF or RIP industry standard protocols in this style of configuration.

❏ B. Because EIGRP is technically categorized as a distance-vector routing protocol, split-horizon causes problems in this configuration.

❏ C. The EIGRP autonomous system 100 is reserved for loopback routing protocol communication.

❏ D. The `no auto-summary` command causes routing issues in this environment because the configuration is using class C subnet masks for the 172.16.0.0 network.

20. Your boss tells you that he read about the RIP routing proto-col and found out that it uses hop count for its metric. He wants to know what the default metric used by IGRP is. What do you tell him?

Quick Answer: **136**
Detailed Answer: **140**

   - ❑ A. Bandwidth and delay
   - ❑ B. Hop count
   - ❑ C. Ticks
   - ❑ D. Bandwidth

21. You are configuring the Ike router on the network shown in the figure below. You would like to use the RIP routing pro-tocol to propagate all the networks to the three routers shown. What configuration would you apply to Ike to have it participate in this objective?

Quick Answer: **136**
Detailed Answer: **140**

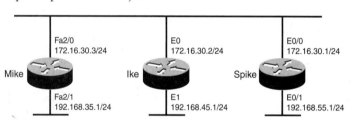

Mike
Fa2/0
172.16.30.3/24
Fa2/1
192.168.35.1/24

Ike
E0
172.16.30.2/24
E1
192.168.45.1/24

Spike
E0/0
172.16.30.1/24
E0/1
192.168.55.1/24

Ike Network router.

   - ❑ A. ```
Ike(config)#router rip
Ike(config-router)#network 172.16.0.0
Ike(config-router)#network 192.168.45.0
```
   - ❑  B.  ```
Ike(config)#router rip
Ike(config-router)#network 172.16.30.0
Ike(config-router)#network 192.168.35.0
Ike(config-router)#network 192.168.45.0
Ike(config-router)#network 192.168.55.0
```
   - ❑ C. ```
Ike(config)#router rip
Ike(config-router)#network 172.16.0.0
Ike(config-router)#network 192.168.35.0
Ike(config-router)#network 192.168.45.0
Ike(config-router)#network 192.168.55.0
```
   - ❑  D.  ```
Ike(config)#router rip
Ike(config-router)#network 172.16.0.0
Ike(config-router)#network 192.168.0.0
```

22. Which of the following is an example of a default static route?

  ❑ A. `ip route 172.16.1.0 255.255.255.0 172.16.2.1`

  ❑ B. `ip route 0.0.0.0 0.0.0.0 172.16.2.2`

  ❑ C. `ip route 172.16.1.0 255.255.255.0 serial 0/0`

  ❑ D. `ip route 172.16.1.0 255.255.255.0 static`

Quick Answer: **136**
Detailed Answer: **140**

23. You need to know what IP routing protocol is in use on your router. Which command should you use?

  ❑ A. `show protocol`

  ❑ B. `show routing protocol`

  ❑ C. `show running-config`

  ❑ D. `show ip protocol`

Quick Answer: **136**
Detailed Answer: **141**

24. This dynamic routing protocol is actually a distance-vector routing protocol, but it acts like a link-state routing protocol in many ways. What is it?

  ❑ A. OSPF

  ❑ B. IGRP

  ❑ C. EIGRP

  ❑ D. RIP version 1

  ❑ E. BGP

  ❑ F. IS-IS

  ❑ G. RIP version 2

Quick Answer: **136**
Detailed Answer: **141**

25. You are configuring a network at your headquarters in Phoenix, Arizona. You decide to use a distance-vector routing protocol. What command do you need to type to activate the mechanisms that stop routing loops? (Choose two.)

  ❑ A. `PhoenixRTR1(config-router)#split-horizon rip`

  ❑ B. `PhoenixRTR1(config-router)#split-horizon distance vector`

  ❑ C. `PhoenixRTR1(config-router)#distance vector`

  ❑ D. `PhoenixRTR1(config-router)#router igrp 100`

  ❑ E. `PhoenixRTR1(config-router)#no routing-loops`

  ❑ F. `PhoenixRTR1(config-router)#router rip`

Quick Answer: **136**
Detailed Answer: **141**

26. In the topology shown here, which of the following statements reflect how these routers send RIP routing updates? (Choose three.)

  ❑ A. Router A updates Router C.

  ❑ B. Router C updates Router B.

  ❑ C. Router B updates Router D.

  ❑ D. Router A updates Router B.

Quick Answer: **136**
Detailed Answer: **141**

27. Your routers do not seem to be sharing routing information. You issue the commands as shown here:

```
ExamCram1#show running-config
<some output text omitted>
interface serial 0/0
    ip address 172.16.12.1 255.255.255.0
    encapsulation PPP
!
router igrp 100
network 172.16.0.0
ExamCram2#show running-config
<some output text omitted>

interface Ethernet 0
    no ip address
    administratively down

interface serial 0
    ip address 10.1.1.1 255.255.255.0
    encapsulation PPP

interface serial 1
    ip address 172.16.12.2 255.255.255.0
    encapsulation PPP
!
router igrp 110
network 172.16.10.0
network 10.0.0.0
```

Why are the routing updates not working?

❑ A. The Ethernet interface does not have an IP address.
❑ B. The interfaces are using the wrong encapsulation.
❑ C. The wrong networks are being advertised.
❑ D. IGRP is incorrectly configured.

28. You have configured an OSPF interface with the `bandwidth 128` command. What is the calculated OSPF cost of this link?

❑ A. 1
❑ B. 781
❑ C. 1562
❑ D. 64000
❑ E. 128000

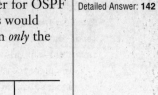

Quick Answer: **136**

Detailed Answer: **142**

29. You are working on the network shown in the figure. You need to configure all interfaces on the Cedar router for OSPF in Area 0. Which of the following syntax examples would accomplish this task and ensure that OSPF runs on *only* the interfaces depicted in the figure below?

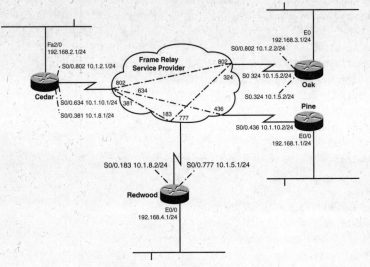

Router network.

- ☐ A. Cedar(config)#router ospf 1
       Cedar(config-router)#network 192.168.2.0 0.0.0.255 area 0
       Cedar(config-router)#network 10.0.0.0 0.255.255.255 area 0

- ☐ B. Cedar(config)#router ospf 1
       Cedar(config-router)#network 192.168.2.0 255.255.255.0 area 0
       Cedar(config-router)#network 10.1.2.0 255.255.255.0 area 0
       Cedar(config-router)#network 10.1.10.0 255.255.255.0 area 0
       Cedar(config-router)#network 10.1.8.0 255.255.255.0 area 0

- ☐ C. Cedar(config)#router ospf 1
       Cedar(config-router)#network 192.168.2.0 255.255.255.0 area 0
       Cedar(config-router)#network 10.0.0.0 255.0.0.0 area 0

- ☐ D. Cedar(config)#router ospf 1
       Cedar(config-router)#network 192.168.2.1 0.0.0.0 area 0
       Cedar(config-router)#network 10.1.2.1 0.0.0.0 area 0
       Cedar(config-router)#network 10.1.10.1 0.0.0.0 area 0
       Cedar(config-router)#network 10.1.8.1 0.0.0.0 area 0

30. Which statements are true regarding the command sequence shown here? (Choose three.)

```
RouterA(config)# interface loopback 0
RouterA(config-if)# ip address 192.168.31.33
255.255.255.255
```

- ❑ A. It creates a virtual interface.
- ❑ B. It uses a subnet mask.
- ❑ C. It ensures that an interface is always active, even if a router is shut off.
- ❑ D. It provides an easier way to identify OSPF routing updates.
- ❑ E. The mask of 255.255.255.255 is called a wildcard mask.
- ❑ F. These commands can be issued only to configure Ethernet interfaces.

31. You are training some new network engineers when one of them asks you the difference between classful and classless routing protocols. What do you tell him?

- ❑ A. They are pretty much the same, except classful protocols have more options.
- ❑ B. Classless supports VLSM, whereas classful supports FLSM.
- ❑ C. Classful can be used only between autonomous systems.
- ❑ D. RIPv1 and IGRP are the standard classless protocols, as they were some of the first protocols in existence.

32. Which of the following commands shows the routing table of EIGRP?

- ❑ A. Show ip route
- ❑ B. Show ip route classless
- ❑ C. Show ip eigrp neighbors
- ❑ D. Show ip route eigrp

33. Which of the following are valid routing protocol troubleshooting commands? (Choose two.)

- ❑ A. ExamCram1#show ip route
- ❑ B. ExamCram1(config-if)#show ip protocols
- ❑ C. ExamCram1>debug ip rip
- ❑ D. ExamCram1#show ip protocols

34. Your senior network administrator wants you to monitor the RIP traffic on your network in real time. Which of the following commands would you issue?

- ❑ A. Show ip route
- ❑ B. Show processes
- ❑ C. Debug ip rip
- ❑ D. Show ip rip

35. You are using a distance-vector routing protocol at your branch office in Boise, Idaho. Because you are using RIP, what can you use to prevent routing loops? (Choose two.)

   ❑ A. Link-state advertisements (LSAs)
   ❑ B. Spanning-Tree Protocol
   ❑ C. A shortest path first tree
   ❑ D. Split-horizon
   ❑ E. Hold-down timers

Quick Answer: **136**
Detailed Answer: **143**

36. Which of the following are considered characteristics of a link-state routing protocol? (Choose three.)

   ❑ A. Provides common view of entire topology
   ❑ B. Exchanges routing tables periodically with neighbors
   ❑ C. Calculates shortest path
   ❑ D. Utilizes event-triggered updates
   ❑ E. Uses routing loop prevention with split-horizon
   ❑ F. Utilizes only periodic updates

Quick Answer: **136**
Detailed Answer: **143**

37. What is the advantage of using VLSM in a routed environment?

   ❑ A. It allows for more hosts than FLSM.
   ❑ B. It allows you to use different subnet masks throughout the network.
   ❑ C. It allows for a standard subnet mask to be used throughout the network.
   ❑ D. It prevents routing loops.

Quick Answer: **136**
Detailed Answer: **143**

38. Which routing protocol has a default administrative distance of 100 on Cisco routers?

   ❑ A. RIP
   ❑ B. IGRP
   ❑ C. OSPF
   ❑ D. EIGRP

Quick Answer: **136**
Detailed Answer: **143**

39. Which of the following commands are required to turn on RIP routing on your network? (Choose two.)

   ❑ A. `ExamCram4(config)#router rip`
   ❑ B. `ExamCram4(config)#router rip 100`
   ❑ C. `ExamCram4(config-router)#network 192.168.0.0`
   ❑ D. `ExamCram4(config-router)#network all`

Quick Answer: **136**
Detailed Answer: **143**

40. Which of the following commands configures a static route on Router 1 to network 192.18.40.0/24 with an administrative distance of 90?

    ❑ A. `Router1(config)# ip route 90 192.18.30.0 255.255.255.0`
              `192.18.20.2`

    ❑ B. `Router1(config)# ip route 90 192.18.20.1 255.255.255.0`
              `192.18.20.2`

    ❑ C. `Router1(config)# ip route 192.18.40.0 255.255.255.0`
              `192.18.30.2 90`

    ❑ D. `Router1(config)# ip route 192.18.30.0 255.255.255.0`
              `192.18.20.1 90`

    ❑ E. `Router1(config)# ip route 192.18.30.0 255.255.255.0`
              `192.18.30.2 90`

Quick Answer: **136**
Detailed Answer: **144**

41. You are checking your router's routing protocols. Your screen shows the following:

What command do you type to see this information?

    ❑ A. `Show ip route`
    ❑ B. `Show version`
    ❑ C. `Show running-config`
    ❑ D. `Show ip protocols`

Quick Answer: **136**
Detailed Answer: **144**

42. Which of the following routing protocols are considered IGPs? (Choose four.)

    ❑ A. RIPv1
    ❑ B. RIPv2
    ❑ C. IGRP
    ❑ D. BGP
    ❑ E. OSPF

Quick Answer: **136**
Detailed Answer: **144**

43. Your new network engineer is curious as to why you are using OSPF in your network versus EIGRP. Which of the following is a valid explanation?

    ❑ A. OSPF has a faster convergence time.
    ❑ B. OSPF is a link-state routing protocol and EIGRP is not.
    ❑ C. OSPF utilizes a better route calculation.
    ❑ D. OSPF is compatible with multiple vendors.

Quick Answer: **136**
Detailed Answer: **144**

44. Which of the following are good candidates for static routes?

    ❑ A. Stub networks
    ❑ B. Large corporations
    ❑ C. Laptop-based networks
    ❑ D. Low-security environments

Quick Answer: **136**
Detailed Answer: **144**

45. You have four dynamic routing protocols running in your environment. A router receives an advertisement for a particular route from all four protocols. When you type the show ip route command on this router, what routing protocol does the router prefer?

   ❑ A. RIP
   ❑ B. IGRP
   ❑ C. OSPF
   ❑ D. EIGRP

46. You need to configure a static route to reach the 172.16.0.0 network. Which of the following is an example of the correct syntax you should use?

   ❑ A. ip route 172.16.0.0 255.255.0.0 172.31.0.1
   ❑ B. ip route 172.16.0.0 255.255.0.0 static
   ❑ C. route 172.16.0.0 255.255.0.0 serial 0 100
   ❑ D. route 172.16.0.0 255.255.0.0 172.31.0.1

47. Split-horizon states that no advertisements will be sent back through the interface on which they were received. What mechanism overrides that behavior?

   ❑ A. Triggered updates
   ❑ B. Hold-down timers
   ❑ C. Poison reverse
   ❑ D. Nothing overrides split-horizon.

48. Which of the following network interfaces can be advertised via OSPF? (Choose three.)

   ❑ A. Ethernet
   ❑ B. Serial
   ❑ C. Loopback
   ❑ D. Console

49. Your boss asks you what "count to infinity" means on a router. Which of the following explanations is the most accurate?

   ❑ A. It is when a router continues to send out packets to an unknown destination.
   ❑ B. It is when a routing table entry continues to increment its metric without stopping.
   ❑ C. It is when a router calculates an unknown destination.
   ❑ D. It is when a router receives a poisoned route.

Quick Check

Quick Answer: **136**

Detailed Answer: **145**

50. Where does OSPF contain the "map" of all the routes it knows about?

❑ A. Neighbor table

❑ B. Topology table

❑ C. Routing table

❑ D. CAM table

Quick Check Answer Key

1. C
2. C, D
3. A
4. D
5. C
6. B
7. B, D, F
8. D
9. D
10. A
11. B
12. A
13. C
14. A
15. B
16. A
17. B
18. D
19. B
20. A
21. A
22. B
23. D
24. C
25. D, F

26. B, C, D
27. D
28. B
29. D
30. A, B, D
31. B
32. D
33. A, D
34. C
35. D, E
36. A, C, D
37. B
38. B
39. A, C
40. C
41. D
42. A, B, C, E
43. D
44. A
45. D
46. A
47. C
48. A, B, C
49. B
50. B

Answers and Explanations

1. **Answer: C.** OSPF uses the highest IP address assigned to a loopback address, which is a logical interface created on a Cisco router. A is incorrect because Router ID is always the highest IP address. B is incorrect, as you have logical loopback interfaces on these routers. Logical interfaces override physical interfaces. If there were no loopback interfaces, the highest IP address on a physical interface would be the router ID. D is incorrect, as the router ID is always the highest IP address on a logical interface. E is incorrect, as the router ID is always the highest IP address on the either the logical or physical interface.

2. **Answers: C and D.** Routed protocols such as IP or IPX are used to help communicate data across network segments by using logical addressing, which identifies both the network and host that need to communicate. D is a correct answer, as routers use routing protocols such as RIP and OSPF to communicate changes in their routing tables. A is incorrect because routed protocols can cross routers. B is incorrect because routing protocols populate only routing tables; they cannot identify data.

3. **Answer: A.** A static route is the most believable route possible (except for being directly connected to a network by a router's interface). Routers use administrative distance (AD) to decide the best route. The lowest AD wins, and in this case, a static route has an AD of 1. B is incorrect, as RIP's AD is 120. C is incorrect, as OSPF's AD is 110. D is incorrect, as a router never "cancels" out routes if it hears from more than one source; that is the function of the AD.

4. **Answer: D.** The show IP route command shows what routes are available for the router. In this case, the information in the brackets is the administrative distance and metric (bandwidth and delay) of the EIGRP route. A is incorrect, as it is not the port number, but the administrative distance. B is incorrect, as EIGRP does not use hops as its metric. C is incorrect, as the first number is the AD of EIGRP, not port number.

5. **Answer: C.** This answer identifies all interfaces on a router with the 0.0.0.0 255.255.255.255 (All addresses) identifier. A is incorrect, as even though you are identifying all interfaces with Area 0, this command does not send out an LSA to the Area. B is incorrect, as the router id command configures a router with a specific router ID. D is incorrect, as this is an invalid command.

6. **Answer: B.** Open Shortest Path First (OSPF) is a link-state routing protocol that contains the entire topology of the network in a database. Because the routers know the entire network topology, they can choose the shortest path to a route's destination. A is incorrect, as RIP is a distance-vector routing protocol that contains only a routing table of routes learned by rumor through directly connected neighbors. C is incorrect, as IGRP is also a distance-vector routing protocol. D is incorrect, as BGP is a path-vector routing protocol used between autonomous systems on WANs and the Internet.

7. **Answers: B, D, and F.** You must specify the autonomous system (AS) number in the `router igrp` command. D is also correct, as you must specify the interface attached to the 192.168.2.0 network. F is correct, as you must specify the interface attached to the 192.168.3.0 network. A is incorrect because you do not give the AS as part of the command. C is incorrect because even though it might advertise for all network interfaces, it's not the approved methodology. E is incorrect because it's not a valid command.

8. **Answer: D.** With all distance-vector routing protocols, split-horizon states that it is not useful to send information back the way it came. A is incorrect, as routers themselves are the devices that split networks, not split-horizon. B is incorrect, as split-horizon is used to solve routing loop issues. C is incorrect because distance-vector routing protocols are notoriously slow in updating, as a result of their periodic nature. This can cause convergence issues.

9. **Answer: D.** The `passive-interface` command is used to control the advertisement of routing information. The command enables the suppression of routing updates over some interfaces while allowing updates to be exchanged normally over other interfaces. A is incorrect, as the actual command to turn off the interface is `shutdown`. B is incorrect, as this answer is the opposite of what the command does. C is incorrect, as keepalives keep up an Ethernet interface but do nothing for a serial interface.

10. **Answer: A.** The `ip route 10.20.0.0 255.255.0.0 10.10.0.1` command establishes a static route in the routing table. B is incorrect, as static routes are specified using subnet masks rather than wildcard masks. Wildcard masks are typically used in access list and OSPF configurations. C and D are incorrect, as you must specify the IP syntax in front of the `route` command.

11. **Answer: B.** EIGRP is considered a hybrid routing protocol, combining the best of the distance-vector and link-state routing protocols. A, C, and D are incorrect, as there are no such classes of routing protocols.

12. **Answer: A.** The administrative distance (AD) of RIP is 120. B is incorrect, as IGRP has an AD of 100. C is incorrect, as OSPF has an AD of 110. D is incorrect, as EIGRP has an AD of 90.

13. **Answer: C.** The distance-vector mechanism to set the metric to the maximum value is called *route poisoning*. A is incorrect, even though route poisoning is part of the split-horizon family. Split-horizon, by definition, does not allow updates to travel back out the interface on which they arrived. B is incorrect, as hold-down timers are not activated by route poisoning. D is incorrect, as triggered updates occur when a change occurs on a network and require an update that is earlier than the default timer.

14. **Answer: A.** Distance-vector routing protocols send the entire routing table to directly connected neighbors. B is incorrect, as the routers send the tables only to their directly connected neighbors. If a router learns of another route from its neighbor, it then passes that information on to another neighbor. C is incorrect, as distance-vector routing protocols send the entire table, not just the changes. D is incorrect, as the routers send the entire table, and they send it only to directly connected neighbors.

15. **Answer: B.** The maximum hop count that RIP allows is 15. Answer C is incorrect because a hop count of 16 is the point that is considered unreachable by the RIP protocol. All other answers are incorrect because they either overshoot or underestimate the maximum hop count.

16. **Answer: A.** Split-horizon is a mechanism in distance-vector routing protocols that prevents routers from sending updates back the way they came. B is incorrect, as hold-down timers are used to prevent routing tables from responding too quickly to sudden changes. C is incorrect, as the Maximum Hop count refers to the maximum metric that RIP can use. D is incorrect, as route poisoning is the process of taking a route and making it the maximum distance, thus "poisoning" the route. E is incorrect, as "counting to infinity" is a problem if a routing update loop occurs.

17. **Answer: B.** The routing table information shown gives the administrative distance (AD) with the metric. A is incorrect, as the [/] shows the AD and metric. Cost is a metric used by OSPF. C is incorrect, as the AD is shown first, then the metric, not the other way around. D is incorrect, as the [AD/Metric] is not shown as cost and hop count.

18. **Answer: D.** The metric shown on this route is 15. If it is passed to a neighboring router, it increments by one, equaling 16, which is unreachable. A is incorrect, as this route could be passed to neighbors. B is incorrect, as this route could be passed to a neighboring router. C is incorrect, as a directly connected network could be advertised to a neighboring router. E is incorrect, as this route is also within the 15-hop limit.

19. **Answer: B.** EIGRP is called many names. Some call it a hybrid routing protocol (primarily Cisco); others call it an advanced distance-vector protocol.
However, technically, it falls under the distance-vector category of protocols,
which causes all the distance-vector loop prevention mechanisms to apply. One
of these mechanisms is split-horizon, which prevents a router from sending an
update back in the same direction from which it was received. By looking at the
diagram, the Nevada router receives updates on its Serial 0/0 interface from
both Washington and New Mexico. It does not send those updates back out,
keeping the Washington and New Mexico routers from learning about each
other. Answer A is incorrect because EIGRP works just fine on frame relay networks. Answer C is incorrect because there are no reserved EIGRP AS numbers. Answer D is incorrect because the no auto-summary command enables
VLSM support for EIGRP.

20. **Answer: A.** Even though IGRP can use up to five different criteria
(Bandwidth, Delay, Load, MTU, and Reliability), it uses only Bandwidth and
Delay by default. B is incorrect, as IGRP has a maximum hop count of 255;
however, it is not the metric it uses. C is incorrect, as ticks are used by RIP for
IPX. D is incorrect, as IGRP uses not only Bandwidth, but also Delay as its
default metrics.

21. **Answer: A.** RIP is considered a classful protocol. From a configuration stand-
point, this means that networks must be entered into the configuration using
their default classes (Class A, B, or C). Because 172.16.0.0 is a class B network,
it must be entered as if it had a class B subnet mask rather than the subnet
mask shown in the figure. In addition, you enter directly connected interfaces
only into a routing process. This concept applies to any routing protocol. In
the case of Ike, it is connected only to the 172.16.0.0 and 192.168.45.0 networks. Answers B and C are incorrect because they enter all the networks
rather than the networks that are directly connected to Ike. Answer D is incorrect because it enters the 192.168.0.0 network in a class B style when this is a
class C address.

22. **Answer: B.** A default route is a static route that contains a unique address and
subnet mask combination of all zeros (0.0.0.0 0.0.0.0). A is incorrect, as it is a
standard static route. C is incorrect, as it is a standard static route using an
interface instead of a next-hop IP address. D is incorrect, as it is not even the
correct syntax for a static route.

23. **Answer: D.** The show ip protocol command lists all routing protocols that are running on your router. A is incorrect because it shows you only the routed protocols, not the routing protocols, on your router. B is incorrect, because this is not a valid command. C is incorrect, as the show running-config command shows you what routing protocols are running, but it also gives you all the other configuration information currently operating in RAM. This is too much information, when all you wanted was to find out which routing protocol was running on the machine.

24. **Answer: C.** EIGRP is a distance-vector routing protocol that uses link-state attributes. A is incorrect, as OSPF is a link-state routing protocol, not a distance-vector routing protocol. B is incorrect, as IGRP is only a distance-vector routing protocol. D is incorrect, as RIPv1 is only a distance-vector routing protocol. E is incorrect, as BGP is a path-vector routing protocol that works between autonomous systems. F is incorrect, as IS-IS is a pure link-state routing protocol. G is incorrect, as RIPv2 is still a distance-vector routing protocol, although it does support VLSM.

25. **Answers: D and F.** You merely need to activate the routing protocols to turn on the routing loop-prevention mechanisms; they are activated by default. A and B are incorrect, as you actually use the no split-horizon command to turn it off and just the split-horizon command to turn it back on. Regardless, it is on by default. C and E are incorrect, as there are no such commands.

26. **Answers: B, C, and D.** Directly connected neighbors update each other when using the RIP routing protocol. A is incorrect, as Router A is not directly connected to Router C and thus does not send an update to Router C.

27. **Answer: D.** The running-config command shows that one router is running IGRP with an AS of 100, while the other is running IGRP with an AS of 110. These two routers do not share routing updates, as IGRP sends updates only to routers that belong to the same AS. A is incorrect, as the routers are connected by serial interfaces. B is incorrect, as the serial interfaces are all using PPP encapsulation. C is incorrect, as both the 172.16.0.0 and 10.0.0.0 networks are being advertised—just not to the other side!

28. **Answer: B.** The formula that OSPF uses to figure the cost of a path is 10^8/bandwidth (bps). In this case, $10^8/128000 = 781.25$. A is incorrect, as that is the cost of a 100Mbps link. C is incorrect, as that is the cost of a 64K link. D and E are invalid costs.

29. **Answer: D.** The configuration shown in answer D is the most precise method to add interfaces to the OSPF routing process. A wildcard mask of 0.0.0.0 tells OSPF to run on the interface that has exactly the IP address that you have typed in before the wildcard mask. In this case, all the IP addresses were typed in exactly as defined on the interfaces with the wildcard mask of 0.0.0.0. This ensures OSPF does not run on any interfaces that are either not shown in the figure or that may be added in the future. Answer A accomplishes part of the objective because OSPF runs on any interface starting with 192.168.2 or 10 (because of the wildcard mask applied); however, in the future, if any interface is added to the router that has an IP address beginning with the number 10, it will automatically begin running OSPF. Answers B and C are incorrect because OSPF network statements require you to enter the wildcard mask rather than the subnet mask.

30. **Answers: A, B, and D.** The command creates a virtual loopback interface with a particular IP address using the 255.255.255.255 subnet mask. When an OSPF router sends a routing update, it includes the router ID to identify itself. In OSPF, the router ID is the highest IP address of a loopback interface. C is incorrect, as a router that is not powered up does not have any active interfaces. E is incorrect, as 255.255.255.255 is typically called a host mask. F is incorrect, as this command sets up a virtual interface, not a physical Ethernet interface.

31. **Answer: B.** One of the main features of classless protocols is to include the subnet mask information in their updates, whereas classful does not. This means that you can use only fixed-length subnet masks (FLSMs), not variable-length subnet masks (VLSMs) in a classful routing environment. A is incorrect, as classless protocols actually have more options. C is incorrect, as both classful and classless protocols can cross autonomous systems. D is incorrect, as RIPv1 and IGRP are actually classful protocols.

32. **Answer: D.** To show the specific routes of EIGRP, you must specify them with the `show ip route EIGRP` command. A is incorrect; although it shows EIGRP routes, it also shows any other routes learned or known by the router, and the question specifically asks for EIGRP routing table information. B is a nonexistent command. C is incorrect, as this command shows you all of the EIGRP neighbors for which the router exchanges information.

33. **Answers: A and D.** The `show ip route` and `show ip protocols` commands give you information on the routing protocols and what routes they have placed into the routing table. B is incorrect, as you cannot issue the `show ip protocols` command from Interface Configuration mode. C is incorrect, as you cannot use `debug` commands from the User EXEC mode. You must be in Privileged EXEC mode.

34. **Answer: C.** Monitoring in real time requires the use of a debug command. Show commands merely grab a snapshot in time, whereas debug commands are in real time. A is incorrect, as it is a show command. B is incorrect, as it is merely another show command. D is also incorrect, as it uses a show command.

35. **Answers: D and E.** Split-horizon ensures that updates are not sent back through the interface on which they arrived; this helps prevent loops. Hold-down timers prevent incorrect updates from propagating throughout the network. A is incorrect, as LSAs are used by link-state protocols to announce changes in the network. B is incorrect, as Spanning-Tree Protocol is used in switched environments, not routing protocols. C is incorrect because the SPF tree is used to help decide the best path to the destination.

36. **Answers: A, C, and D.** Link-state routing protocols have the entire network mapped in their topology database. From this database, it calculates the shortest path using Dijkstra's algorithm. They also send small update announcements called LSAs when there is a change in the topology. B is incorrect because link-state routing protocols exchange their routing information with their neighbors once and then send only changes. E is incorrect, as link-state routing protocols do not use split-horizon. F is incorrect, as link-state protocols exchange a periodic update, but only if no LSAs have been sent over a long period of time.

37. **Answer: B.** The use of VLSM in a routed network allows you to use different subnet masks throughout the network. You can also use route aggregation (also called route summarization), which shrinks the size of routing tables. A is incorrect, as you actually lose host addresses when you use subnetting. C is incorrect, as you can use different size subnet masks such as /30 and /12 and /26 masks in the same network. D is incorrect, as VLSM is not a loop-routing preventive mechanism.

38. **Answer: B.** IGRP has a default administrative distance (AD) of 100. A is incorrect, as the administrative distance of RIP is 120. C is incorrect, as OSPF has an AD of 110. D is incorrect, as EIGRP has an AD of 90.

39. **Answers: A and C.** You must turn on the routing protocol with the router rip command from Global Configuration mode. You must then specify interfaces to advertise; the network command accomplishes this. B is incorrect, as you do not need to specify an autonomous system for RIP, as you would IGRP. D is incorrect, as it is not a valid network command.

40. **Answer: C.** The correct syntax for a static route is `ip route [destination network] [subnet mask] [interface or next hop ip address] [administrative distance(optional)]`. Increasing the AD from the default of 1 to 90 allows the static route to be less believable than some routing protocols. This is known as a *floating static route*, which is used for backup paths. In this case, you are trying to reach the 192.18.40.0 network. You are telling the router to send packets for that network to 192.18.30.2, which is the next-hop IP address. You are also setting the AD to 90. A and B are incorrect, as the AD parameter does not go in front of the destination network parameter. D is incorrect, as you are trying to reach the 192.18.40.0 network, not the 192.18.30.0 network.

41. **Answer: D.** The `show ip protocols` command shows all currently configured routing protocols in use on your router. A is incorrect, as it shows you the routing table. B is incorrect, as it shows you the version of the IOS and the configuration register settings. C is incorrect, as it shows you all of the currently configured settings in RAM.

42. **Answers: A, B, C, and E.** A is correct, as RIPv1 is an Interior Gateway Protocol (IGP), meaning it exchanges routing information with routers in the same autonomous system (AS). B is correct, as RIPv2 is also an IGP. C is correct, as IGRP actually gets its name from being an IGP. E is correct, as OSPF is an industry standard IGP. D is incorrect, as Border Gateway Protocol is an External Gateway Protocol (EGP), which means it exchanges routing information between autonomous systems.

43. **Answer: D.** EIGRP is a proprietary Cisco routing protocol that does not function on other vendors' routers. OSPF, however, is an industry standard. A is incorrect, as EIGRP is actually a bit faster than OSPF in converging. B is incorrect, as EIGRP, although not technically a link-state protocol, uses link-state behavior. C is incorrect, as EIGRP's DUAL algorithm is equally capable of route calculation as OSPF's Dijkstra's algorithm.

44. **Answer: A.** Stub networks have only one way in and one way out. Static routes serve well in this environment. B is incorrect, as large corporations typically have hundreds of routers, which make static routes inappropriate. C is incorrect, as laptops versus desktops typically do not affect routing choices. D is incorrect, as static routes are typically used in high-security environments.

45. **Answer: D.** EIGRP has a default administrative distance of 90, which is the lowest of all of these protocols. A is incorrect, as RIP has an administrative distance of 120, which is the highest of all the protocols. B is incorrect, as IGRP has an administrative distance of 100. C is incorrect, as OSPF has an administrative distance of 110.

46. **Answer: A.** The `ip route 172.16.0.0 255.255.0.0 172.31.0.1` command establishes a static route in the routing table. B is incorrect, as you do not have to specify that it is a static route with the word `static`. Instead, there should be an interface or next-hop router address parameter. C and D are incorrect, as you must specify the `IP` in front of the `route` command.

47. **Answer: C.** Poison reverse, or "reverse poisoning," overrides split-horizon and sends a route poison broadcast back out the interface on which the poisoned route came in. A is incorrect, as triggered updates override the periodic update behavior of distance-vector protocols. B is incorrect, as hold-down timers maintain stability of the routing table by waiting before making any changes. D is incorrect, as poison reverse overrides split-horizon.

48. **Answers: A, B, and C.** They are capable of being advertised with OSPF. D is incorrect, as the console interface is merely for local machine configuration and is not a valid network interface.

49. **Answer: B.** A router without active default mechanisms could theoretically increment its metric forever if a routing update loop occurs, thus the phrase "counting to infinity." All distance-vector routing protocols now have built-in mechanisms to stop this behavior. A is incorrect, as a router, if it does not know where to send a packet, either discards the packet or sends it to a "default route." C is incorrect, as a router does not run a calculation on a route it does not know. D is incorrect, as a router marks a route as "possibly down" when it receives a poisoned route update. It then activates a hold-down timer until it either receives an update that the route is back up, or it hears nothing and flushes the route from its table.

50. **Answer: B.** An OSPF router contains all known routes in its Topology table. It then runs the SPF algorithm for all the routes to decide the best path based on cost. A is incorrect, as the Neighbor table is merely the list of routers with which the OSPF router has a neighbor relationship. C is incorrect, as the Routing table merely contains the *best* routes calculated from the Topology table. D is incorrect, as the Content Addressable Memory Table is also known as the MAC address table. The CAM table is located on Catalyst switches.

Access Lists and Network Address Translation

1. An administrator creates an access list prohibiting Telnet on his router. He then successfully initiates a Telnet session from the router. What is the most likely reason the access list failed?

   ❑ A. The access list should be changed to stop UDP traffic.
   ❑ B. The access list should be changed to stop TCP traffic.
   ❑ C. The access list should be changed to block port 23 traffic.
   ❑ D. The access list cannot stop the administrator's action.

2. Which of the following are valid reasons to implement access lists? (Choose three.)

   ❑ A. Priority queuing
   ❑ B. Route filtering
   ❑ C. Dial-on-demand routing
   ❑ D. Console port security

3. Which of the following are types of access lists? (Choose three.)

   ❑ A. Standard
   ❑ B. Extended
   ❑ C. Restricted
   ❑ D. Static
   ❑ E. Named
   ❑ F. Unnamed

4. Which types of access lists can filter traffic based on the source port? (Choose two.)

   ❑ A. Standard
   ❑ B. Extended
   ❑ C. Restricted
   ❑ D. Static
   ❑ E. Named
   ❑ F. Unnamed

5. Which type of access list can filter based only on the source address of a packet?

- ❑ A. Standard
- ❑ B. Extended
- ❑ C. Dynamic
- ❑ D. Static
- ❑ E. Named
- ❑ F. Unnamed

Quick Answer: **161**
Detailed Answer: **162**

6. Which of the following identifiers can be used for standard access lists? (Choose two.)

- ❑ A. 91
- ❑ B. 107
- ❑ C. 1270
- ❑ D. 1902

Quick Answer: **161**
Detailed Answer: **162**

7. Which of the following identifiers can be used for extended access lists? (Choose two.)

- ❑ A. 99
- ❑ B. 100
- ❑ C. 2500
- ❑ D. 2700

Quick Answer: **161**
Detailed Answer: **162**

8. Which access list type allows you to delete entries in a specific access list?

- ❑ A. Standard
- ❑ B. Extended
- ❑ C. Named
- ❑ D. Unnamed

Quick Answer: **161**
Detailed Answer: **163**

9. You are filtering traffic to an FTP site and you want only FTP traffic to reach the server. You do not want additional traffic to reach the server. Which traffic should be allowed?

- ❑ A. TCP on ports 20 and 21
- ❑ B. UDP on ports 20 and 21
- ❑ C. TCP on port 21
- ❑ D. TCP and UDP on ports 20 and 21

Quick Answer: **161**
Detailed Answer: **163**

10. You have established a DNS server on one of your networks. You need to permit traffic, including queries and zone transfers, to the DNS server using access lists. Which traffic should be allowed?

Quick Answer: **161**
Detailed Answer: **163**

❑ A. TCP and UDP on ports 53
❑ B. TCP and UDP on port 69
❑ C. TCP and UDP on port 67
❑ D. TCP on port 67

11. What happens to a packet that does not meet the conditions of any access list filters?

Quick Answer: **161**
Detailed Answer: **163**

❑ A. The packet is routed normally.
❑ B. The packet is flagged and then routed.
❑ C. The packet is dropped.
❑ D. The administrator is notified.

12. Which of the following statements regarding outbound access lists are correct? (Choose two.)

Quick Answer: **161**
Detailed Answer: **163**

❑ A. Outbound access lists cannot filter packets originating from the router.
❑ B. Outbound access lists filter packets before a routing decision has been made.
❑ C. Outbound access lists drop packets that are not routable.
❑ D. Outbound access lists can drop packets based on protocol numbers.

13. Which of the following statements regarding inbound access lists are correct? (Choose three.)

Quick Answer: **161**
Detailed Answer: **163**

❑ A. Inbound access lists cannot filter packets originating from the router.
❑ B. Inbound access lists filter packets before a routing decision has been made.
❑ C. Inbound access lists drop packets that are not routable.
❑ D. Inbound access lists can drop packets based on protocol numbers.

14. You create an access list with a single entry to deny all FTP traffic. Which of the following is the most accurate statement regarding this access list?

Quick Answer: **161**
Detailed Answer: **163**

❑ A. Only FTP traffic is denied.
❑ B. All traffic is denied.
❑ C. All traffic is permitted.
❑ D. All traffic except FTP traffic is denied.

15. You have an IP address and wildcard mask of 172.16.99.25 0.0.255.255. Which of the following IP addresses are affected by this rule? (Choose two.)
    - ❑ A. 172.16.99.1
    - ❑ B. 192.168.99.25
    - ❑ C. 172.30.99.25
    - ❑ D. 172.16.1.1

Quick Answer: **161**
Detailed Answer: **163**

16. You have an IP address and wildcard mask of 10.0.20.5 255.255.0.0. Which of the following IP addresses are affected by this rule? (Choose two.)
    - ❑ A. 10.0.0.10
    - ❑ B. 192.168.20.5
    - ❑ C. 172.30.20.5
    - ❑ D. 10.2.1.1

Quick Answer: **161**
Detailed Answer: **164**

17. Which of the following is an abbreviation for the access list entry 172.16.32.3 0.0.0.0?
    - ❑ A. Single 172.16.32.3
    - ❑ B. Host 172.16.32.3
    - ❑ C. 172.16.32.3 0
    - ❑ D. One 172.16.32.3

Quick Answer: **161**
Detailed Answer: **164**

18. What is the abbreviation for the wildcard mask of all ones?
    - ❑ A. all
    - ❑ B. none
    - ❑ C. any
    - ❑ D. full

Quick Answer: **161**
Detailed Answer: **164**

19. You want to create an access list to filter all traffic from the 172.16.16.0 255.255.240.0 network. What wildcard mask is appropriate?
    - ❑ A. 0.0.7.255
    - ❑ B. 0.0.15.255
    - ❑ C. 0.0.31.255
    - ❑ D. 0.0.63.255

Quick Answer: **161**
Detailed Answer: **164**

20. You want to create an access list to filter all traffic from the 10.0.64.0 255.255.224.0 network. What wildcard mask is appropriate?
    - ❑ A. 0.0.7.255
    - ❑ B. 0.0.15.255
    - ❑ C. 0.0.31.255
    - ❑ D. 0.0.63.255

Quick Answer: **161**
Detailed Answer: **164**

21. Regarding access lists, which of the following statements is correct?

   ❑ A. Only one access list per protocol, per direction, per interface

   ❑ B. Only one access list per port number, per protocol, per interface

   ❑ C. Only one access list per port number, per direction, per interface

   ❑ D. Only one access list per port number, per protocol, per direction

22. Which of the following is accurate regarding the ordering of access lists?

   ❑ A. Named access list lines can be added anywhere in an access list.

   ❑ B. The ordering of an access list is not important, as all rules are checked.

   ❑ C. More specific rules in an access list should be placed lower in the list.

   ❑ D. Access lists are processed from the top of the access list to the end.

23. You have an internal web server that must be accessed from the corporate Internet connection. This internal web server has the IP address 172.16.55.10. The router accesses the Internet through the FastEthernet0/1 interface. What NAT syntax is necessary to forward HTTP requests to the internal web server?

   ❑ A. `ip nat outside destination tcp 80 fastEthernet0/1 172.16.55.10 80`

   ❑ B. `ip nat inside source static tcp 172.16.55.10 80 interface fastEthernet 0/1 80`

   ❑ C. `ip nat outside source tcp 80 172.16.55.10 80 interface fastEthernet0/1 80`

   ❑ D. `ip nat inside destination static tcp 172.16.55.10 80 interface fastEthernet 0/1 80`

Quick Answer: **161**

Detailed Answer: **165**

Quick Check ✓

24. You would like to configure NAT for a small office DSL connection, as shown in the figure below. Users on the 192.168.254.0/24 network should share the public address assigned to the router's Ethernet 0/3 interface for public access. In addition, one of the internal users (192.168.254.32) is running an FTP server containing files that need to be accessed from the Internet. Which of the following configurations accomplishes these objectives?

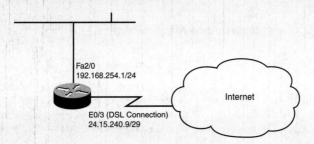

Small office DSL connection.

❑ A.   `interface fastethernet 2/0`
      `ip nat inside`
   `interface Ethernet 0/3`
      `ip nat outside`
   `ip nat inside source interface Ethernet 0/3 interface`
   `fastethernet 2/0 overload`

❑ B.   `interface fastethernet 2/0`
      `ip nat inside`
   `interface Ethernet 0/3`
      `ip nat outside`
   `ip nat inside source static 192.168.254.32 interface`
   `fastethernet 2/0`
   `ip nat inside source interface ethernet 0/3 interface`
   `fastethernet 2/0 overload`

❑ C. `interface fastethernet 2/0`
      `ip nat inside`
   `interface Ethernet 0/3`
      `ip nat outside`
   `access-list 50 permit 192.168.254.0 0.0.0.255`
   `ip nat inside source static tcp 192.168.254.32 21`
   `interface fastethernet 2/0 21`
   `ip nat inside source list 50 interface fastethernet 2/0`
   `overload`

❏ D. `interface fastethernet 2/0`

   `ip nat inside`

`interface Ethernet 0/3`

   `ip nat outside`

`access-list 50 permit 192.168.254.0 0.0.0.255`

`ip nat inside source static tcp interface ethernet 0/3`
`21 interface fastethernet 2/0 21`

`ip nat inside source list 50 interface fastethernet`
`2/0`

25. You create an access list in Notepad in preparation to apply it to an interface. Before you add the lines to the access list, you apply the list to the intended interface. What is the result?

   ❏ A. You receive an error message to create the access list.

   ❏ B. You permit all traffic through the interface.

   ❏ C. All traffic through the interface is denied.

   ❏ D. You receive a syntax error message.

Quick Answer: **161**
Detailed Answer: **165**

26. Network Address Translation (NAT) typically translates between one or more internal private addresses to public Internet addresses. What ranges are defined in RFC 1918 as internal private addresses? (Choose three.)

   ❏ A. 10.0.0.0/8

   ❏ B. 172.16.0.0/16

   ❏ C. 169.254.0.0/16

   ❏ D. 172.16.0.0/16–172.31.255.255/16

   ❏ E. 192.168.0.0/24–192.168.255.255/24

   ❏ F. 224.0.0.0/24

Quick Answer: **161**
Detailed Answer: **166**

27. You are troubleshooting a NAT configuration on your 2514 router. It seems that all of the syntax is in place, but users are not able to access the Internet. You are able to ping Internet websites from your router successfully. What is the most likely cause of the problem?

Quick Answer: **161**
Detailed Answer: **166**

Relevant router configuration:

```
interface fastethernet 0
  ip address 192.168.1.1 255.255.255.0
interface fastethernet 1
  ip address dhcp
  ip nat outside
ip route 0.0.0.0 0.0.0.0 fastethernet 1
access-list 50 permit 192.168.1.0 0.0.0.255
ip nat inside source static tcp 192.168.1.50 80 inter-
face fastethernet 1 80
ip nat inside source list 50 interface fastethernet 1
overload
```

❑ A. The static route is incorrect. It needs to be pointed to the ISP next-hop address rather than the router's local interface.

❑ B. The NAT configuration is incomplete.

❑ C. Static NAT features cannot be combined with the NAT Overload features.

❑ D. All of the above.

28. Which of the following creates a standard access list that allows traffic from the 172.16 subnet?

Quick Answer: **161**
Detailed Answer: **166**

❑ A. `access-list 1 permit 172.16.0.0 0.0.255.255`

❑ B. `access-list 100 permit 172.16.0.0 255.255.0.0`

❑ C. `access-list 1 permit 172.16.0.0 255.255.0.0`

❑ D. `access-list 100 permit 172.16.0.0 0.0.255.255`

29. Which of the following access list lines denies access to a computer with an IP of 172.16.0.5?

Quick Answer: **161**
Detailed Answer: **166**

❑ A. `access-list 1 172.16.0.5 0.0.0.0 deny`

❑ B. `access-list 1 deny host 172.16.0.5`

❑ C. `access-list 1 deny 172.16.0.5 255.255.255.255`

❑ D. `access-list 101 deny 172.16.0.5 0.0.0.0`

30. You want to create an access list that denies port 23 TCP traffic from the 172.30.10.0 network and that is destined for the 172.30.20.0 network. Which of the following commands accomplishes this?

❑   A. `access-list 101 tcp deny 172.30.10.0 0.0.0.255`
        `172.30.20.0 0.0.0.255 eq 23`

❑   B. `access-list 91 tcp deny 172.30.10.0 0.0.0.255`
        `172.30.20.0 0.0.0.255 eq 23`

❑   C. `access-list 101 deny tcp 172.30.10.0 0.0.0.255`
        `172.30.20.0 0.0.0.255 eq 23`

❑   D. `access-list 91 deny tcp 172.30.10.0 0.0.0.255`
        `172.30.20.0 0.0.0.255 eq 23`

Quick Answer: 161
Detailed Answer: 166

31. You want to create an access list that denies all outbound traffic to port 80 from the 10.10.0.0 network. Which access list entry meets your requirements?

❑   A. `access-list 101 deny tcp 10.10.0.0 0.0.255.255 eq 80`

❑   B. `access-list 91 deny tcp 10.10.0.0 0.0.255.255 any eq`
        `80`

❑   C. `access-list 101 deny tcp 10.10.0.0 0.0.255.255 all eq`
        `80`

❑   D. `access-list 101 deny tcp 10.10.0.0 0.0.255.255 any eq`
        `80`

Quick Answer: 161
Detailed Answer: 166

32. Which of the following forms of NAT allows you to translate one group of IP addresses to another in a 1:1 relationship with minimal configuration?

❑   A. Port Address Translation
❑   B. Static NAT
❑   C. NAT Overload
❑   D. Dynamic NAT

Quick Answer: 161
Detailed Answer: 167

Quick Check ✓

Quick Answer: **161**
Detailed Answer: **167**

33. You are configuring the Internet connection for the network pictured in the figure below. The initial NAT Overload configuration has been set up; you must now publish the internal FTP and web server to the Internet. What commands accomplish this? (Choose two.)

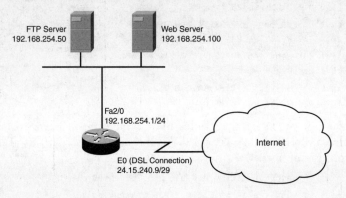

FTP Server
192.168.254.50

Web Server
192.168.254.100

Fa2/0
192.168.254.1/24

Internet

E0 (DSL Connection)
24.15.240.9/29

Internet network connection.

❑ A. `ip nat inside source static tcp 80 192.168.254.100 80 24.15.240.9`

❑ B. `ip nat inside source static tcp 192.168.254.50 20 24.15.240.9 20`

❑ C. `ip nat inside source static tcp 192.168.254.50 21 24.15.240.9 21`

❑ D. `ip nat inside source static tcp 192.168.254.100 80 24.15.240.9 80`

❑ E. `ip nat inside source static tcp 21 192.168.254.50 21 24.15.240.9`

Quick Answer: **161**
Detailed Answer: **167**

34. You want to use `access list 1` to filter traffic on your inbound vty lines. What command do you enter?

❑ A. `access-group 1 in`
❑ B. `access-group 1 vty in`
❑ C. `access-list 1 in`
❑ D. `access-class 1 in`

Quick Answer: **161**
Detailed Answer: **167**

35. Which of the following statements are correct regarding the placement of access lists? (Choose two.)

❑ A. Place extended access lists close to the source.
❑ B. Place extended access lists close to the destination.
❑ C. Place standard access lists close to the source.
❑ D. Place standard access lists close to the destination.

36. What command allows you to view access lists applied to interface `serial 0/1`?

Quick Answer: **161**
Detailed Answer: **167**

    ❑ A. `show access list serial 0/1`
    ❑ B. `show access-group serial 0/1`
    ❑ C. `show ip interface serial 0/1`
    ❑ D. `show ip access-lists serial 0/1`

37. You want to view all entries in all access lists on your router. What is the appropriate command to enter?

Quick Answer: **161**
Detailed Answer: **167**

    ❑ A. `show ip access-lists`
    ❑ B. `show all access-lists`
    ❑ C. `show access-lists`
    ❑ D. `show all ip access-lists`

38. You need to link an extended access list to an Ethernet interface on your router. What command properly configures the interface?

Quick Answer: **161**
Detailed Answer: **168**

    ❑ A. `ip access-group 120 e0`
    ❑ B. `ip access-group 120 out`
    ❑ C. `access-list 120 e0`
    ❑ D. `access-list 120 in e0`

39. You need to permit SSH traffic. What port do you need to allow in your access lists?

Quick Answer: **161**
Detailed Answer: **168**

    ❑ A. 22
    ❑ B. 23
    ❑ C. 69
    ❑ D. 443

40. You are hosting a POP3-based email server that users need to access. You need to deny all traffic except to the POP3 server. What port must you allow?

Quick Answer: **161**
Detailed Answer: **168**

    ❑ A. 25
    ❑ B. 143
    ❑ C. 110
    ❑ D. 443

41. You want to prevent Telnet access to your router. After the access list is created, what configuration mode is appropriate to apply it?

Quick Answer: **161**
Detailed Answer: **168**

    ❑ A. Privileged EXEC mode
    ❑ B. Global Configuration mode
    ❑ C. Interface Configuration mode
    ❑ D. Line Configuration mode

42. You want to prevent Telnet access through your router. What configuration mode is appropriate?

    ❑ A. Privileged EXEC mode
    ❑ B. Global Configuration mode
    ❑ C. Interface Configuration mode
    ❑ D. Line Configuration mode

Quick Answer: **161**
Detailed Answer: **168**

43. You want to create access lists for vty lines. You also want to create an admin access list and a regular user access list. You've been told you should use the same access list for each line. Why should the same access lists be applied to all vty lines?

    ❑ A. To keep intruders out.
    ❑ B. To apply equal levels of security.
    ❑ C. You have to apply the same lists to each line.
    ❑ D. External users can't choose which lines they connect to.

Quick Answer: **161**
Detailed Answer: **168**

44. You are troubleshooting a standard access list and realize that an incorrect entry has been made. You want to remove the incorrect entry. What steps must you take?

    ❑ A. Delete all the lines starting from the last one until the incorrect line; then add the necessary lines.
    ❑ B. Delete all the lines starting from the first one until the incorrect line; then add the necessary lines.
    ❑ C. Delete all the lines and re-create the list.
    ❑ D. Delete the incorrect line.

Quick Answer: **161**
Detailed Answer: **168**

45. You are troubleshooting a named access list and realize that an incorrect entry has been made. You want to remove the incorrect entry. What steps must you take?

    ❑ A. Delete all the lines starting from the last one until the incorrect line; then add the necessary lines.
    ❑ B. Delete all the lines starting from the first one until the incorrect line; then add the necessary lines.
    ❑ C. Delete all the lines and re-create the list.
    ❑ D. Delete the incorrect line.

Quick Answer: **161**
Detailed Answer: **168**

46. You are configuring an office to use a Cisco router to connect to the Internet. The onsite network administrator would like to publish an internal email server, two internal web servers, and an internal FTP server to the Internet so outside users can access them. What is necessary for this configuration?

   ❑ A. You need a public Internet IP address for each internal server. These addresses can be mapped using Static NAT features.

   ❑ B. You need a single public Internet IP address for this configuration and use NAT Overload to share it among all four internal servers.

   ❑ C. You need a single public Internet IP address for this configuration and use Static NAT to map specific ports to all four internal servers.

   ❑ D. You need two public Internet IP addresses to accommodate the internal web servers. The FTP and email server can be mapped to individual ports on either of the addresses.

47. You are creating an access list entry to control access to a vty line. Which configuration mode should you be in to create the entry?

   ❑ A. Privileged EXEC mode
   ❑ B. Global Configuration mode
   ❑ C. Interface Configuration mode
   ❑ D. Line Configuration mode

48. Which keyword, when used with the `access-list` command, sends a message to the console?

   ❑ A. `console`
   ❑ B. `log`
   ❑ C. `report`
   ❑ D. `send`

49. You want to remove access restrictions on your vty lines, after previously applying access list filters. What command should you enter?

   ❑ A. `no access-list 1`
   ❑ B. `no access-group 1`
   ❑ C. `no access-class 1`
   ❑ D. `access-group 1 delete`

50. You need to devise a wildcard mask that checks the first four bits of an octet. Which of the following is correct?
    - ❏ A. 00001111
    - ❏ B. 11110000
    - ❏ C. 11000000
    - ❏ D. 00000011

Quick Answer: **161**
Detailed Answer: **169**

Quick Check Answer Key

1. D

2. A, B, C

3. A, B, E

4. B, E

5. A

6. A, D

7. B, C

8. C

9. A

10. A

11. C

12. A, D

13. A, B, D

14. B

15. A, D

16. B, C

17. B

18. C

19. B

20. C

21. A

22. D

23. B

24. C

25. B

26. A, D, E

27. B

28. A

29. B

30. C

31. D

32. D

33. C, D

34. D

35. A, D

36. C

37. C

38. B

39. A

40. C

41. D

42. C

43. D

44. C

45. D

46. D

47. B

48. B

49. C

50. A

Answers and Explanations

1. **Answer: D.** Access lists stop traffic going through the router—not traffic originating from the router, as in this scenario. Therefore, the administrator's Telnet session is able to connect. A is incorrect because Telnet uses TCP. B is incorrect. Telnet does use TCP traffic, but this is not the most likely cause of the problem. C is incorrect. Telnet connects to remote port 23 by default; however, the issue here is that the session initiated from the router, and access lists filter only traffic going through the router.

2. **Answers: A, B, and C.** Access lists can be used with QoS in implementing priority and custom queuing. Access lists can filter routing protocol updates. Access lists can also specify interesting traffic to trigger dial-on-demand routing. D is incorrect because access lists aren't used for console port security.

3. **Answers: A, B, and E.** Standard access lists check the packet's source address. Extended access lists check both source and destination packet addresses and other parts of the packets. Named access lists allow the use of a friendly name for the access list. C is incorrect because there are no restricted access lists. D is incorrect because there are no static access lists. F is incorrect, as there are no unnamed access lists.

4. **Answers: B and E.** Extended access lists can use source and destination information, including the source port, and named access lists can be either extended or standard, so they have the capability to filter based on the source port. A is incorrect because standard access lists can filter on source address information, but not source port. C is incorrect, as there are no restricted access lists. D is incorrect because there are no static access lists. F is incorrect because there are no unnamed access lists.

5. **Answer: A.** Standard access lists can filter based only on the source address, subnet, or source host IP address of a packet. B is incorrect because extended access lists can use source and destination information, including the source port. C is incorrect, as there are no dynamic access lists. D is incorrect because there are no static access lists. E is incorrect; if the named access list is an extended access list, this does not hold true. F is incorrect because there are no unnamed access lists.

6. **Answers: A and D.** Standard access lists can range from 1–99 and IP Standard Expanded ranges from 1300–1999. B is incorrect because this value is in the range for extended access lists. C is incorrect, as this is not a valid identifier for access lists.

7. **Answers: B and C.** Extended access lists can range from 100–199 and IP Extended Expanded ranges from 2000–2699. A is incorrect, as this is a standard access list identifier. D is incorrect, as this is outside the range of standard and extended access lists.

8. **Answer: C.** Named access lists allow the deletion of individual lines anywhere in the access list. The newer IOS versions support a named access list that can even add lines in between other lines. A is incorrect because standard access lists do not allow the deletion of specific lines. B is incorrect because extended access lists do not allow the deletion of specific lines. D is incorrect, as there are no unnamed access lists.

9. **Answer: A.** FTP uses TCP and ports 20 and 21. B is incorrect, as FTP uses TCP. C is incorrect because port 20 is required as well. D is incorrect, as UDP is not necessary.

10. **Answer: A.** TCP and UDP traffic need to be allowed on port 53. TCP is used typically by zone transfers, whereas UDP is used for queries. B is incorrect because port 69 is used by `finger`. C is incorrect, as port 67 is used by DHCP. D is incorrect because DNS queries use UDP and port 53.

11. **Answer: C.** A packet that does not meet any filters is dropped. A is incorrect because the packet is discarded instead of being routed. B is incorrect, as there is no mechanism to flag the packet. D is incorrect; although it is conceivable that an administrator could be notified, by default the packet is simply dropped.

12. **Answers: A and D.** No access list can filter packets originating from the router, and outbound access lists, if they are extended, can drop packets based on protocol numbers. B is incorrect because the filtering takes place after a routing decision has been made. C is incorrect because as the routing decision has made, the router has already dropped packets that are not routable.

13. **Answers: A, B, and D.** No access lists can filter packets originating from a router; a routing decision has not been made until after the access list is processed; and extended access lists can be used as inbound access lists and can therefore filter packets based on protocol number. C is incorrect because the routeability of packets has not yet been determined, and access lists do not make routing judgments.

14. **Answer: B.** Because there is no `permit` statement and access lists end with an implicit `deny all`, no traffic is permitted. A is incorrect; this statement is true, but all traffic is denied, not just FTP traffic. C is incorrect because no traffic is permitted. D is incorrect, as all traffic is denied because of the lack of any `permit` statements.

15. **Answers: A and D.** The indicated mask affects the 172.16.0.0 network, so 172.16.99.1 and 172.16.1.1 are affected. B and C are incorrect, as 192.168.0.0 and 172.30 don't match the bits that matter—those set to 0 in the mask.

16. **Answers: B and C.** The significant bits are the last 16, indicated by the wild-card mask of 255.255.0.0. The IP addresses 192.168.20.5 and 172.30.20.5 match the last two octets, or 16 bits, of the 10.0.20.5 IP address. A and D are incorrect; although the first portions of the IP address match, it is the last two octets that are significant.

17. **Answer: B.** To abbreviate the all-0 wildcard mask, use the keyword host to specify a single host. A and D are incorrect, as this is invalid syntax. C is incorrect because this syntax results in an error message.

18. **Answer: C.** You can replace 255.255.255.255 with the keyword any. A, B, and D are all invalid syntax options.

19. **Answer: B.** The wildcard mask 0.0.15.255 affects the 172.16.16.0 255.255.240.0 network. In the third octet, the first four bits are checked in binary, resulting in 00000000.00000000.00001111.11111111. A is incorrect, as this does not match the given problem, checking too many bits (five) in the last octet. C is incorrect because this mask checks only three bits in the third octet. D is incorrect because this mask checks only two bits in the third octet.

20. **Answer: C.** The subnet mask, in the third octet as binary, is 1110 0000. This indicates that the first three bits are significant in the wildcard mask, and the last five bits of the third octet are not checked. This gives 00011111 in the third octet, which is 31 in decimal notation. A is incorrect, as this wildcard mask checks too many bits (five) in the third octet. B is incorrect because this choice checks four bits in the IP, which are too few. D is incorrect because this choice considers only two bits significant in the third octet, which are too few for the example.

21. **Answer: A.** You may create only one access list per protocol, per direction, per interface. B is incorrect because you can have multiple access lists for a single port number and only one per direction. C is incorrect, as you may have only one access list per protocol, not per port number. D is incorrect because you may not have more than one access list per interface, which is not listed.

22. **Answer: D.** Access lists are processed from the top down, so ordering is very important. A is incorrect, as named access list lines can be deleted from any-where, but insertions are at the end. B is incorrect; ordering is important, because after a rule is matched, processing ends. C is incorrect. More general rules should be placed at the end; otherwise, traffic might be unintentionally affected by the filter, whereas specific rules might not be applied because they are never processed.

23. **Answer: B.** The `ip nat` syntax can be quite cryptic because the Cisco router gives you plenty of flexibility with the form and directions of NAT translation. In this case, you are looking to create a static NAT translation to allow TCP port 80 (HTTP) to pass through the Cisco router to the internal web server. There are two ways to accomplish this: You can create a static NAT translation from the `inside` perspective or from the `outside` perspective. In this question, the only correct answer is the translation performed from the inside: `ip nat inside source static tcp 172.16.55.10 80 interface fastEthernet 0/1 80`. If you were to perform the static NAT translation from the outside perspective, you would not be given the option to choose to translate from an interface (`fastEthernet 0/1`, in this case). All other answers result in an invalid syntax message.

24. **Answer: C.** This is a fairly complex NAT configuration that combines both static NAT and NAT Overload features into a single configuration. First, all interfaces on the router are marked as either inside or outside NAT interfaces. Second, a standard access list needs to be created that shows the router what addresses should be translated. Third, the NAT Overload configuration is applied as coming from the addresses in `access-list 50` going to the `fastEthernet 2/0` interface. Finally, the static NAT translation is defined for port 21 (FTP) from the internal host (192.168.254.32) to the `fastEthernet 2/0` interface. Answer A is incorrect because it is missing the static NAT translation. It also uses invalid syntax on the NAT Overload configuration. The Cisco router cannot translate from one interface to another; it always needs an access list defining the internal range. Answer B is incorrect because it is missing the protocol (TCP) and port number (21) for the static NAT translation and also uses the same invalid NAT Overload configuration as answer A. Answer D is incorrect because the static NAT translation goes between interfaces rather than to an internal IP address. The `overload` keyword is also missing from the NAT Overload syntax. This means only one IP address at a time can access the Internet.

25. **Answer: B.** If an empty access list is applied to an interface, all traffic is permitted through the interface. C is incorrect because traffic is allowed through the interface, not blocked. A and D are incorrect because you do not receive an error message.

26. **Answers: A, D, and E.** RFC 1918 defines a private address range for each of the three classes of usable addresses: Class A: 10.0.0.0/8, Class B: 172.16.0.0/16–172.31.255.255/16, and Class C: 192.168.0.0/24–192. 168.255.255/24. Answer B is incorrect because it defines only one of the Class B ranges that are considered private; any address from the range 172.16.0.0/16–172.31.255.255/16 is considered a private address. Answer C is incorrect because this range represents addresses that are automatically assigned to a computer when it cannot obtain a valid address through DHCP (these are called *local link addresses*). They are not defined in RFC 1918 as a private address. Answer F is incorrect because this is the first range of Class D addresses, which are used for multicast.

27. **Answer: B.** The NAT configuration is missing the `ip nat inside` command under the `fastethernet 0` interface. Without this command, the router does not know the interface it should use when translating internal, source addresses. Answer A is incorrect because static routes can be pointed to an exit interface or a next-hop address. Answer C is incorrect because Static NAT is commonly combined with NAT Overload features to accomplish required objectives. Answer D is incorrect because…well, this should be pretty obvious.

28. **Answer: A.** This answer has the correct syntax of the `access-list` command followed by the list number, permit/deny, and IP address, and a wildcard mask. B and D are incorrect because they indicate an extended access list. C is incorrect because the wildcard mask has been reversed.

29. **Answer: B.** This command uses the `host` keyword to specify a single host. A is incorrect, as deny follows the access list number. C is incorrect because the wildcard mask should be all zeros. D is incorrect because the access list number represents an extended access list.

30. **Answer: C.** An extended access list is required, and 101 fits. Additionally, this answer shows deny properly preceding `tcp` in the syntax. A is incorrect because deny should precede `tcp`. B and D are incorrect because the access list numbers are for a standard access list.

31. **Answer: D.** Use the any keyword to specify all destinations. A is incorrect because no destination is specified. B is incorrect, as this specifies a standard access list. C is incorrect because `all` is not the proper keyword.

32. **Answer: D.** Dynamic NAT allows you to configure multiple pools of IP addresses and translate between them. The router dynamically matches each IP address to one another as a request is made. Answer A is incorrect because Port Address Translation (PAT) is just another name for NAT Overload. Answer B is incorrect. Although Static NAT could perform this task, it would take quite a bit of configuration to manually map IP addresses in large pools. Answer C is incorrect because NAT Overload takes a group of IP addresses and translates them to a single (overloaded) IP address.

33. **Answers: C and D.** The generic Static NAT syntax for TCP translations is `ip nat inside source static tcp <inside_ip> <inside_port> <outside_ip/outside_interface> <outside_port>`. In this case, only answers C and D match this syntax. Answers A and E flip the IP address and port numbers in the wrong location, which produce a syntax error. Answer B uses port 20, which is used by FTP; however, only port 21 is used to initiate an FTP session. After a client initiates the incoming FTP session on port 21, the FTP server establishes an outgoing FTP data connection using port 20. Because of this, no incoming NAT translation is necessary for TCP port 20.

34. **Answer: D.** The `access-class 1 in` command is used to apply `access-list 1` inbound to the vty interface. A is incorrect because the `access-group` command is used on physical interfaces. B is incorrect because the `vty` keyword is invalid. C is incorrect because the `access-list` command is used to create access list entries.

35. **Answers: A and D.** Extended access lists should go near the source of the traffic, and standard access lists should go close to the destination. B is incorrect because extended access lists close to the destination cause routers to process more packets than necessary. C is incorrect because standard access lists close to the source may drop too much traffic and prohibit network communications.

36. **Answer: C.** The correct syntax is `show ip interface serial 0/1`, which displays detailed information about the interface, including the applied access lists. A is incorrect, as this is invalid syntax and results in an error. B and D are invalid commands.

37. **Answer: C.** The `show access-lists` command is correct and displays each access list defined on the device, as well as its entries. A is incorrect because the keyword `ip` is used only if you want to see the IP standard and extended access lists. It does not show you any MAC address, IPX, or AppleTalk access lists, and the question specifically states you would like to see *all* access lists. B and D are incorrect because the keyword `all` is invalid.

38. **Answer: B.** To apply the access list to an interface, enter Interface Configuration mode and use the `ip access-group` command, specifying the list and direction. A is incorrect, as the interface is not specified in the command, but by entering Interface Configuration mode. C is incorrect, as `access-group` is the correct command, and the direction is not specified. D is incorrect because the command is `access-group`, not `access-list`.

39. **Answer: A.** SSH uses port 22. B is incorrect, as port 23 is used by Telnet. C is incorrect, as port 69 is used by `finger`. D is incorrect because port 443 is used by HTTPS.

40. **Answer: C.** POP3 uses TCP port 110. A is incorrect, as SMTP uses port 25. B is incorrect, as IMAP uses port 143. D is incorrect because port 443 is used by HTTPS.

41. **Answer: D.** You need to apply the access list to a vty line in Line Configuration mode for it to be effective. A is incorrect because even though you are in Privileged EXEC mode, this answer is too general. B is incorrect, as the access list is created in Global Configuration mode. C is incorrect because vty access is controlled by Line Configuration mode, not Interface Configuration mode.

42. **Answer: C.** You need to restrict Telnet traffic through the appropriate interfaces. A is incorrect because Privileged EXEC mode is not specific. B is incorrect because Global Configuration mode is used to create the access list. D is incorrect because Line Configuration mode can be used to control Telnet access to the router, but not through it.

43. **Answer: D.** You cannot choose which line you connect to when telnetting from an outside location, so it is typically best to apply the same rules for each line. A is incorrect because although you do want to keep intruders out, this is not the best reason. B is not correct, as this is effectively what you are doing, but it is not a compelling reason to do so. C is incorrect because you do not have to apply the same list to each line.

44. **Answer: C.** You must delete the list and re-create it entirely. The remaining responses are incorrect because you cannot selectively delete lines.

45. **Answer: D.** You can selectively delete lines in named access lists, and only in named access lists. C is incorrect because although you could re-create the entire list, it is much more work than is necessary. A and B are incorrect because you cannot selectively delete lines.

46. **Answer: D.** NAT can accomplish some pretty amazing feats; however, sharing an IP address for two servers that use the same port number is not one of them. In this case, you need two public Internet addresses to allow both internal web servers to be accessed on TCP port 80. The other servers can use port 21 (FTP) and port 25 (SMTP) on either of the public Internet IP addresses. Answer A could be used to solve this problem, but it is not the best solution because it is more costly to deploy than answer D. B is incorrect because NAT Overload allows the servers to share only a single IP address when accessing the Internet, not when the requests originate *from* the Internet. Answer C is incorrect because you can map only TCP port 80 on the single IP address to one of the internal web servers. The other cannot be accessed from the Internet.

47. **Answer: B.** Access list entries are created and defined in Global Configuration mode. A is incorrect because Privileged EXEC mode is too general. C is incorrect, as vty lines are configured in Line Configuration mode, but access list entries are created in Global Configuration mode. D is incorrect because Line Configuration mode is for applying the access list.

48. **Answer: B.** The `log` option sends a message to the console. A, C, and D are all invalid keywords.

49. **Answer: C.** The `no access-class 1` command removes the access list from the vty line. A and B are incorrect, as they are not valid commands on the vty line. D is incorrect, as there is no delete switch in the syntax.

50. **Answer: A.** A 0 indicates the bit is checked or significant. B is incorrect because the first four bits are ignored. C is incorrect because the first two bits are ignored. D is incorrect because the first six bits are checked.

Serial WAN and Frame Relay Connections

Quick Check ✓

1. Your junior network administrator asks what type of frame relay encapsulation should be used for your branch office, which contains 25 routers: 15 are Cisco 2611s, 5 are Cisco 3640s, and 5 are a mix of other vendors. What do you tell her?

   ❑ A. Cisco
   ❑ B. Q.333a
   ❑ C. IETF
   ❑ D. ANSI

Quick Answer: **185**
Detailed Answer: **186**

2. What function does a frame relay DLCI provide with respect to a router and a frame relay switch?

   ❑ A. Defines the signaling standard between a router and the frame relay switch
   ❑ B. Identifies the signaling between a router and the destination router
   ❑ C. Identifies the circuit between a router and the frame relay switch
   ❑ D. Identifies the encapsulation used between two routers

Quick Answer: **185**
Detailed Answer: **186**

3. What is the default Local Management Interface (LMI) frame type used by a Cisco router?

   ❑ A. ANSI
   ❑ B. Cisco
   ❑ C. IETF
   ❑ D. Q.933a
   ❑ E. Modified cut-through

Quick Answer: **185**
Detailed Answer: **186**

Quick Check

4. You are required to troubleshoot the WAN link between the Acme, Inc., main office in Baltimore and the Acme, Inc., remote office in Taiwan. A Cisco router that was providing frame relay connectivity at the Taiwan site is replaced with a different vendor's frame relay router. Connectivity is now down between the Baltimore and Taiwan site, but you can still get to the Phoenix remote site using frame relay. What is the most likely cause of the problem?

Quick Answer: **185**
Detailed Answer: **186**

❑ A. Mismatched LMI types

❑ B. Incorrect DLCI

❑ C. No authentication

❑ D. Incorrect IP address mapping

5. You are having routing table issues because of RIP running over your frame relay connections. Your router is not updating other remote sites as a result of split-horizon issues. What can you do to alleviate this problem?

Quick Answer: **185**
Detailed Answer: **186**

❑ A. Create frame relay maps

❑ B. Configure frame relay proxies

❑ C. Configure LMI to update the router

❑ D. Create sub-interfaces on the interface the updates come in on

6. Frame relay is an ITU-T and ANSI standard that defines the process of sending data over a _____.

Quick Answer: **185**
Detailed Answer: **186**

❑ A. Packet-switched line

❑ B. Circuit-switched line

❑ C. Leased-line

❑ D. Local area network

7. Frame relay primarily encapsulates information from the upper layers of the OSI Model at the _____ layer.

Quick Answer: **185**
Detailed Answer: **187**

❑ A. Application

❑ B. Transport

❑ C. Session

❑ D. Data-link

❑ E. Physical

8. Which of the following is the signaling standard between the router device and the frame relay switch that is responsible for managing the connection and maintaining the status between the devices?

    ❑ A. DLCI

    ❑ B. LMI

    ❑ C. PVC

    ❑ D. IETF

Quick Answer: **185**
Detailed Answer: **187**

9. In which frame relay topology do all routers have virtual circuits to all other destinations?

    ❑ A. Star

    ❑ B. Hub and spoke

    ❑ C. Bus

    ❑ D. Partial mesh

    ❑ E. Full mesh

Quick Answer: **185**
Detailed Answer: **187**

10. The nonbroadcast multi-access nature of frame relay causes issues with what routing loop preventative mechanism?

    ❑ A. Route poisoning

    ❑ B. Hold-down timers

    ❑ C. Triggered updates

    ❑ D. Split-horizon

Quick Answer: **185**
Detailed Answer: **187**

11. If you are unable to support Inverse ARP to map DLCIs to network layer addresses, what method do you need to use?

    ❑ A. Static routes

    ❑ B. Static maps

    ❑ C. DHCP

    ❑ D. LMI mapping

Quick Answer: **185**
Detailed Answer: **187**

12. Which of the following commands configures a static map of the remote IP address 172.16.12.2 to the DLCI of 100?

    ❑ A. `Frame relay map dlci 100 ip 172.16.12.2`

    ❑ B. `Frame relay rarp ip 172.16.12.2 100`

    ❑ C. `Frame relay lmi dlci 172.16.12.2 100 broadcast`

    ❑ D. `Frame relay map ip 172.16.12.2 100 broadcast`

Quick Answer: **185**
Detailed Answer: **187**

13. Which of the following commands gives you the current frame relay map entries?

    ❑ A. Show ip frame
    ❑ B. Show ip route
    ❑ C. Show frame relay map
    ❑ D. Show ip interfaces brief

Quick Answer: **185**
Detailed Answer: **187**

14. What are issues to consider if you turn off split-horizon in a frame relay environment? (Choose two.)

    ❑ A. You cannot turn off split-horizon on an IP network.
    ❑ B. Routing updates can no longer get through.
    ❑ C. Not all Layer 3 protocols allow you to disable split-horizon.
    ❑ D. You can open up your network to routing loops.

Quick Answer: **185**
Detailed Answer: **188**

15. When you are setting up frame relay for point-to-point sub-interfaces, which of the following must not be configured?

    ❑ A. The frame relay encapsulation on the physical interface
    ❑ B. The local DLCI on each sub-interface
    ❑ C. An IP address on the physical interface
    ❑ D. The sub-interface type as point-to-point

Quick Answer: **185**
Detailed Answer: **188**

16. The frame relay circuit illustrated in the figure below is experiencing congestion. Which of the following techniques could be used to help alleviate the congestion and notify the routers? (Choose three.)

Quick Answer: **185**
Detailed Answer: **188**

    ❑ A. FECN
    ❑ B. BECN
    ❑ C. DE bit
    ❑ D. LMI
    ❑ E. CIR

17. Which frame relay mechanism is responsible for transmitting keepalives to ensure that the PVC does not shut down because of inactivity?

 ❑   A. LMI
 ❑   B. BECN
 ❑   C. FECN
 ❑   D. DLCI

18. You are the network administrator of a frame relay network topology that consists of a high-speed (1.544Mbps) connection at the central site and low-speed (64Kbps) connections at the branch sites. Because of the speed mismatch, a bottleneck often exists for traffic on a virtual circuit when the central site tries to communicate with the branch offices. What can you do to resolve this issue without spending more money?

 ❑   A. Use a slower link at the branch offices
 ❑   B. Use a faster link at the branch offices
 ❑   C. Use frame relay traffic shaping
 ❑   D. Use more PVCs

19. Your junior network administrator asks you what the CIR is with regard to frame relay. What do you tell her?

 ❑   A. It's the value that specifies the maximum average data rate that the network undertakes to deliver under "normal conditions."
 ❑   B. It's a 10-bit number in the address field of the frame relay frame header that identifies the VC.
 ❑   C. It's a method of dynamically associating the remote router network layer address with a local DLCI.
 ❑   D. It's a signaling standard between the router (DTE device) and the local frame relay switch (DCE device).

20. You are the network administrator for a medium-size corporation with eight branch offices. Each office is running frame relay to your central site and is running connections to the other offices for a full mesh topology. You are told that you have just added two new branch offices that need to be fully meshed. How many total PVCs must you have in your full mesh?

 ❑   A. 10
 ❑   B. 20
 ❑   C. 25
 ❑   D. 45

21. X.25 was the predecessor to frame relay and is still used in certain parts of the world. What is the main difference between X.25 and frame relay?

   ❑   A.   X.25 is faster and more expensive than frame relay.
   ❑   B.   Frame relay does not carry the overhead of X.25.
   ❑   C.   X.25 is cell-switched and frame relay is packet-switched.
   ❑   D.   X.25 is standards-based and frame relay is proprietary.

Quick Answer: **185**
Detailed Answer: **189**

22. Which of the following statements is true regarding virtual circuits?

   ❑   A.   Virtual circuits are single-streamed data links over a service provider's network.
   ❑   B.   Switched virtual circuits are the most popular of the virtual circuits.
   ❑   C.   Permanent virtual circuits are used when you need periodic use of the frame relay circuit.
   ❑   D.   Switched virtual circuits require call setup and teardown.

Quick Answer: **185**
Detailed Answer: **189**

23. For Inverse ARP to work, which of the following must be in place? (Choose three.)

   ❑   A.   A virtual circuit must be in place.
   ❑   B.   LMI must be operating correctly.
   ❑   C.   Your routing protocol must support Inverse ARP.
   ❑   D.   You must be running Cisco IOS 11.2 or higher.

Quick Answer: **185**
Detailed Answer: **189**

24. You are running frame relay in your network, in a star topology. All of your equipment at your central site is Cisco. Your branch offices are running Cisco routers, but one of your branch offices does not have a Cisco router. How can you enable a frame relay connection to this branch office?

   ❑   A.   Use a static frame map and specify IETF as the encapsulation.
   ❑   B.   Use IETF as your encapsulation at the central site.
   ❑   C.   You must purchase a Cisco router.
   ❑   D.   You can use a frame relay proxy.

Quick Answer: **185**
Detailed Answer: **189**

25. You have two routers connected over a frame relay network. The router in Arizona has the IP address 10.1.1.1/24 and uses a local DLCI of 512. The router in Michigan has the IP address 10.1.1.2/24 and uses a local DLCI of 598. Which of the following syntax correctly creates a static map that allows Arizona to reach Michigan and allows routing protocol functionality?

Quick Answer: **185**
Detailed Answer: **189**

❏ A. `frame-relay map ip 10.1.1.2 512 broadcast`

❏ B. `frame-relay map ip 10.1.1.1 512 broadcast`

❏ C. `frame-relay map ip 10.1.1.2 598 broadcast`

❏ D. `frame-relay map ip 10.1.1.1 598 broadcast`

26. You are troubleshooting your frame relay connections. After you type in the show `frame-relay pvc` command, one of your PVCs shows up as DELETED. What causes this message?

Quick Answer: **185**
Detailed Answer: **189**

❏ A. Your router is incorrectly configured. You need to add the right DLCI information, and the circuit should come up.

❏ B. The remote router is incorrectly configured.

❏ C. You are physically disconnected from the service provider.

❏ D. You need to switch from a multipoint configuration to a point-to-point configuration and create a sub-interface for each PVC you plan on using.

27. You are having connectivity problems with your frame relay connection. Which of the following commands displays information regarding the encapsulation, Layer 1, and Layer 2 status?

Quick Answer: **185**
Detailed Answer: **190**

❏ A. `Show frame relay pvc`

❏ B. `Show interface serial`

❏ C. `Show encapsulation frame relay`

❏ D. `Show running-config`

28. You are troubleshooting your frame relay connection and have called your service provider. The technician asks you for your circuit number. What is the significance of this circuit number?

Quick Answer: **185**
Detailed Answer: **190**

❏ A. It is the local loop identifier.

❏ B. It is the DLCI.

❏ C. It is the LMI.

❏ D. It is the CIR.

Quick Check ✓

Quick Answer: **185**
Detailed Answer: **190**

Quick Answer: **185**
Detailed Answer: **190**

29. What command do you type to receive the output generated here?

```
LMI Statistics for interface Serial0 (Frame Relay DCE)
LMI TYPE = CISCO
  Invalid Unnumbered info 0        Invalid Prot Disc 0
  Invalid dummy Call Ref 0         Invalid Msg Type 0
  Invalid Status Message 0         Invalid Lock Shift 0
  Invalid Information ID 0         Invalid Report IE Len 0
  Invalid Report Request 0         Invalid Keep IE Len 0
  Num Status Enq. Rcvd 72          Num Status msgs Sent 71
  Num Update Status Sent 0         Num St Enq. Timeouts 0
Router1#
```

❑ A. Show frame relay
❑ B. Show frame relay pvc
❑ C. Show frame relay lmi
❑ D. Show frame relay encapsulation

30. What command do you type to see the following output on your Cisco router?

```
Jul 12 14:21:45.667: Serial0(in): StEnq, myseq 112
Jul 12 14:21:45.671: RT IE 1, length 1, type 1
Jul 12 14:21:45.671: KA IE 3, length 2, yourseq 115,
myseq 112
Jul 12 14:21:45.675: Serial0(out): Status, myseq 113,
yourseen 115, DCE up
Jul 12 14:21:55.587: Serial0(in): StEnq, myseq 113
Jul 12 14:21:55.587: RT IE 1, length 1, type 1
Jul 12 14:21:55.591: kA IE 3, length 2, yourseq 116,
myseq 113
Jul 12 14:21:55.591: Serial0(out): Status, myseq 114,
yourseen 116, DCE up
```

❑ A. Show frame relay
❑ B. Show frame relay lmi
❑ C. Debug frame relay
❑ D. Debug frame relay lmi
❑ E. Debug all

31. By default, LMI signaling is sent every _____ seconds.
    - ❏ A. 10
    - ❏ B. 20
    - ❏ C. 30
    - ❏ D. 60

32. Which two implementation agreements were made between the ATM and Frame Relay Forums to make communications possible between them? (Choose two.)
    - ❏ A. FRF.1
    - ❏ B. FRF.5
    - ❏ C. FRF.8
    - ❏ D. FRF.11

33. Which of the following is an accurate statement regarding frame relay?
    - ❏ A. Frame relay is an ITU-T and ANSI standard that defines the process for sending data over the public, packet-switched network.
    - ❏ B. The core aspects of frame relay function at the middle two layers of the OSI Model.
    - ❏ C. Frame relay allows you to connect your sites with a star topology only.
    - ❏ D. Frame relay operates in a VLAN environment.

34. Your boss asks you about the significance of the OSI Model to frame relay. What do you tell her?
    - ❏ A. Frame relay operates at all layers of the OSI Model.
    - ❏ B. Frame relay operates at the top layers of the OSI Model.
    - ❏ C. Frame relay operates at the middle layers of the OSI Model.
    - ❏ D. Frame relay operates at the bottom two layers of the OSI Model.

35. What command do you type on Router1 to see the following output?

Quick Answer: **185**
Detailed Answer: **191**

```
PVC Statistics for interface Serial0 (Frame Relay DCE)

       Active    Inactive  Deleted   Static
       Local  1          0        0        0
       Switched  0        0        0        0
       Unused  0          0        0        0

DLCI = 101, DLCI USAGE = LOCAL, PVC STATUS = ACTIVE,
INTERFACE = Serial0

  input pkts 207      output pkts 239      in bytes 15223
  out bytes 14062     dropped pkts 0       in FECN pkts 0
  in BECN pkts 0      out FECN pkts 0      out BECN pkts 0
  in DE pkts 0        out DE pkts 0
  out bcast pkts 17   out bcast            bytes 3264
  PVC create time 00:11:32, last time PVC status changed
  00:11:32
  Router1#
```

- ❏ A. Show frame relay lmi
- ❏ B. Show frame relay pvc
- ❏ C. Show frame relay virtual circuit
- ❏ D. Show frame relay all

36. Which of the following frame relay topologies is the least expensive of them all?

Quick Answer: **185**
Detailed Answer: **191**

- ❏ A. Full mesh
- ❏ B. Partial mesh
- ❏ C. Hub and spoke
- ❏ D. NBMA

37. You have been assigned a CIR of 64Kbps. Your network has been occasionally sending traffic that exceeds your CIR. What does the service provider do?

Quick Answer: **185**
Detailed Answer: **191**

- ❏ A. Nothing
- ❏ B. Discard all extra data over 64Kbps
- ❏ C. Allow the traffic but charge you an extra fee
- ❏ D. Mark extra frames with a DE bit and do its best to deliver the packets

38. Which of the following is implemented to inform the receiving DTE that there is congestion on the network?

   ❑ A. FECN
   ❑ B. BECN
   ❑ C. DE
   ❑ D. CIR

Quick Answer: **185**
Detailed Answer: **191**

39. What are the requirements of a service provider for a frame relay connection to be made? (Choose four.)

   ❑ A. PVC
   ❑ B. CIR
   ❑ C. Inverse ARP
   ❑ D. LMI
   ❑ E. DLCI

Quick Answer: **185**
Detailed Answer: **191**

40. You are discussing frame relay with your service provider, and your representative asks you whether you prefer EIA/TIA-530 or V.35. To what is she referring?

   ❑ A. The signaling standard for frame relay
   ❑ B. The protocol for sending frame relay across the frame cloud
   ❑ C. The cable that connects you to the DCE
   ❑ D. The connector for the Cisco router

Quick Answer: **185**
Detailed Answer: **191**

41. Which two devices are necessary for frame relay connection? (Choose two.)

   ❑ A. Data terminal equipment
   ❑ B. Data termination equipment
   ❑ C. Data transport equipment
   ❑ D. Data communications equipment
   ❑ E. Data clocking equipment
   ❑ F. Data circuit equipment

Quick Answer: **185**
Detailed Answer: **191**

42. Which of the following can solve the problem of split-horizon in a frame relay environment? (Choose three.)

   ❑ A. Use a fully meshed topology
   ❑ B. Use sub-interfaces
   ❑ C. Turn off split-horizon
   ❑ D. Use RIPv2 as your routing protocol

Quick Answer: **185**
Detailed Answer: **192**

43. What is the primary purpose of using sub-interfaces for frame relay?

Quick Answer: **185**
Detailed Answer: **192**

- ❏ A. To allow more than one frame relay connection on the router
- ❏ B. To allow you to use more than one physical interface
- ❏ C. To overcome split-horizon
- ❏ D. To save IP addresses

44. You are troubleshooting your frame relay connection and notice that LMI reports the PVC is in an "inactive state." What does this mean?

Quick Answer: **185**
Detailed Answer: **192**

- ❏ A. The virtual circuit connection is active and the routers can exchange data.
- ❏ B. The local connection to the frame relay switch is working, but the remote router's connection to the remote frame relay switch is not working.
- ❏ C. No LMI is being received from the frame relay switch, or no service exists between the router and the local frame relay switch.
- ❏ D. The interface has been shut down.

45. Which of the following states represents a virtual circuit connection that is active and data is being exchanged over the frame relay network?

Quick Answer: **185**
Detailed Answer: **192**

- ❏ A. Inactive state
- ❏ B. Deleted state
- ❏ C. Blocked state
- ❏ D. Active state

46. Which of the following are valid LMI signaling types? (Choose three.)

Quick Answer: **185**
Detailed Answer: **192**

- ❏ A. Cisco
- ❏ B. ANSI
- ❏ C. ITU-T
- ❏ D. Q.933a

Quick Answer: **185**
Detailed Answer: **192**

47. You type the following configuration into a router. When you execute the show ip route command, however, you do not notice any new routes. What is wrong with the configuration?

```
router rip
 network 10.0.0.0
 network 172.19.0.0
 version 2
interface serial 0/0
 ip address 10.0.0.1 255.0.0.0
 frame-relay map ip 10.0.0.2 100
 frame-relay interface-dlci 100
 no frame-relay inverse-arp
interface ethernet 0/0
 ip address 172.19.0.0 255.255.0.0
```

- ❏ A. The frame-relay map command is missing the broadcast keyword.
- ❏ B. RIP should be running version 1, not version 2.
- ❏ C. Inverse ARP should be enabled.
- ❏ D. RIP is not activated on the interfaces.

48. How often do routers send Inverse ARP packets on all active DLCIs by default?

- ❏ A. Every 10 seconds
- ❏ B. Every 60 seconds
- ❏ C. Every 90 seconds
- ❏ D. Every 120 seconds

Quick Answer: **185**
Detailed Answer: **192**

49. On a frame relay switch, what is the first step that the switch performs on the incoming frame?

- ❏ A. It adds the two DLCI values in the header of the frame relay frame.
- ❏ B. It forwards the frame to the appropriate *switch.slot.port*.
- ❏ C. It checks the inbound DLCI number.
- ❏ D. It looks up the corresponding DLCI number for the remote router interface.

Quick Answer: **185**
Detailed Answer: **193**

Quick Check

Quick Check

Quick Answer: **185**
Detailed Answer: **193**

50. Which of the following topologies is shown in the figure below?

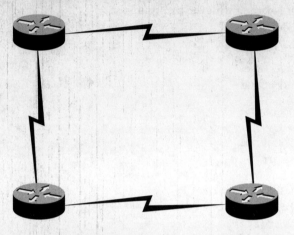

- ❑   A.   Partial mesh
- ❑   B.   Full mesh
- ❑   C.   Ring mesh
- ❑   D.   Hub and spoke

Quick Check Answer Key

1. C
2. C
3. B
4. A
5. D
6. A
7. D
8. B
9. E
10. D
11. B
12. D
13. C
14. C, D
15. C
16. A, B, C
17. A
18. C
19. A
20. D
21. B
22. D
23. A, B, D
24. A
25. A

26. A
27. B
28. A
29. C
30. D
31. A
32. B, C
33. A
34. D
35. B
36. C
37. D
38. A
39. A, B, D, E
40. C
41. A, D
42. A, B, C
43. C
44. B
45. D
46. A, B, D
47. A
48. B
49. C
50. A

Answers and Explanations

1. **Answer: C.** Your environment has non-Cisco routers. Although some newer vendors support Cisco's version of frame relay encapsulation, most do not. You have to use the standards-based IETF (Internet Engineering Task Force—the forum that oversees the evolution of the Internet architecture and the smooth connectivity across the Internet). A is incorrect, as you have non-Cisco routers. B is incorrect, as Q.933a is an LMI signaling standard developed by the CCITT (Comité Consultatif International Téléphonique et Télégraphique— the forum that defines many standards for data communication). D is incorrect, as ANSI (American National Standards Institute—an organization that administers the voluntary standardization of many different standards) is also an LMI signaling standard.

2. **Answer: C.** A DLCI identifies a logical circuit between the router and the frame relay switch. A is incorrect, as your router either autosenses the signaling, or you assign it manually. B is incorrect, as the DLCI does not decide the signaling. D is incorrect, as a DLCI is used by frame relay encapsulation, not used to define the encapsulation.

3. **Answer: B.** The Cisco LMI type is turned on by default. It is not proprietary to Cisco, as Northern Telecom and other companies helped develop it. A is incorrect, as the ANSI T1.617.D is not the default LMI type. D is incorrect, as Q.933a is not the default type. E is incorrect, as modified cut-through is a frame-forwarding convention.

4. **Answer: A.** Typically, you have different LMI types on different vendors. B is incorrect, as the LMI provides signaling between the router and the frame relay switch. It also assigns the DLCI. C is incorrect, as frame relay does not handle authentication. D is incorrect, as you typically have Inverse ARP handling IP address mapping.

5. **Answer: D.** The problem with split-horizon is its refusal to broadcast routes out the physical interface it came in on. When logical sub-interfaces are created, the router thinks the sub-interfaces are "separate" interfaces. A is incorrect, as frame relay maps help map DLCIs to IP addresses. B is incorrect, as there are no such things as frame relay proxies. C is incorrect, as LMI is a signaling standard similar to keepalives.

6. **Answer: A.** Frame relay uses packet-switched technology. B is incorrect, as circuit-switched technology is used by asynchronous serial and ISDN connections. C is incorrect, as leased lines are dedicated TDM lines that are given dedicated bandwidth and dedicated connections. D is incorrect, as LANs do not run frame relay.

7. **Answer: D.** Frame relay primarily works at Layer 2 of the OSI Model, which is the Data-link layer. A is incorrect, as frame relay is not involved with the Application layer. B is incorrect, as frame relay is not involved at the Transport layer. C is incorrect, as frame relay is not involved at the Session layer. E is incorrect as well; although frame relay does have involvement at the Physical layer, encapsulation does not occur there.

8. **Answer: B.** The Local Management Interface (LMI) is responsible for maintaining the connection between the router and the frame relay switch. A is incorrect, as the DLCI is responsible for identifying the virtual circuit between a router and the frame relay switch. C is incorrect, as the permanent virtual circuit is the logical path that data travels over in a frame relay environment. D is incorrect, as the Internet Engineering Task Force is not a signaling standard; it's a standards committee.

9. **Answer: E.** A full mesh topology has virtual circuits to all other routers involved in the topology. A is incorrect, as the star topology has a central router that has single virtual circuits to the other routers. B is incorrect, as the hub-and-spoke topology is the same as a star topology. C is incorrect, as the bus topology is sometimes called peer-to-peer and has a connection between two routers. D is incorrect, as a partial mesh topology has some redundant links, but not to every destination.

10. **Answer: D.** Split-horizon prevents routing updates (broadcasts) from going back out the interface they came in on. If you have multiple virtual circuits coming in on a physical interface, this causes issues. A is incorrect, as route poisoning still functions. B is incorrect, as hold-down timers do not affect frame relay. C is incorrect, as triggered updates still occur.

11. **Answer: B.** Static map statements need to be entered if Inverse ARP is not supported or is not working correctly. A is incorrect, as static routes do not give you correct DLCI-to-Layer 3 address mappings. C is incorrect, as DHCP assigns IP addresses to host interfaces. D is incorrect, as there is no such thing as LMI mapping. LMI does assist in the Inverse ARP process, however.

12. **Answer: D.** The Cisco IOS command is `frame relay map [protocol]` `[network address] [dlci number] [broadcasts allowed or not` `(optional)]`. A is incorrect, as you do not specify the DLCI before the IP address. B is incorrect, as RARP is not involved. C is incorrect, as the LMI is not involved in the `frame relay map` command.

13. **Answer: C.** The command shows all the current entries, dynamic or static, in the frame relay map table. A is incorrect, as there is no such command. B is incorrect, as this command shows you the routing table entries. D is incorrect, as this command shows you an overview of settings on all IP interfaces.

14. **Answers: C and D.** IPX and AppleTalk do not allow you to turn off split-horizon, and split-horizon is in place to prevent routing loops from occurring. A is incorrect, as you can turn off split-horizon in an IP network. B is incorrect, as routing updates are still transferred.

15. **Answer: C.** You do not want to have an IP address configured on the physical interface. A is incorrect, as you do need to specify frame relay on the physical interface. B is incorrect, as each sub-interface needs a DLCI to identify the virtual circuit assigned to the sub-interface. D is incorrect, as you must specify whether a sub-interface is multipoint or point-to-point.

16. **Answers: A, B, and C.** Forward Explicit Congestion Notifications (FECNs) and Backward Explicit Congestion Notifications (BECNs) are used to notify routers of congestion occurring on the frame relay circuit. Discard Eligible (DE) bits are used to mark packets that exceed the CIR and are dropped if congestion occurs. D is incorrect, as LMI maintains the circuit between the router and the frame relay switch. E is incorrect, as the Committed Information Rate does nothing to control congestion but merely states the promised bandwidth from the service provider.

17. **Answer: A.** LMI is the protocol used between a DCE and DTE to manage the connection. Signaling messages for SVCs, PVC status messages, and keepalives are all LMI messages. B is incorrect, as BECN is the bit in the frame relay header that signals to anyone receiving the frame that congestion is occurring in the backward direction of the frame. Switches and DTEs can react by slowing the rate by which data is sent in that direction. C is incorrect, as FECN is the same as BECN, only in a different direction. D is incorrect, as DLCI is the frame relay address used in the headers to identify the virtual circuit.

18. **Answer: C.** Frame Relay Traffic Shaping (FRTS) allows you to control the flow of traffic over your virtual circuits. It is included as part of the Cisco IOS and does not cost any additional money. A is incorrect, as you already have a slow link at the branch office. B is incorrect, as the criteria state you cannot spend more money, and faster links require more money. D is incorrect as well because you have to purchase each PVC, and this would require spending more money.

19. **Answer: A.** The Committed Information Rate is the value that sets the maximum data rate that the frame relay network tries to deliver under "normal conditions." B is incorrect, as this identifies the DLCI. C is incorrect, as this defines Inverse ARP. D is incorrect, as it defines LMI.

20. **Answer: D.** You have added two offices to your existing eight, bringing the total number of nodes to 10. Using the formula of $n(n-1)/2$ to figure out the total number of PVCs, you arrive at 45. A is incorrect, as this works only for a

star topology. B is incorrect, as this is only a partial mesh. C is incorrect; this provides only a partial mesh, as there are not enough connections for a full mesh.

21. **Answer: B.** Frame relay improved on X.25 by relying on applications, or upper layers, to provide error correction and reliability of transmission. A is incorrect, as frame relay is faster than X.25 because of the lack of overhead. C is incorrect, as X.25 is packet-switched as well. D is incorrect, as both X.25 and frame relay are standards-based.

22. **Answer: D.** Switched virtual circuits (SVCs) are temporary connections. A is incorrect, as VCs are multiplexed logical data conversations. B is incorrect, as SVCs are not widely supported by all frame relay providers. C is incorrect, as PVCs are used for always-on permanent connections.

23. **Answers: A, B, and D.** A PVC must be in place with LMI operating correctly. To use Inverse ARP, you must be running Cisco IOS 11.2 or higher. C is incorrect, as you do not need your routing protocol to support Inverse ARP for it to work.

24. **Answer: A.** The `frame relay map` command allows you to specify a different encapsulation (IETF or Cisco) to be used rather than the general encapsulation given in the interface command `encapsulation frame relay [ietf/cisco]`. B is incorrect, as you are using Cisco equipment elsewhere in your environment, and it is better to use the Cisco version of frame relay if possible. C is incorrect, as it is unnecessary to purchase new equipment. D is incorrect, as there is no such thing as a frame relay proxy.

25. **Answer: A.** The correct syntax of the frame relay map command is `frame-relay map ip [remote_ip_address] [local_dlci] broadcast`. The `broadcast` keyword allows routing protocol updates to function. In this case, Arizona is trying to reach the remote IP address 10.1.1.2 in Michigan and uses the local DLCI of 512 to get there. All other answers are incorrect because they use either the wrong DLCI or IP address.

26. **Answer: A.** Three primary PVC states indicate the status of the line. ACTIVE means there are no problems. Answer B is incorrect, as INACTIVE means that there is a problem with the remote router; DELETED means that there is a problem with your local router. Typically, this is caused by using the incorrect DLCI information. Answer D is eliminated because multipoint and point-to-point designs use DLCI information in the same way. If the DLCI shows up as DELETED under a multipoint configuration, it shows up as DELETED under a point-to-point configuration. Finally, if you are physically disconnected from the service provider, you do not see DLCI information (because LMI is used to send the DLCI status to your router); thus, answer C is incorrect as well.

27. **Answer: B.** The `show interface serial [port]` command gives you information about the Physical and Data-link layer on your interface. A is incorrect, as this command displays the status of each configured connection, but more importantly, it shows the traffic statistics. C is incorrect, as there is no such command. D is incorrect, as this command gives you the existing configuration of the router that is currently running in RAM.

28. **Answer: A.** The circuit number is the local loop identifier given by the service provider. It is typically on the label attached to your CSU/DSU. B is incorrect, as the DLCI identifies the virtual circuit to the router and is given by the LMI. C is incorrect, as the LMI is the signaling technology that maintains the virtual circuits. D is incorrect, as the CIR is the minimum agreed bandwidth between the provider and your company.

29. **Answer: C.** The output shown is from the `show frame relay lmi` command. A is incorrect, as this command is ambiguous and needs another parameter. B is incorrect, as this command displays the status of each configured connection with traffic statistics. D is incorrect, as there is no such command.

30. **Answer: D.** The `debug frame relay lmi` command gives you the output shown. A is incorrect, as it is ambiguous and requires another parameter. B is incorrect, as this command displays the LMI traffic statistics in a static manner. C is incorrect, as it gives you *all* frame relay statistics in real time, not just the output shown. E is incorrect, as you never issue this command on a production router.

31. **Answer: A.** LMI multicasts are sent every 10 seconds by default. B, C, and D are incorrect timers for LMI signaling.

32. **Answers: B and C.** FRF.5 allows for frame relay to cross ATM networks. FRF.8 allows a frame relay user to communicate with an ATM user. A is incorrect, as FRF.1 defines UNI implementations. D is incorrect, as FRF.11 defines voice-over-frame relay.

33. **Answer: A.** Both the ITU-T and ANSI groups help define frame relay. B is incorrect, as frame relay operates at the lower two layers of the OSI Model. C is incorrect, as frame relay allows for star, partial mesh, and full mesh topologies. D is incorrect, as VLANs are a Layer 2 Switch capability to segment your network into logical sub-networks or virtual LANs.

34. **Answer: D.** Frame relay's core aspects function at the two lowest layers of the OSI Reference Model: Physical and Data-link. A is incorrect, as frame relay does not have aspects at all layers. B is incorrect, as well, because despite frame relay relying on upper layers for functionality of data, it does not operate there. C is incorrect, as frame relay does not operate at the Session and Transport layers of the OSI Model.

35. **Answer: B.** The show frame relay pvc command provides you with statistics of each configured connection, as well as traffic statistics. A is incorrect, as the output is not for LMI statistics. C and D are incorrect, as there are no such commands.

36. **Answer: C.** You need only a connection from the hub to each of the spokes. A is incorrect, as each router needs a separate connection for each and every other router in the topology. This would be quite expensive in a large topology. B is incorrect, as you still have more connections than a hub-and-spoke topology. D is incorrect, as nonbroadcast multi-access (NBMA) does not affect the cost of frame relay.

37. **Answer: D.** A service provider marks extra frames with a Discard Eligible (DE) bit in the header that allows the service provider to discard frames if necessary when there is congestion. A is incorrect, as the service provider marks extra traffic. B is incorrect, as providers allow occasional "bursting," as long as it doesn't affect the network. C is incorrect, as service providers typically do not charge extra fees when there is bursting, depending on the type of contract you have.

38. **Answer: A.** A frame relay switch sends Forward Explicit Congestion Notification (FECN) marked frames to the destination DTE if there is congestion on the frame network. B is incorrect, as BECNs are sent back to the source DTE after FECNs are received. C is incorrect, as Discard Eligible (DE) frames are discarded if the network becomes too congested. D is incorrect, as the CIR sets the maximum average data rate that the network undertakes to deliver under "normal conditions."

39. **Answers: A, B, D, and E.** For a frame relay connection to be in place, you must have a virtual circuit identified by a DLCI. The DLCI is given to you via LMI, which also maintains the circuit. The service provider wants a CIR for each of the virtual circuits. C is incorrect, as you do not need Inverse ARP if you use static frame relay maps.

40. **Answer: C.** The cable that connects you to the DCE is specified by the service provider. It can be a form of EIA/TIA, V.35, or X.21. A is incorrect, as the signaling standard is specified by the LMI. B is incorrect, as the encapsulation for crossing the cloud is either IETF or Cisco. D is incorrect, as Cisco routers use a DB-60 connector on their end.

41. **Answer: A and D.** DTE is on the customer end and is the data terminal equipment. The DCE is on the service provider's equipment, typically called data communication equipment. It's usually a device like a CSU/DSU. B and C are incorrect, as these describe equipment not used in frame relay or any serial communication. E is incorrect as well; even though the DCE does provide

clocking, it is not called data clocking equipment. F is also incorrect; although these devices help provide the logical circuits, they are not called data circuit equipment.

42. **Answers: A, B, and C.** A is correct, as you can use a full mesh topology, which solves the issue. B is correct, as you can use sub-interfaces. C is also correct; however, you must be running a routing protocol that uses split-horizon. D is incorrect because RIPv2 still has split-horizon mechanisms, although it does improve over RIPv1 by using multicasts to update other routers and is a class-less routing protocol.

43. **Answer: C.** Sub-interfaces allow you to overcome split-horizon issues if you use point-to-point sub-interfaces. A is incorrect, as you can use more than one physical interface if necessary for more frame relay connections. B is incorrect, as sub-interfaces don't require you to use more than one physical interface. D is incorrect, as you still need to assign IP addresses to the sub-interfaces. In fact, you increase the number of IP addresses.

44. **Answer: B.** A virtual circuit is "inactive" when the remote side is not sending, but you are okay on your side of the connection. A is incorrect, as this represents a working connection, or active state. C is incorrect, as this represents a deleted state. D is incorrect, as a shutdown interface shows up as administratively down.

45. **Answer: D.** This describes a virtual circuit in an active state. A is incorrect, as an inactive state shows a problem on the opposite side of the connection. B is incorrect, as this shows a circuit that is not receiving any LMI signaling. C is incorrect, as this is a port state in Spanning-Tree Protocol.

46. **Answers: A, B, and D.** They are all valid signaling types for Local Management Interface (LMI). C is incorrect, as the ITU-T is a standards organization that actually created the Q.933a standard.

47. **Answer: A.** Without the broadcast keyword, broadcast and multicast-based routing updates are not sent across the link. Answer B is incorrect because the RIP version is irrelevant to getting RIP working across frame relay. Answer C is incorrect because Inverse ARP has nothing to do with getting your routing updates across a frame relay network. Finally, answer D is incorrect because RIP is activated on the interfaces. When you enter in the network statements under the RIP configuration mode, it automatically enables RIP on the interfaces where those networks reside.

48. **Answer: B.** Routers send Inverse ARP messages every 60 seconds by default. The rest of the answers are not the default timer values for Inverse ARP messages.

49. **Answer: C.** The frame relay switch checks the incoming frame's inbound DLCI number. A is incorrect, as it is the last step. B is incorrect, as it is part of the last step. D is incorrect, as it is the second step.

50. **Answer: A.** There are redundant links between the routers; however, there are not redundant links between all of the routers. B is incorrect, as there are not redundant links between all of the routers. C is incorrect, as even though the connections form a ring as shown in the figure, if it is in the cloud, it does not look like this. D is incorrect, as it is not a star or hub-and-spoke topology; there is no central point.

ISDN

Quick Check

1. What is the data transfer rate for an ISDN bearer channel?

   ❏ A. 12Kbps
   ❏ B. 16Kbps
   ❏ C. 56Kbps
   ❏ D. 64Kbps
   ❏ E. 128Kbps

Quick Answer: **206**
Detailed Answer: **207**

2. What is the data transfer rate for a BRI ISDN delta channel?

   ❏ A. 12Kbps
   ❏ B. 16Kbps
   ❏ C. 56Kbps
   ❏ D. 64Kbps
   ❏ E. 128Kbps

Quick Answer: **206**
Detailed Answer: **207**

3. Which protocol recommends telephone network standards for ISDN?

   ❏ A. A-series
   ❏ B. E-series
   ❏ C. I-series
   ❏ D. Q-series

Quick Answer: **206**
Detailed Answer: **207**

4. Which protocol deals with concepts, terminology, and methods?

   ❏ A. A-series
   ❏ B. E-series
   ❏ C. I-series
   ❏ D. Q-series

Quick Answer: **206**
Detailed Answer: **207**

5. Which protocol covers switching and signaling in ISDN?

    ❏ A. A-series

    ❏ B. E-series

    ❏ C. I-series

    ❏ D. Q-series

Quick Answer: **206**
Detailed Answer: **207**

6. How many bearer channels are provided in BRI?

    ❏ A. 1

    ❏ B. 2

    ❏ C. 16

    ❏ D. 23

Quick Answer: **206**
Detailed Answer: **207**

7. How many bearer channels are provided in PRI for North America?

    ❏ A. 1

    ❏ B. 2

    ❏ C. 16

    ❏ D. 23

Quick Answer: **206**
Detailed Answer: **207**

8. What is the data transfer rate for a PRI ISDN delta channel?

    ❏ A. 12Kbps

    ❏ B. 16Kbps

    ❏ C. 56Kbps

    ❏ D. 64Kbps

    ❏ E. 128Kbps

Quick Answer: **206**
Detailed Answer: **207**

9. How many bearer channels are provided in PRI for Europe?

    ❏ A. 16

    ❏ B. 24

    ❏ C. 30

    ❏ D. 32

Quick Answer: **206**
Detailed Answer: **207**

10. Which channel provides setup, signaling, and termination in ISDN?

    ❏ A. B channel

    ❏ B. D channel

    ❏ C. S channel

    ❏ D. T channel

Quick Answer: **206**
Detailed Answer: **207**

Quick Check ✓

11. Which channel in ISDN is used for the transfer of data and the bulk of network traffic?

   ❑ A. B channel

   ❑ B. D channel

   ❑ C. S channel

   ❑ D. T channel

Quick Answer: **206**
Detailed Answer: **207**

12. Which of the following designates a router or ISDN telephone as a device having a native ISDN interface?

   ❑ A. TE1

   ❑ B. NT-2

   ❑ C. NT-1

   ❑ D. TE2

   ❑ E. TA

Quick Answer: **206**
Detailed Answer: **207**

13. Which of the following is the point at which all ISDN lines at a customer site are aggregated and switched using a customer-switching device?

   ❑ A. TE1

   ❑ B. NT-2

   ❑ C. NT-1

   ❑ D. TE2

   ❑ E. TA

Quick Answer: **206**
Detailed Answer: **208**

14. Which of the following converts the four-wire BRI signals from an S/T interface into two-wire signals of a U interface?

   ❑ A. TE1

   ❑ B. NT-2

   ❑ C. NT-1

   ❑ D. TE2

   ❑ E. TA

Quick Answer: **206**
Detailed Answer: **208**

15. Which of the following designates a device such as a PC or router requiring a TA to adapt communication for BRI signals?

   ❑ A. TE1

   ❑ B. NT-2

   ❑ C. NT-1

   ❑ D. TE2

Quick Answer: **206**
Detailed Answer: **208**

16. Which of the following converts EIA/TIA-232, V.35, and other signals into BRI signals?
    - ❏ A. TE1
    - ❏ B. NT-2
    - ❏ C. NT-1
    - ❏ D. TE2
    - ❏ E. TA

Quick Answer: **206**
Detailed Answer: **208**

17. Which of the following reference points refers to the connection between a non–ISDN-compatible device and a terminal adapter?
    - ❏ A. R
    - ❏ B. S
    - ❏ C. T
    - ❏ D. U

Quick Answer: **206**
Detailed Answer: **208**

18. Which of the following reference points refers to the point that connects into the NT-2, or customer-switching device?
    - ❏ A. R
    - ❏ B. S
    - ❏ C. T
    - ❏ D. U

Quick Answer: **206**
Detailed Answer: **209**

19. Which of the following reference points refers to the outbound connection from the NT-2 to the ISDN network?
    - ❏ A. R
    - ❏ B. S
    - ❏ C. T
    - ❏ D. U

Quick Answer: **206**
Detailed Answer: **209**

20. Which of the following reference points refers to the connection between the NT-1 and the ISDN network owned by the telephone company?
    - ❏ A. R
    - ❏ B. S
    - ❏ C. T
    - ❏ D. U

Quick Answer: **206**
Detailed Answer: **209**

21. Which of the following components is supplied by the end user in the United States and by the provider in Europe?

Quick Answer: **206**
Detailed Answer: **209**

- ❑ A. TE1
- ❑ B. NT-2
- ❑ C. NT-1
- ❑ D. TE2
- ❑ E. TA

22. Which of the following designations indicates that the NT-1 is built in?

Quick Answer: **206**
Detailed Answer: **209**

- ❑ A. TE1
- ❑ B. NT-2
- ❑ C. S/T
- ❑ D. U
- ❑ E. TA

23. Which of the following is a series of characters that identifies you to the switch at the central office?

Quick Answer: **206**
Detailed Answer: **209**

- ❑ A. UID
- ❑ B. SID
- ❑ C. SPID
- ❑ D. Terminal ID

24. You need to specify the type of ISDN switch you are using to configure ISDN BRI. You are using a National ISDN-1. Which command is correct?

Quick Answer: **206**
Detailed Answer: **209**

- ❑ A. `switch-type ni1`
- ❑ B. `switch-type basic-ni1`
- ❑ C. `isdn switch-type ni1`
- ❑ D. `isdn switch-type basic-ni1`

25. You have configured the switch type; however, your ISDN BRI connection is not working. What else should you do?

Quick Answer: **206**
Detailed Answer: **209**

- ❑ A. Re-enter the switch type.
- ❑ B. Reload the router configuration.
- ❑ C. Restart the router.
- ❑ D. Flush NVRAM.

Quick Check

26. You've set the switch type to AT&T 5ESS for your BRI connection. Your provider has given you your SPID. What is your next step?

❑ A. Configure only the SPID on the first B channel.
❑ B. Configure only the SPID on the second B channel.
❑ C. Configure the SPID on both B channels.
❑ D. Configure the SPID on neither B channel.

Quick Answer: **206**
Detailed Answer: **209**

27. You need to configure the SPID for your router. What command is appropriate?

❑ A. `isdn spid1 spid-number`
❑ B. `isdn spid spid-number`
❑ C. `spid spid-number`
❑ D. `spid1 spid-number`

Quick Answer: **206**
Detailed Answer: **210**

28. You are reviewing your device's current configuration. You notice that you have configured different switch type settings for your switch in both Global Configuration mode and Interface Configuration mode. What is the effective switch type?

❑ A. The global setting overrides all settings.
❑ B. The interface setting overrides the global setting for that interface.
❑ C. Neither setting takes effect.
❑ D. This configuration cannot be created.

Quick Answer: **206**
Detailed Answer: **210**

29. You have a T1 interface that needs to have ISDN PRI configured on all 24 channels. After you set the switch type and controller, what command should you enter next?

❑ A. `pri-group timeslots 1-24`
❑ B. `pri-group timeslots 0-23`
❑ C. `timeslots 0-23`
❑ D. `timeslots 1-24`

Quick Answer: **206**
Detailed Answer: **210**

30. You type the following configuration into a router:

Quick Answer: **206**
Detailed Answer: **210**

```
access-list 110 permit tcp any any eq www
dialer-list 1 protocol ip list 110
isdn switch-type basic-5ess
interface bri0
 ip address 10.0.0.1 255.0.0.0
 dialer-group 1
 dialer map ip 10.0.0.2 5551111
 isdn spid1 55511110101 5551111
```

Next, you test the ISDN connection by attempting to send HTTP traffic. The line comes up successfully, and the HTTP traffic is transmitted across the ISDN connection. You then send SMTP traffic and notice that SMTP traffic is also being permitted. Why is SMTP traffic going across the ISDN connection?

- ❏ A. The access list is configured wrong.
- ❏ B. The dialer list is not applied correctly.
- ❏ C. The `dialer-list` command specifies only what traffic brings up the ISDN connection, not what traffic is allowed across after the connection is up.
- ❏ D. SMTP traffic is a subset of HTTP; therefore, it is allowed across the ISDN connection.

31. You want to display statistics for the BRI interface configured on the router. What command should you enter?

Quick Answer: **206**
Detailed Answer: **210**

- ❏ A. `show isdn statistics`
- ❏ B. `show isdn bri`
- ❏ C. `show interfaces bri0`
- ❏ D. `show isdn status`

32. You want to ensure the router is communicating properly with the switch by viewing the status of both Layer 1 and Layer 2, as well as by viewing the number of active calls. What command permits this?

Quick Answer: **206**
Detailed Answer: **210**

- ❏ A. `show isdn layers`
- ❏ B. `display isdn layers`
- ❏ C. `show isdn status`
- ❏ D. `show isdn info`

33. You need to examine Layer 2 messages regarding the D channel. Which command displays this information?

- ❑ A. debug isdn q921
- ❑ B. debug show isdn
- ❑ C. show isdn layer2
- ❑ D. show isdn q921

Quick Answer: **206**
Detailed Answer: **210**

34. You need to view Layer 3 messages regarding the setup and teardown of the ISDN network connection. Which command is appropriate?

- ❑ A. show isdn q931
- ❑ B. show isdn layer3
- ❑ C. debug isdn q931
- ❑ D. debug isdn layer3

Quick Answer: **206**
Detailed Answer: **210**

35. You want to view CHAP and PAP information for your ISDN connection. Which command shows you the packet exchange information?

- ❑ A. debug isdn authentication
- ❑ B. debug ppp authentication
- ❑ C. debug authentication
- ❑ D. show isdn ppp

Quick Answer: **206**
Detailed Answer: **210**

36. You enter the following configuration into a router, but when you test it, you are unable to initiate the ISDN call. What is wrong?

Quick Answer: **206**
Detailed Answer: **210**

```
Router#config terminal
Router(config)#hostname Arizona
Arizona(config)#router rip
Arizona(config-router)#network 10.0.0.0
Arizona(config-router)#network 192.168.200.0
Arizona(config-router)#version 2
Arizona(config-router)# no auto-summary
Arizona(config-router)#passive-interface default
Arizona(config-router)# no passive-interface eth0
Arizona(config-router)#exit
Arizona(config)#interface ethernet0
Arizona(config-if)#ip address 10.0.0.1 255.0.0.0
Arizona(config-if)#interface bri0
Arizona(config-if)#ip address 192.168.200.93
255.255.255.252
Arizona(config-if)#encapsulation ppp
Arizona(config-if)#ppp authentication chap
```

Quick Check

```
Arizona(config-if)#dialer map ip 192.168.200.94 name
Indiana 5553333
Arizona(config-if)# isdn spid1 55511110101 5551111
Arizona(config-if)#isdn spid2 55522220101 5552222
Arizona(config-if)# dialer-group 40
Arizona(config-if)#dialer idle-timeout 30
Arizona(config-if)#isdn switch-type basic-ni
Arizona(config-if)#exit
Arizona(config)#ip route 192.168.200.96 255.255.255.224
192.168.200.94
Arizona(config)#dialer-list 4 protocol ip permit
Arizona(config)#username Indiana password sanjose
```

- ❑ A. The dialer group is applied wrong.
- ❑ B. The RIP configuration is wrong.
- ❑ C. The PPP authentication is configured wrong.
- ❑ D. The dialer map is configured wrong.
- ❑ E. The configuration is incomplete.

37. You want to monitor PPP traffic and exchanges, including Link Control Protocol and Network Control Protocol. What command shows this information?

- ❑ A. `debug ppp traffic`
- ❑ B. `show ppp traffic`
- ❑ C. `debug ppp negotiation`
- ❑ D. `show ppp negotiation`

Quick Answer: **206**
Detailed Answer: **210**

38. Dial-on-demand routing (DDR) is designed for which of the following types of connections?

- ❑ A. Low-volume periodic connections
- ❑ B. High-volume periodic connections
- ❑ C. Low-volume persistent connections
- ❑ D. High-volume persistent connections

Quick Answer: **206**
Detailed Answer: **211**

39. In DDR operation, what is "interesting traffic"?

- ❑ A. Traffic signaling a possible attack
- ❑ B. Traffic that should be blocked
- ❑ C. Traffic that should initiate the connection
- ❑ D. Traffic that initiates from the router

Quick Answer: **206**
Detailed Answer: **211**

40. Which command allows you to specify interesting traffic for DDR?

  ❏   A. `dialer-list`
  ❏   B. `accesslist`
  ❏   C. `dial list`
  ❏   D. `dial-list`

Quick Answer: **206**
Detailed Answer: **211**

41. What command associates a port with a dial list?

  ❏   A. `dialer-group`
  ❏   B. `dial port`
  ❏   C. `dialer port`
  ❏   D. `dialer-port`

Quick Answer: **206**
Detailed Answer: **211**

42. What command associates a dialer string with a dial list?

  ❏   A. `dialer-map`
  ❏   B. `dialer-list`
  ❏   C. `dial map`
  ❏   D. `dial list`

Quick Answer: **206**
Detailed Answer: **211**

43. What three things are necessary to complete a DDR ISDN call? (Choose three.)

  ❏   A. Static routes
  ❏   B. Dialer information
  ❏   C. Interesting traffic
  ❏   D. Routing protocols
  ❏   E. SPID numbers
  ❏   F. DLCIs

Quick Answer: **206**
Detailed Answer: **211**

44. You've configured static routes for use with your DDR connection. You want to review the routes the router is using. What command displays these routes?

  ❏   A. `show ip static`
  ❏   B. `show ip route`
  ❏   C. `show route`
  ❏   D. `show route static`

Quick Answer: **206**
Detailed Answer: **211**

45. What BRI command displays statistics for the ISDN DDR call, including the source and destination information for the packet initiating the call?

  ❏   A. `show ddr`
  ❏   B. `show dialer interface bri0`
  ❏   C. `show dialer interface`
  ❏   D. `show interface bri0`

Quick Answer: **206**
Detailed Answer: **211**

Quick Check

46. Which command allows you to receive debugging information about the packets received on a dialer interface?

    ❏ A. `debug packets`
    ❏ B. `debug dialer`
    ❏ C. `debug interface`
    ❏ D. `debug dialer interface`

Quick Answer: **206**
Detailed Answer: **211**

47. You need to disable the interface. Disconnecting any call in progress is acceptable. What command should you issue?

    ❏ A. `no isdn`
    ❏ B. `shutdown isdn`
    ❏ C. `disable isdn`
    ❏ D. `shutdown`

Quick Answer: **206**
Detailed Answer: **211**

48. You need to configure the line to disconnect if it has been idle for two minutes. What command should you use?

    ❏ A. `dialer timeout 120`
    ❏ B. `dialer idle-timeout 120`
    ❏ C. `dialer idle 120`
    ❏ D. `dialer line idle 120`

Quick Answer: **206**
Detailed Answer: **212**

49. You have set the dialer load threshold value to 25. What is the minimum percentage load that will cause the line to initiate another call to the destination?

    ❏ A. 2.5%
    ❏ B. 10%
    ❏ C. 25%
    ❏ D. 100%

Quick Answer: **206**
Detailed Answer: **212**

50. Which of the following types of traffic are acceptable for ISDN BRI bearer channels? (Choose three.)

    ❏ A. Voice
    ❏ B. Data
    ❏ C. Signaling
    ❏ D. Acknowledgments
    ❏ E. Video

Quick Answer: **206**
Detailed Answer: **212**

Quick Check Answer Key

1. D	26. D
2. B	27. A
3. B	28. B
4. C	29. A
5. D	30. C
6. B	31. C
7. D	32. C
8. D	33. A
9. C	34. C
10. B	35. B
11. A	36. A
12. A	37. C
13. B	38. A
14. C	39. C
15. D	40. A
16. E	41. A
17. A	42. A
18. B	43. A, B, C
19. C	44. B
20. D	45. B
21. C	46. B
22. D	47. D
23. C	48. B
24. D	49. B
25. C	50. A, B, E

Answers and Explanations

1. **Answer: D.** The transfer rate of the bearer channel is 64Kbps. A, B, C, and E all feature incorrect bearer channel transfer rates.

2. **Answer: B.** The transfer rate for the delta channel is 16Kbps. A, C, D, and E all feature incorrect delta channel transfer rates.

3. **Answer: B.** The E-series specifies telephone network standards. A is incorrect because this is not a valid specification. C is incorrect, as the I-series specifies concepts, terminology, and methods for ISDN. D is incorrect, as the Q-series specifies switching and signaling in ISDN.

4. **Answer: C.** The I-series specifies concepts, terminology, and methods for ISDN. A is incorrect because this is not a valid specification. B is incorrect because the E-series specifies telephone network standards. D is incorrect, as the Q-series specifies switching and signaling in ISDN.

5. **Answer: D.** The Q-series specifies switching and signaling in ISDN. A is incorrect because this is not a valid specification. B is incorrect because the E-series specifies telephone network standards. C is incorrect because the I-series specifies concepts, terminology, and methods for ISDN.

6. **Answer: B.** There are only two bearer channels in BRI. A, C, and D all feature the incorrect number of bearer channels in BRI.

7. **Answer: D.** There are 23 bearer channels in PRI for North America as well as 1 delta channel. A, B, and C all feature the incorrect number of bearer channels.

8. **Answer: D.** The PRI D channel has a 64Kbps transfer rate to handle the larger number of bearer channels. Each bearer channel also has a 64Kbps transfer rate. A, B, C, and E all feature incorrect transfer rates.

9. **Answer: C.** There are 30 bearer channels in Europe for PRI. A, B, and D all feature the incorrect number of bearer channels for Europe.

10. **Answer: B.** This is provided by the D channel in ISDN. A is incorrect because the bearer channel carries data. C and D are not valid ISDN channels.

11. **Answer: A.** The bearer channel carries the bulk of network traffic and data. B is incorrect, as this is provided by the D channel in ISDN. C and D are not valid ISDN channels.

12. **Answer: A.** TE1 designates a router or ISDN telephone as a device having a native ISDN interface. B is incorrect because NT-2 indicates the point at which all ISDN lines at a customer site are aggregated and switched. C is incorrect because NT-1 converts the four-wire BRI signals from an S/T interface into the two-wire signals of a U interface. D is incorrect because TE2 is a

device such as a PC or router that requires a TA to adapt communication for BRI signals. E is incorrect, as the TA converts EIA/TIA-232 and other signals into BRI signals.

13. **Answer: B.** NT-2 indicates the point at which all ISDN lines at a customer site are aggregated and switched. A is incorrect because TE1 designates a router or ISDN telephone as a device having a native ISDN interface. C is incorrect, as NT-1 converts the four-wire BRI signals from an S/T interface into the two-wire signals of a U interface. D is incorrect, as TE2 is a device such as a PC or router that requires a TA to adapt communication for BRI signals. E is incorrect because the TA converts EIA/TIA-232 and other signals into BRI signals.

14. **Answer: C.** NT-1 converts the four-wire BRI signals from an S/T interface into the two-wire signals of a U interface. A is incorrect because TE1 designates a router or ISDN telephone as a device having a native ISDN interface. B is incorrect because NT-2 indicates the point at which all ISDN lines at a customer site are aggregated and switched. D is incorrect, as TE2 is a device such as a PC or router that requires a TA to adapt communication for BRI signals. E is incorrect because the TA converts EIA/TIA-232 and other signals into BRI signals.

15. **Answer: D.** TE2 is a device such as a PC or router that requires a TA to adapt communication for BRI signals. A is incorrect because TE1 designates a router or ISDN telephone as a device having a native ISDN interface. B is incorrect because NT-2 indicates the point at which all ISDN lines at a customer site are aggregated and switched. C is incorrect because NT-1 converts the four-wire BRI signals from an S/T interface into the two-wire signals of a U interface.

16. **Answer: E.** The TA converts EIA/TIA-232 and other signals into BRI signals. A is incorrect because TE1 designates a router or ISDN telephone as a device having a native ISDN interface. B is incorrect because NT-2 indicates the point at which all ISDN lines at a customer site are aggregated and switched. C is incorrect, as NT-1 converts the four-wire BRI signals from an S/T interface into the two-wire signals of a U interface. D is incorrect because TE2 is a device such as a PC or router that requires a TA to adapt communication for BRI signals.

17. **Answer: A.** The R reference point refers to the connection between a non–ISDN-compatible device and a terminal adapter. B is incorrect because S refers to the point that connects into the NT-2 or customer-switching device. C is incorrect because the T reference point refers to the outbound connection from the NT-2 to the ISDN network. D is incorrect; this refers to the connection between the NT-1 and ISDN network owned by the telephone company.

18. **Answer: B.** S refers to the point that connects into the NT-2 or customer-switching device. A is incorrect because the R reference point refers to the connection between a non–ISDN-compatible device and a terminal adapter. C is incorrect because the T reference point refers to the outbound connection from the NT-2 to the ISDN network. D is incorrect; this refers to the connection between the NT-1 and ISDN network owned by the telephone company.

19. **Answer: C.** The T reference point refers to the outbound connection from the NT-2 to the ISDN network. A is incorrect because the R reference point refers to the connection between a non–ISDN-compatible device and a terminal adapter. B is incorrect, as S refers to the point that connects into the NT-2 or customer-switching device. D is incorrect; this refers to the connection between the NT-1 and ISDN network owned by the telephone company.

20. **Answer: D.** This reference point refers to the connection between the NT-1 and ISDN network owned by the telephone company. A is incorrect because the R reference point refers to the connection between a non–ISDN-compatible device and a terminal adapter. B is incorrect, as S refers to the point that connects into the NT-2 or customer-switching device. C is incorrect because the T reference point refers to the outbound connection from the NT-2 to the ISDN network.

21. **Answer: C.** The NT-1 is supplied by the end user in the United States and by the provider in Europe. A, B, and D are not correct because they are all end-user devices.

22. **Answer: D.** U indicates that the NT-1 is built in. C is incorrect, as this indicates the NT-1 is not built in. A, B, and E are all incorrect, as they have no bearing on the NT-1.

23. **Answer: C.** This is the service profile identifier (SPID) assigned by the provider. D is incorrect, as the terminal ID is not a designation assigned by the ISDN provider. A and B are not valid ISDN acronyms.

24. **Answer: D.** the correct format to specify a national ISDN-1 switch is `isdn switch-type basic-ni1`. B is incorrect because this is not the proper syntax. A and C use invalid syntax.

25. **Answer: C.** Setting the switch type requires a router reboot to take effect. A is incorrect, as this is not the most likely problem. B is incorrect because reloading the router configuration does not force the setting to take effect. D is incorrect, as this problem is not indicative of an NVRAM problem.

26. **Answer: D.** The 5ESS switch does not require you to configure the SPID. A and B are incorrect, as these are rarely the proper configurations. Typically, both channels are configured, or neither channel is configured. C is incorrect because this is not valid for this switch type.

27. **Answer: A.** This is the proper syntax to configure the SPID. B is incorrect, as you need to specify spid1 or spid2, for instance. C and D are incorrect because isdn should precede the command.

28. **Answer: B.** An interface setting overrides the global setting. A is incorrect because you can override the global setting at the interface level. C is incorrect because both settings are effective. D is incorrect, as this is a valid configuration.

29. **Answer: A.** The proper syntax is pri-group timeslots 1-24. B is incorrect, as the values are 1–24, not 0–23. C is incorrect because the values are wrong, and the pri-group command precedes the timeslots keyword. D is incorrect because the pri-group command has been left out.

30. **Answer: C.** The dialer list in the configuration references access list 110. Access list 110 causes any HTTP traffic to bring up the ISDN connection. This access list is not used as a packet filter, however; so after the ISDN line is up, all traffic (including non-HTTP traffic) is allowed across the link. A and B are incorrect because the configuration is configured correctly. D is incorrect because SMTP is not a subset of HTTP.

31. **Answer: C.** The proper command is show interfaces bri0. D is incorrect, as this does not show the requested information. A and B are invalid IOS commands.

32. **Answer: C.** The show isdn status command displays Layer 1 status and Layer 2 status information. A, B, and D are all invalid IOS commands.

33. **Answer: A.** The debug isdn q921 command shows Layer 2 information for the D channel. B, C, and D are all invalid IOS commands.

34. **Answer: C.** The debug isdn q931 command is the correct command to view Layer 3 debugging information. A, B, and D are invalid IOS commands.

35. **Answer: B.** The debug ppp authentication command allows you to view authentication protocol information, such as that from CHAP and PAP. D is incorrect, as it does not show the requested information. A and C are not valid IOS commands.

36. **Answer: A.** The dialer list is 4 but is applied as number 40. B, C, and D are incorrect because there is nothing wrong with the remaining configuration. E is incorrect because the configuration is complete.

37. **Answer: C.** The debug ppp negotiation command shows PPP traffic exchanges and negotiation information, including LCP and NCP information. A, B, and D are all invalid IOS commands.

38. **Answer: A.** DDR is ideal for low-volume periodic connections and can help keep costs down when cost is tied to the amount of bandwidth used. B is incorrect because high-volume connections can be better served with a persistent high-bandwidth connection. C is incorrect, as persistent connections don't require DDR. D is incorrect because high-volume persistent connections are not served well by DDR.

39. **Answer: C.** Interesting traffic activates the link, causing it to connect and the traffic to be delivered. A is incorrect because this is not interesting traffic as defined by DDR. B is incorrect because interesting traffic should be delivered, not blocked. D is incorrect because interesting traffic does not necessarily initiate at the router.

40. **Answer: A.** The `dialer-list` command is used to specify interesting traffic by applying an access list to an interface. C is incorrect, as this is not the appropriate command. B and D are invalid IOS commands.

41. **Answer: A.** You use the `dialer-group` command to associate a port with a dial list. B, C, and D are all invalid IOS commands.

42. **Answer: A.** To associate a dialer string with a dial list, you use the `dialer-map` command. B is incorrect because this is not the correct command. C and D are both invalid IOS commands.

43. **Answers: A, B, and C.** You must have a static route, you must have dialer information to call the opposite-side router, and you must specify what interesting traffic will initiate the call. D is incorrect, as dynamic routing protocols can cause issues with dial-on-demand routing. E is incorrect because SPIDs are optional and not all switch types or service providers require them. F is incorrect, as Data-link connection identifiers (DLCIs) are used by frame relay to identify virtual circuits.

44. **Answer: B.** The `show ip route` command shows the static and dynamic routes on the router. C is incorrect, as this is not the appropriate command. A and D are invalid IOS commands.

45. **Answer: B.** The correct command to display statistics is `show dialer interface bri0`. C is incorrect because it's an incomplete IOS command. A and D are both invalid IOS commands.

46. **Answer: B.** The `debug dialer` command displays debugging information for the packets on a dialer interface. A and D are invalid IOS commands. C is incorrect; although this is a valid command, it does not show the requested information.

47. **Answer: D.** You use the `shutdown` command on the interface to disable it. A, B, and C are all invalid IOS commands.

48. **Answer: B.** The correct syntax is `dialer idle-timeout 120`. A, C, and D are all invalid IOS commands.

49. **Answer: B.** The value can range from 1 to 255, so 25 is roughly 10%. A is incorrect; 25 is around 10% of the maximum of 255. C is incorrect; the value can range up to 255, not 100. D is incorrect; the value can range up to 255, not 25.

50. **Answers: A, B, and E.** ISDN can be used to transfer not only data, but also voice and video. This makes it an excellent choice for a backup WAN connection. C is incorrect, as signaling occurs only on the delta (D) channel, not the bearer channel (B). D is incorrect, as acknowledgments are a function of Transmission Control Protocol (TCP). Although some of the data being sent may contain acknowledgments, it is not a specific item carried by the B channels.

CD Contents and Installation Instructions

The CD features an innovative practice test engine powered by MeasureUp that includes all the questions from the book, as well as two router simulations, giving you yet another effective tool to assess your readiness for the exam. Cisco simulations validate a person's hands-on skills in addition to knowledge. MeasureUp's Cisco simulations model real-life networking scenarios by requiring the user to perform tasks on simulated Cisco networking devices. MeasureUp's simulations measure troubleshooting and problem-solving skills to address realistic networking problems. The CD also includes a helpful "Need to Know More?" appendix that will break down by chapter extra resources you can visit if some of the topics in this book are still unclear to you.

Multiple Test Modes

MeasureUp practice tests are available in Study, Certification, Custom, Missed Question, and Non-Duplicate question modes.

Study Mode

Tests administered in Study Mode enable you to request the correct answer(s) and explanation to each question during the test. These tests are not timed. You can modify the testing environment *during* the test by selecting the Options button.

Certification Mode

Tests administered in Certification Mode closely simulate the actual testing environment you will encounter when taking a certification exam. These tests do not enable you to request the answer(s) and/or explanation to each question until after the exam.

Custom Mode

Custom Mode enables you to specify your preferred testing environment. Use this mode to specify the objectives you want to include in your test, the timer length, and other test properties. You can also modify the testing environment *during* the test by selecting the Options button.

Missed Question Mode

Missed Question Mode enables you to take a test containing only the questions you have missed previously.

Non-Duplicate Mode

Non-Duplicate Mode enables you to take a test containing only questions not displayed previously.

Random Questions and Order of Answers

This feature helps you learn the material without memorizing questions and answers. Each time you take a practice test, the questions and answers appear in a different randomized order.

Detailed Explanations of Correct and Incorrect Answers

You'll receive automatic feedback on all correct and incorrect answers. The detailed answer explanations are a superb learning tool in their own right.

Attention to Exam Objectives

MeasureUp practice tests are designed to appropriately balance the questions over each technical area covered by a specific exam.

Installing the CD

The minimum system requirements for the CD-ROM are

➤ Windows 95, 98, Me, NT 4.0, 2000, or XP

➤ 7MB disk space for the testing engine

➤ An average of 1MB disk space for each test

If you need technical support, please contact MeasureUp at 678-356-5050 or email support@measureup.com. Additionally, you'll find Frequently Asked Questions (FAQs) at www.measureup.com.

To install the CD-ROM, follow these instructions:

1. Close all applications before beginning this installation.

2. Insert the CD into your CD-ROM drive. If the setup starts automatically, go to step 5. If the setup does not start automatically, continue with step 3.

3. From the Start menu, select Run.

4. In the Browse dialog box, double-click Setup.exe. In the Run dialog box, click OK to begin the installation.

5. On the Welcome screen, click Next.

6. To agree to the Software License Agreement, click Yes.

7. On the Choose Destination Location screen, click Next to install the software to C:\Program Files\Certification Preparation.

8. On the Setup Type screen, select Typical Setup. Click Next to continue.

9. After the installation is complete, verify that Yes, I Want to Restart My Computer Now is selected. If you select No, I Will Restart My Computer Later, you will not be able to use the program until you restart your computer.

10. Click Finish.

11. After restarting your computer, choose Start, Programs, MeasureUp Practice Tests.

12. Select the practice test and click Start Test.

Creating a Shortcut to the MeasureUp Practice Tests

To create a shortcut to the MeasureUp practice tests, follow these steps:

1. Right-click on your Desktop.

2. From the shortcut menu, select New, Shortcut.

3. Browse to C:\Program Files\MeasureUp Practice Tests and select the MeasureUpCertification.exe or Localware.exe file.

4. Click OK.

5. Click Next.

6. Rename the shortcut MeasureUp.

7. Click Finish.

After you have completed step 7, use the MeasureUp shortcut on your Desktop to access the MeasureUp practice test.

Technical Support

If you encounter problems with the MeasureUp test engine on the CD-ROM, please contact MeasureUp at 678-356-5050 or email support@measureup.com. Technical support hours are from 8:00 a.m. to 5:00 p.m. EST Monday through Friday. Additionally, you'll find Frequently Asked Questions (FAQs) at www.measureup.com.

If you'd like to purchase additional MeasureUp products, call 678-356-5050 or 800-649-1MUP (1687), or visit www.measureup.com.

Notes

Notes

Notes

Notes

Notes

Notes

Notes

Notes

Notes

Notes

Notes

Notes